SUNRISE ON THE SOUTHBOUND SLEEPER

SUNRISE ON THE SOUTHBOUND SLEEPER

THE NEW *TELEGRAPH* BOOK OF
GREAT RAILWAY JOURNEYS

Edited by Michael Kerr

First published 2011 by
Aurum Press Limited
7 Greenland Street
London NW1 0ND
www.aurumpress.co.uk

A catalogue record for this book is available from the British Library.

ISBN 978 1 84513 668 0
Ebook ISBN 978 1 84513 743 4

1 3 5 7 9 10 8 6 4 2
2011 2013 2015 2014 2012

Typeset by SX Composing DTP, Rayleigh Essex

Printed and bound in Great Britain byClays Ltd, St Ives plc

*IN MEMORY OF ANNIE KERR, WHO TALKED OF
A TRAIN 'THAT STOPPED AT EVERY
HOLE IN THE HEDGE'*

CONTENTS

INTRODUCTION

———————

Two pieces in this anthology neatly book-end the story of man's 200-year-old relationship with the railways. One recalls the early days of steam, when even minor accidents scared the life out of passengers and gave rise to an early form of post-traumatic stress: railway spine. The other was written at the start of 2011, after earthquake, tsunami and nuclear accident, when the bullet train, punctual as ever, was clung to by the Japanese as a source of reassurance.

In between, of course, came the jet aircraft, and confident predictions (yes, even in the *Daily Telegraph*) that the train would soon go the way of the penny farthing. But those were in the first half of the twentieth century – before the advent of high-speed trains through the Channel Tunnel and high-altitude terrorism in the United States. When aircraft in much of Europe were grounded last year following the eruption of a volcano in Iceland, British holidaymakers turned to the train to make their way to and from the Continent. For many, used to travelling by rail only as far as the office, it will have been a moment of conversion. The daily commute from suburbia to the city might be something to be done with as quickly as possible, blotted out with newspaper, book or headphones, but the train from a grand mainline station to the South of France or Istanbul is still an experience worth savouring. 'Railway termini are our gates to the glorious and the unknown,' as E.M. Forster put it. 'Through them we pass out into adventure and sunshine . . .'

As I was finishing the editing of this book, I kept coming across reports of two kinds on developments in railway travel. The first kind, full of firm figures, trumpeted the journey-shrinking capabilities of new high-speed trains: 90 minutes instead of three and a half hours from Madrid to Valencia; four hours instead of seven between Munich and Berlin; four hours instead of ten from Shanghai to Beijing. The second kind of report, much vaguer, was about lines that had just opened or reopened or were still being sketched on plans; lines that would take you where you couldn't have gone before, and on which, instead of shrinking the journey, you could stretch it: the reopened North Borneo Railway, on which trains can take four hours to cover the 84 miles between Tanjung Aru and Tenom; 'Corridor 10', a pan-European road-and-rail link between central and south-eastern Europe; a railway carving a path through the northern tip of South America, from Cartagena on Colombia's Caribbean coast to an unspecified site on the Pacific . . .

This volume, like its predecessor, *Last Call for the Dining Car*, is a celebration of the second kind of development. It's about the journey not as a necessary inconvenience between points A and B but as an end in itself. It's for people who like to spin things out; people who don't just want to get there and back but who want to *travel*. The Swiss are currently building through the Alps what will be the world's longest and deepest railway tunnel. For James Bedding, taking a hard-hat tour, the development is something to cheer not because it will bring the Latin and Teutonic realms within commuting distance of each other (which it will) but because it will send underground both freight and braying business passengers, leaving the Alpine air fresher and the clanking old trains that he loves so much quieter.

When I'm in a hurry, I have nothing against high-speed trains. When I'm not, I want to look out the window and enjoy the passing show. You can't do much of that on a TGV (That looks interesting . . . Could it be? . . . Too late. It's gone). There are times, I reckon, when I have seen more of France on taking off and landing in an aircraft than I did on my last trip through the country by train. Not that I'd swap the TGV for a plane. I'm with Chris Heath, one of my contributors, on this one: 'Despite the real-time sky map on your seatback TV, and the occasional glance through an aeroplane window at the terrain far below, flying is about being somewhere and then, magically, reappearing somewhere else. It is *Star Trek* teleportation, albeit in a slightly more sluggish form.' He had been planning to take a trip on the Trans-Siberian Express. Then, while doing some research, he discovered how much farther the railway line could be extended at either end. He could go all the way from Highgate in north London to Hanoi in Vietnam – a third of the way round the globe. The possibility was irresistible.

So it was for many other contributors to this anthology. It is the '*New Telegraph* Book of Great Railway Journeys' because nearly 20 of the articles have been specially commissioned for it (and are being used at shorter length for a series, 'The Rail World', in the travel section of the *Daily Telegraph*). Several of those do justice to the long run. Among them are Stephen McClarence's 2,000-mile trip across India, from the parched salt flats of Gujarat to the lush semi-tropics of Assam, and Fionnuala McHugh's from China's 'Special Administrative Region' in the south – Hong Kong – to what the Chinese government likes to call the 'Tibetan Autonomous Region' in the far west. The remainder of the pieces have been unearthed from the archives since I completed the first book (including John Betjeman's tribute to the Great Western), or have been published in one of the *Telegraph* titles since that appeared in 2009*.

There is soft travelling here and hard. The former is at its most luxurious on the Maharajas' Express through the desert of Rajasthan, where passengers alight at one stop to have lunch with a maharana and at another to play a few chukkas of elephant polo. The presidential suite is a carriage in its own right, complete with sitting room and two bedrooms, the second of which has not only a double bed but an en suite bathroom complete with a tub. At the other extreme are the public trains that the tireless Dervla Murphy took through Cuba in her late seventies, with loos in such a state that this redoubtable woman suffered a bad case of 'penis envy'. With only the light of the moon to guide her on a night train, she pushed open the door of a *baño* and almost stepped to her death ('not exactly a premature death but an unpleasant and rather silly way to go') through a hole in the floor. So bad were the trains that Murphy, fearing her account might read like fiction, gives a guarantee that it isn't.

In a year when John Steinbeck has come in for a posthumous whipping over alleged fabrications in *Travels with Charley*, I should point out that there *is* a little fiction in this anthology, in the shape of a chapter from an online novel that Alexander McCall Smith wrote for the *Daily Telegraph*, and in which he is about to send two characters on a sleeper from London to Edinburgh. *The Railway Children* and *Thomas the Tank Engine* put in a few appearances as well. Thomas's creator, the Rev W. Awdry, shares space, in a chapter devoted to steam trains, with that notorious petrolhead James May, presenter of *Top Gear*. Which is just as it should be: on a train you might bump into anyone. Fionnuala McHugh, travelling through China, finds the experience 'as safe and as sociable as a sleepover with people whose names you just don't happen to know'. Jenny Diski, who prefers to be solitary, succumbs with a little more reluctance:

> Just because we all happen to be going in the same direction, an us has been formed. And I discover that however much I wish to justify my private daydreaming and pleasurable alienation . . . this random collection of strangers has become a group to which I belong, here and now and unavoidably.

What do you do, though, when one of those strangers makes it clear that she would like to prolong the encounter once the train has arrived at your destination? That's the question that Anthony Peregrine was faced with at the end of a trip from Fontainebleau to Paris.

And what do you do when your travelling companions ask if you have any good train stories, and you are in possession of one that will fascinate them but might also ruin their trip? Pamela Petro had to deal with that one. Her secret: that she had survived one of America's worst train crashes.

Throwing you into unexpected company is just one of the more obvious functions that the railways can perform, but their capabilities go far beyond that. In this anthology, the train serves as a church, bringing the Orthodox faith to remote parts of Russia; as a mobile disco in North Wales; as Santa's sleigh-on-rails through outback Australia; and as a time machine, transporting Nicholas Shakespeare back to the Nazi-occupied France that his aunt endured in the 1940s. Then the train was exploited for evil ends: between 1941 and 1944, the SNCF, the French railway company, was to carry a total of 76,000 European Jews in 76 cattle cars to the French-German border, and thence to Auschwitz. In the twenty-first century, after another war, this time in Bosnia, the train – as Adrian Bridge discovered – has become in the Balkans a symbol of optimism, the reopening of the line between Sarajevo and Belgrade a proof that life is returning to normal for the people of the former Yugoslavia. Surely, though, the greatest repair job the railways have performed is to the image of Michael Portillo: when he lost his parliamentary seat on a 14 per cent swing to Labour in 1997 he seemed all but friendless; having presented in the meantime several television series about great train journeys, he now has strangers rushing up to shake his hand.

If we think better of Portillo, then his programmes make us think better of Britain's railways – at least until the following morning when we are on the 7.57 into Waterloo. Then, at the first pause for a signal failure, we'll be grumbling that this doesn't happen in France or Germany; that our Continental neighbours do everything – everything – so much better. An item from our Peterborough diary of 16 December 1980 sums it up nicely for me: 'About half of Switzerland's train drivers and ticket collectors marched through Berne on Sunday in a protest rally to demand better pay and working conditions. The other half kept the trains running because they believe they can't win their case without the goodwill of the travelling public. Comments, please, to NUR and ASLEF, not to me.'

The Rev W. Awdry, while appalled by some of the developments (and the destruction) that had taken place in his lifetime, took a sunnier view. 'Railways and the Church have their critics,' he would say, 'but both are the best ways of getting man to his ultimate destination.' Commentary on the Church is beyond the scope of this anthology, but I'm with him on the railways.

---

* Articles that are undated in these pages have yet to appear in print or online.

CHAPTER I
EUROPE

———————————

5 FEBRUARY 2011

STAYING ON THE SUNNY SIDE OF THE TRACKS

THE TRAIN FROM MONTPELLIER TO ROME: AN INEBRIATING PROSPECT – UNTIL **ANTHONY PEREGRINE** FACTORED IN THE RAILWAY NETWORKS, THEIR STAFF, AND THE SERIAL KILLER AMONG HIS FELLOW PASSENGERS

'All roads lead to Rome' is a blatant lie. Some of them lead to Blackburn. And those that do lead to Rome are not necessarily enjoyable. They take forever and, once you get into Italy, confirm that life is cheap and your life cheapest of all. The plane is no better. From my home in the south of France, the least expensive way to fly to Rome is via London. I reject this on the grounds of absurdity. So the train is the reasonable option.

It is also desirable. You're going to Rome because it is the most civilised and sensual of capital cities. It makes sense to travel in a manner that sets the tone. And a railway trip round the Mediterranean surely cannot fail. Someone else will do the driving. You have no worries about the proper packaging for your toothpaste or falling out of the sky. You may sit back and soak up suitable subjects preparatory for Rome. Classical culture expanded all round this coast. There's plenty of it about. You might also dip in and out of the Renaissance: Tuscany is on the itinerary. And then there's the beauty of the Riviera (you're doing both the French and Italian ones), which gave rise to mass tourism in the 1800s.

The prospect is inebriating. In practice, of course, reality kicks in with distractions. That is the way of public transport. There are the imperatives of the timetable – and delays. In handing yourself over to the railway network, you offload all responsibility for your short-term future. This is terrifically liberating – until it isn't, until you're becalmed in a field and the time of your connection at La Spézia is getting closer and closer and there's not a damned thing you can do about it and everything, up to and including your whole life, is about to go wrong. In Italian.

Then there are the other passengers. They can be noisy and one – a muscular, scarred fellow sitting directly opposite – is, according to my wife, a serial killer. ('Serial killers never look like serial killers,' I whisper. 'This one does,' she says.)

But that lies in the future. For the time being, we are waiting at Lunel station, near Montpellier. 'I can barely contain myself,' I tell my wife. 'Do try,' she replies, moving slightly farther along the platform than seems necessary.

DAY 1

Lunel station, like all French stations, has the dignified bearing of a bastion of the Republic. 'The train for Marseille?' I asked the chap in a cap. 'Over there,' he barked, pointing vaguely towards the rest of the world. He did not lift his head from documents dealing with, I'd guess, plans to ensure public order in case of a points failure.

We are now standing with early-morning people going just down the line to work or school. One teenage schoolgirl is carrying two rats in a cage. What is this: bring-your-own dissection classes? I long to ask her but don't, either on the platform or in the train. Except in unusual circumstances, or unless a child shows off a drawing, people on a train don't speak to strangers, even though many are available.

We skirt the Camargue and the Etang de Berre lagoon, and I see little of either. The train is as packed as a field of wheat. I'm jammed against a bulbous lady. Bending down to look out of the window would mean plunging my nose into her cleavage – something that few women appreciate, on trains or elsewhere.

So it's a relief to pull into Marseille's St Charles station. I never thought I'd say that. In the past, St Charles offered the traveller an opportunity to study a comprehensive cross-section of France's disadvantaged in one tight-knit area. There were drunks, beggars, beggars' dogs, whores, drug addicts, and happy madmen of many nations peeing in corners. These days, it's been redone with glass and metal and open-fronted fast-food outlets and is, thank heavens, indistinguishable from any other big modern station. It also has those flip-up destination boards from which you dare not take your eyes lest they flip up your destination and then flip it down again, unseen. This never happens, but it might.

As expected, the boards indicate that we have no time to visit Marseille. We have, though, minutes enough – 19 – to nip out onto the station's rather grand new terrace and survey France's oldest, most boisterous city. By this hour it is being out-stared by a sun that renders it monumental and pure, while also casting shadows enough for skulduggery.

Now it is 12h59 and the real French Mediterranean train – to Nice – is pulling out of the station. It's a TGV, so we have numbered seats. Talk about contentment. Soon we're rolling along the coast, like the European elites before us. The opening of the line in the 1860s meant that crowned heads could whisk in to winter in the Riviera in even greater numbers than before. Tsar Alexander III was on the train into Nice shortly after the rails reached the city. Napoleon III of France followed shortly. So did King Leopold of Belgium and, later, our own Victoria, in a carriage with Louis XVI furniture covered in blue silk. She travelled with an entourage of 60 and, so it is said, her own supplies of Irish stew.

We have ham sandwiches, but the views are essentially the same. They are the stuff of arias. You know the views I mean. You've seen the photographs or been there yourself. Rocks plunge straight to a sea spangled by light so clear that it must have come direct from the Creation. Here and there, they grant beaches and bays. For mile after mile, this seascape remains powerful, elegant and immense. It enters through the eyes and gladdens the whole being. The journey is, in short, coming right.

Then it goes wrong. Somewhere around Toulon, the SNCF halts the train for an hour, then two. 'Difficulties on the line,' we are told. In other words, the problem is that there's a problem. The carriage swells with mutterings and barking into mobile phones. The French demand perfection but anticipate anarchy, and are well-schooled in amplifying it. After two hours, nine minutes, the train starts moving, but backwards. 'Perfect,' the lady across the way screeches into a phone. 'We're going backwards!' Then we stop again. ('We've stopped again!') Wisely, no SNCF representative makes an appearance, for there is a sharp tang of Great Terror in the air. But then, on two hours, 23 minutes, we move forwards – and keep going. ('Here's a novelty – a train that's moving bloody forwards.' She must be talking to her husband. Anyone else would have hung up ages ago.)

And the thing is that the relief is commensurate with the previous anguish. This is something that trains do well – both locking you up in the Black Hole of Despair, and then releasing you back to the sunlit uplands. It is included in the price of the ticket. But you can see that it takes your mind off Caesar's Gallic campaigns, which you maybe should be considering as you cross this landscape.

Nevertheless, we are light-hearted as we roll across the Provençal plain, more so still when we hit the real Côte-d'Azur – surprised, as always, that names as famous as St Tropez, St Raphaël and Cannes appear on railway signs. The train scoots along, hemming the coast. No other travellers – whether they be in open-topped limos, helicopters or 300-foot yachts – have quite this constant, close-up experience of life-affirming splendour. Nor do they have the fun of being enshrouded in a tunnel and then bursting forth to another creek, another view across sea and mountains, another beach speckled with families. We flit through their lives as if flipping through holiday snaps. For miles, *The Girl With the Dragon Tattoo* lies unread on my lap.

We approach Nice. This involves the usual palaver of everyone standing up far too soon, either elbowing fellow passengers or clouting them on the head as suitcases are wrestled from the rack, then standing around for long tense minutes, cornered by one's luggage, before being hurled across the knees of the odd passenger who hasn't stood up as the train brakes with unexpected abruptness. As in Nice, so it is across the world. There's nothing to be done about it.

Nice station is heaving with people as disorientated as people always are in the grips of mass transport. We neither trust the transport providers to do what they say they are going to do, nor do we trust ourselves to understand what this might be. The result is low-level frenzy and a hefty cuff to the back of my legs from a break-away wheelie case.

For minutes, I hate everybody, but mostly the half-baked morons with push-chairs blocking the pavement. It's a long way from the station to the Promenade-des-Anglais with a case and a limp. You need to keep the momentum going. 'We should have taken a taxi,' my wife says. 'We should have taken a tank,' I cry, sweeping aside a mother and child. But then we burst out to the Bay of Angels. You have to be very grumpy indeed to keep grumpiness going here.

The bay opens up like, well, like what I expect to see on passing through the Pearly Gates: vast acreage of sea and sky, mountains behind, palms before and a suggestion of frisky sophistication in the palaces fronting the prom. Into one of which we are booked. It's a good one, too. The Palais de la Méditerranée has a fabulously ornate Art Deco-cum-classical façade soaring white above the sea-front. It went to the brink of demolition late last century after a picaresque episode involving a disputed succession, a murdered heiress and a Niçois former lawyer (now in jail). Glamour rendered all the more alluring by undercurrents of scandal: that's Nice in a nutshell.

The lobby – all marble, wood and light – is the size of a hamlet. The welcome has been well-learned. In the bedroom are a large platter of fruit and a note of greetings from the manager. I unpack a bottle of Scotch from my bag. (After too many muggings by mini-bar, I always take my own.) We settle on the balcony, overlooking the large terrace and pool directly below, the Promenade and sea just beyond.

'On a clear day, you can hear Russian billionaires from here,' I say. 'Perhaps,' she replied, 'but why is there a telephone in the loo?' It's a good question. We both struggle to imagine a phone call so urgent that it cannot wait until you have finished in the lavatory.

DAY 2

A brilliant morning starts with an early sprint to the flower market, a later bus-ride up to the Cézanne museum. This means we can tick one cultural box (two, if you count gladioli). But that's it. There is a train to catch. It is a friendly local item threading us along towards high-rise Monaco, which disappears abruptly. The line through the principality, and Monaco station itself, are wholly underground. We emerge to skim Roquebrune and Menton and, well, I mustn't go on about the views or we'll never get through, but there is a sense that, once you've arrived among these rocks, sea and sky, there's nowhere better to go. It's a sort of full stop to experience.

That's why so very many very rich people have ended up here. Their presence is not generally disruptive (though if you've sat next to big-spending Russians in a bar, you're entitled to disagree). Villas, gardens and generations of well-dressed, well-bred decadence enhance the lustre.

At Ventimiglia station, the lustre runs out. Though it's the entrance to Italy for thousands, the place has lost the will to live. Station buildings look shot at, the public toilets are filthily squat, the sandwiches proto-historic and the staff clearly filling in time between more important missions, conceivably for the UN. Except for the border guards, who are extremely focused – and have that Italian gift for looking terrific in uniforms that wouldn't disgrace a Venezuelan field-marshal. They patrol the platform as the train pulls in from France, looking for suspicious passengers from behind their shades. Naturally, they pick the only black chap aboard.

The onward train is as you would expect of such a station – a much-battered symphony of light blues and lighter blues, of internal doors that don't shut and windows that don't open. It is the sort of train you would put into a retirement home, if there were retirement homes for trains.

And it has the serial killer sitting opposite us. He rolls an unlit Marlboro around his mouth in Dodge City fashion. On the window above his head is scratched the word 'Amen'– the last gasp, my wife assumes, of a former victim, conceivably a clergyman. Thus it is not until the killer gets off, somewhere around Imperia, that I sit back and realise. Italy! The Italian Riviera! Then we enter a tunnel. That happens a lot in Liguria. The place is more tunnels than place. What with all those mountains, it has to be. Applause, then, for Italian civil engineering, but it does mean that, instead of looking out upon celebrated coast, sunny romance and flowers, we're entombed in a rock tube for many miles. The landscape scoots intermittently into view, as in a peep-show.

So Genoa comes as a relief, and not solely because it's above ground. After hours, days, of elemental beauty, it's kind of bracing to see the seaside grow suddenly productive and menacing. The pandemonium of the great port stretches endlessly to the right, a gigantic tangle of cranes and wasteland, of mountains of rusting metal, warehouses, containers and big boats promising much. The Lord only knows how anyone ever makes sense of it all.

The resultant city swirls into our carriage – through Genoa, the train becomes the local tram service – and out again, in a flurry of shopping bags and high-octane conversation. But it takes a full hour from one end of Genoa to the other, so I rejoin Lisbeth Salander. Southern Liguria slides past unnoticed. I'm still grappling with the Vanger family tree when the train expires in the middle of a field. As noted, our connection in La Spézia is now in terrible danger. And there seems a serious possibility that, having been on these uncomfortable, very light blue seats for upwards of five hours now, we might remain on them until the end of time.

We don't. The train eventually revives and we arrive in La Spézia with moments to spare. We dash. I knock old Italian ladies out of the way. My wife offers them apologies and, for all I know, compensation. We hurl ourselves onto the Pisa train. Then I hurl myself off it again, hare back down the underpass and sprint to the platform entrance. I have neglected to validate the tickets in those machines that continentals place precisely so as to maximise the panic of the forgetful.

Why do they do this to me? What possible purpose can such validation serve? The ticket is already dated and timed. In the train, the guard will come round and clip it. The potential for some rogue passenger to return from Pisa to La Spézia and surreptitiously use the same ticket for a second La Spézia-Pisa journey is nil. Obliging the passenger to validate the ticket cannot reduce it further, for there is nothing lower than nil. The only conclusion must be that the practice indulges a public service's taste for pointless bossiness. Plus, of course, it affords railway staff a little light entertainment as a sweating foreign imbecile legs it along the platform and leaps for the train as the whistle blows.

Still and all, a dash of desperation, once overcome, is no bad thing. We enter the Tuscan plain in heightened spirits. The hills shimmer off to the left. The sea is mainly out of view to the right as we skirt the untended backs of Carrara and Viareggio. But it *is* Carrara – the place where Michelangelo came for his marble before whacking it into David shape. Carrara marble is the marble of the Pantheon, Trajan's column and our own Marble Arch. It's said to be the best in the world – and, glory be, here are masons' yards right by the track absolutely full of it. It's stacked up, or packed in crates, as if it were as common as breeze-blocks.

I scrutinise closely – or as closely as a faster train will permit – some fellows walking round one of the yards. I've read that Carrara in general, and the marble workers in particular, have a traditional taste for anarchism. The International of Anarchist Federations was apparently set up in the town in 1968. But the fellows look calm enough and the surrounds are as tidy as any others outside Italian towns – which isn't very, but doesn't quite qualify as anarchy.

So to Pisa, where friends holidaying in the area have come to meet us. I cannot tell you how wonderful it is to see friendly faces amid the madding scrum of a foreign station. It turns arrival into a proper event rather than simply a journey's end.

We dump the bags and skitter across town to the Field of Miracles. We've never been before. I am pumped up to the max. The monuments apparently shut at 8 p.m. It's now around 7.25, which should allow enough time, if not to climb the leaning tower, then at least to scan the cathedral interior, and Pisano's pulpit, which is what I'm really excited about.

I career into the ticket office. The guy is smiling. 'We are closed,' he says. 'The ticket office closes at 7.30.' By my watch, it is 7.28. By his, it is 7.31. His wins. 'You're not going to fail me for one minute. I have travelled from England specially,' I lie.

'Signor, much people has travelled from England for centuries. They arrive on time. Return tomorrow morning.' He smiles again and brings down the little shutter.

We can't return tomorrow morning. We have a train to catch. I exit the office minded to kick someone. The fat bloke taking a picture of his fatter wife pretending to hold up the tower seems an ideal candidate.

This is deemed unproductive by my wife when I rejoin our little group. She's right. We are among the greatest collection of medieval buildings in Italy. OK, we can't go in, but that's no reason to take it out on the obese. We should appreciate what we have. The tower, for a start. As advertised, it leans.

But then it occurs that the campanile, with its layers of 190 marble and granite columns, is also an item of considerable beauty. And – I may be going out on a limb here – it might still be beautiful even if it were straight. The fact of toppling has perhaps obscured the loveliness of the conception. Mussolini agreed. He wanted the tower straightened. I'm not sure he was entirely wrong, not about towers, anyway.

Across the way, the cathedral is more magnificent still. As very often before, I wonder how the Middle Ages – otherwise so brutal and disgusting – could have bequeathed majesty that still uplifts 900 years on. And then there's the Baptistry and the Campo Santo and it's perhaps as well we couldn't get inside them, or I'd be rabid. It also leaves a little extra money for aperitivos.

DAY 3

The carriage from Pisa to Rome is colonised by two unrelated groups of American women. At the back, a middle-aged bunch considers this an appropriate time for a hoedown. They sprawl, hoot and holler; they pass bottles of Coke back and forth, and snack unremittingly. Italian passengers eye them with puzzlement. There is much about the etiquette of continental European railway travel that these ladies have yet to grasp. Apart from anything else, 24/7 snacking just doesn't happen on trains in southern Europe.

Nearer to us, a much younger US group – college girls, perhaps – are smartly dressed, pretty and hold themselves well. They discuss their progress in the learning of Italian, they fill in journals and then two of them, at a guess around 20 years old, take out embroidery and start sewing. 'Where do you find girls like that these days?' I whisper to my wife. 'I don't know,' she replies, 'but I wish they'd go and give lessons to their elders.'

The excitement of arriving in the Italian capital is always tempered by the need to scramble through initial mayhem. As we make from mainline to metro station, it is as if, 1,600 years on, Alaric and his Visigoths have lately revisited Rome. Tunnels and stairways have evidently been recently sacked. They are long, scruffy, dark, menacing and set about with works, and signs doubling us back where we've just come from. Finally, though, we are released into the light near the Spanish Steps. We walk along the Via Condotti and, like notable English-speakers before us – Byron, Hemingway, Prince Philip – sheer off down a tiny street for the Hotel d'Inghilterra.

'Just once, I'd like to stay in a posh European hotel where Hemingway hadn't been,' I say. My wife isn't listening. She's smiling at the concierge and he's smiling back. Though (or perhaps 'because') owned by a university professor, the Inghilterra comes on like a gentleman's club run by contemporary Italian nobility. The public anonymity of the railway service is replaced by the warmest possible concern for our welfare. Nothing is ruffled. This is one of the great pleasures of mixing with the moneyed.

So, for two full days, we have Rome before us. We are ready. Our aesthetic sensibilities are both battered and buffed. We start with a bottle of prosecco in the bedroom.

SLOW TRAIN TO THE EDGE OF EUROPE

ELIZABETH GRICE ENJOYS IDLING THROUGH THE LUSH, GREEN SCENERY OF CANTABRIA – BUT FINDS THE GYMNASTICS AT BEDTIME A CHALLENGE

The serpent can swallow its tail, and I start at the end of my journey because the final flourish, Santiago de Compostela, is somebody else's beginning. We've left the train behind after five days of pootling and whistling through northern Spain and now our boastful coach is inching its way down a side street towards the cathedral square like a foot trying to get into the wrong-sized shoe.

Pilgrims are funnelling down to join the Saturday festival, pressing against our flanks, claiming priority. Across the mouth of the road, a procession of multi-coloured silk banners, tassels nodding, pours into the square, and the bearers take up positions on three sides. The driver gives up. We climb down into the melee.

'It's nice the square is full,' a Spanish member of our group says, 'but eez a mess.' It is to become a lot messier as the day wears on and St James's Cathedral, tufted with lichens, fills up over and over again for pilgrims' services. The city is fit to burst. Prayerful beggars squat at the foot of the baroque pillars. As Chaucer knew well, religious feasts are good for business. We watch cheeses being rolled through the open market on small trolleys and fish-sellers slapping their produce into submission. Girls in traditional costume are offering trays of tiny cakes to passers-by, a stream of pilgrims in capes, hats and hiking boots. The hollow tap-tap of stick on cobbles is the sound of Santiago as much as the scallop shell is its visual symbol.

It looks as if it could be hours before we can get inside the cathedral, so we retreat to a quiet street café outside the Facultade de Geografia Historia for a glass of Nero d'Avola to help us take stock. Five days earlier, we had joined El Transcantábrico at Santander, on the third day of its week-long journey from León to Santiago, a distance of about 400 miles with abundant stops and detours. We had slept in railway sidings, woken to the sound of a school bell and a new place each morning, and yattered through a Spain we didn't know existed. Along the way, the train's maroon-liveried coach took us for excursions and increasingly calorific meals.

It was a moment to congratulate ourselves on still being on speaking terms. No one tells you that the polished wood cabin where you sleep and shower seems to have been been fitted out by a Sylvanian Families' interior designer and you will need to be in a strong relationship to survive.

El Transcantábrico is billed as a five-star 'cruise on rails'. There was indeed a pleasant whiff of exclusivity each time we passed through a separate gate onto the platform where the train was waiting. Staff in uniform stood in line to see us off when we crossed the tracks into town for an excursion and they were there again when we returned, looking as if they might break out into a salute at any moment. Once, I caught sight of someone wiping the brass handles of the doors just before we embarked.

On some stretches, men leaned on their forks to watch us pass. We idled through people's backyards and farmsteads, examining their washing and their husbandry. Five days of sedate travelling took us through the green bucolic landscape of Cantábrica to the mountains of Asturias and the wild inlets of Galicia. A cyclist could have kept up.

The inspiration for this laid-back tour of 'Green Spain' was a thundering monster known as the Hullero, or coal train, that used to transport coal from the city of León to the iron and steelworks of Bilbao. In 1980, the writer Juan Pedro Aparicio travelled rough on the Hullero, sharing the cooking pots and the stories of the men who drove and rode in her. His romantic account of that journey, *The Transcantabrican*, started a movement to save the line.

He was struck by how the wily British and French had turned their narrow-gauge railways into popular attractions. 'If Spain were a less uncouth place,' he wrote, 'the route . . . would be one of the most important tourist attractions in the country; the Hullero would be one of Spain's major tourist trains. In this valley [the Mena] you will find archaeological remains, historical relics, unique landscapes, vistas only possible from the Hullero, places that are integral to this country's origins, and which have remained exactly as they were more than a thousand years ago.'

Aparicio is an entertaining companion on the way to Santiago, but his journey is not ours. There are few points of contact between the Hullero's urgent route and the much longer, coast-hugging one we are taking through Arriondas, Gijón, Oviedo, Luarca, Ribadeo and Viveiro. We travel lazily, resting up in a siding overnight and starting to roll again just before breakfast. Our schedule allows us to break away from the train, explore a town or a cave, eat a four- or five-course meal and saunter back for another burst of cow-gazing before the train pulls in for the night. Unlike the Hullero, we don't have a mission. We don't have coal.

What we do have is an odd assortment of 46 mainly middle-aged passengers. Most are Spanish, six are Mexican and of the four other couples, one is German-speaking Swiss, one French, one Australian and one English. Our guide is busy in four languages. By the time we join the group at Santander, allegiances have been formed.

One of the peculiarities of the Transcantabrian journey is that we appear to be travelling as many coach miles as railway miles. So it's bye-bye Santander in the morning; hello Llanes in the afternoon. In between, the coach trundles us inland to see the teeming cave paintings at Altamira – prehistoric bison, deer and horses that were discovered in 1879 by a man and his daughter when they were out walking.

It's known as 'the Sistine chapel of Palaeolithic times' because the artists probably lay on their backs as they worked. There is a waiting list of five years for restricted access to the original cave a little way up the hill. We don't have the time. Yet we don't feel short-changed. Human breath was destroying the paintings. How can we argue for direct emotional engagement with the originals when the cavalcade of animals is rendered so magnificently in a stone replica of the cave and its paintings, here in the Museo de Altamira?

The nearby Santillana del Mar sounds like a seaside town but it is a long way from the sea. They call it the town of three lies because it is neither holy nor flat – and there's no sea. Founded on monastic wealth and landowner rivalry, it's such a jumble of styles that it looks as if it was created to illustrate a mediaeval architectural primer. Sartre called it 'the most beautiful village in Spain'. The result is that it's certainly one of the most visited: a pretty mishmash of coats of arms, belltowers, balconies, herringboned redbrick houses and a baroque town hall.

While our group crocodiled off into the distance, we slipped into a cobbled courtyard for a *vino branco* in the sunshine. From here, we could admire Santillana's other oddities – the statue of a bison in the market square and hanging carnations that grow into a ball, without soil, apparently thriving on thin air. The biggest flower balls, begun as a single dangling cutting, had taken 20 years to reach the size of a football.

Back on the train, we headed for Covadonga and the tumbling white-grey peaks of the Picos de Europa. The beauty of this kind of lordly locomotion is that it allows you to flick through the living brochure of a whole swathe of northern Spain: that place you could cheerfully pass over; this one you'll return to another day.

Covadonga is where the Christian reconquest of the peninsula supposedly began. From the pinky, limestone walls of its great basilica, we see people snaking down to a small cave in the valley below. Our group is urged not to miss this focus of devotion: King Pelayo, the Asturian leader, is buried at the scene of his victory in AD 718, or so they say. His sarcophagus is kept in a niche in a small chapel by a waterfall. But the sun is on our backs. With limited time to wander, why trail down to the grotto when we can see it, all mystery preserved, from the ramparts of the basilica?

Perverse little stands for independence give spice to the day. We'll see the church instead of the cave. We'll fork left when the others fork right. We won't join the group tonight for the second five-course meal of the day. But once in the majestic Asturian Picos, we are happy to adopt the group mentality. The coach hairpins up through the wilds of the national park, coming to a satisfied stop by a lake where biscuit-coloured cows nuzzle their calves and more cows graze the skyline where mountain goats should be.

We stop for *chorizos a la sidra*, cider-cooked sausage, and sheep's cheese at a jolly rustic *sidreria*. Serrano ham and roasted tomatoes arrive on a baguette. Cider is being poured into a glass from a great height, like a circus trick, while the waiter affects to look elsewhere. It has to be drunk quickly while still oxygenated and cloudy.

As we subside into an afternoon haze, someone mentions that there are about 170 bears left in Asturias – not a comfortable statistic when you are lunching al fresco within sight of the forest. Numbers are rising thanks to the work of two preservation trusts set up in 1992 to protect the bear population – but hunting lore is still a vivid folk memory. One of our group, a Spaniard, is telling fellow drinkers that a bear cannot use its paws to clasp its prey. 'It puts its forepaws up and the hunter slashes it in the chest with a small blade,' he says, jabbing an imaginary knife. 'He wears a metal plate on his forearm for protection – that is all he needs – and he slashes again and again in the same place.'

While breakfast is being served in Gijón the next morning, the train starts to pull out towards Oviedo, capital of Asturias. Every now and then, we catch sight of its bullet nose and centipedal body as it takes a bend. Two great churches demand our attention here: Santa Iglesia Catedral de Oviedo, with its Holy Chamber of relics, and St Julian de los Prados, where a twelfth-century crucifix hangs free, suspended from the centre of the transept. Christ wears a golden crown, not thorns, and among all the geometric patterns and pastoral frescoes there is not a single depiction of a human being. The cathedral's silver ark contains relics almost too insalubrious to name, including a piece of the true cross, bread from the Last Supper, some of Christ's 'nappies' (let's hope a mistranslation) and milk from the Virgin Mary.

Will we have the stomach for lunch? Somehow, despite the occasional mutterings ('I'm a big eater, but we're eating way too much'), we always do. The meals are lavish. In El Raitán restaurant in Oviedo, waitresses in Asturian costume glide over the stone floors with armfuls of local dishes – crab soup, fried egg and spicy minced sausage on corncake; butter beans in tomato and oil; bacon, black sausage, pork and chorizo; cinnamon rice pudding and cherry liqueur. Our Swiss table-companion, Sylvie, carries a large tube of mayonnaise in her handbag for those moments when the local flavours are a little too robust.

The train shakes it all down on the way to Luarca through the sleepy late afternoon. 'We are eating too much food,' someone says, 'but it's all right, it's OK.' The Swiss couple, the only seasoned

Transcantabricans on the trip, seem to be having a domestic at the hilltop cemetery where we have stopped to look down on the fishing village. Fishing boats are streaming into the harbour at dusk, one after another like planes coming in to land, their pilots calling out to one another. Kurt and Sylvie march down the hill, some distance apart. Next time we see them they are sitting companionably outside a small café, watching the sea while the coach sweeps the rest of us to a restaurant beyond the town. They wave. We wave back. Another small victory for independence.

'Have you ever been camping?' Sylvie wanted to know at our first dinner. We must have sounded tentative. 'Well', she replied. 'I don't think you'll be doing this again.' So why did they? They'd done Santiago to León; now they said they wanted to experience the journey in reverse. An endorsement, then, from which we were mysteriously excluded.

At this point, we were still captivated by the microcosmic ingenuity of our quarters. All those tiny shelves and cupboards. The craftily backward-tilting overhead bookshelf. The shower cubicle like a transparent cigar tube. Floral china knobs on the washroom cabinets. What charm.

The operational challenges didn't become clear until it was time for bed. We had to take turns dressing and undressing in the narrow channel beside the double bed. Getting up in the night was best not attempted by the person sleeping trapped against the wall. Some couples said they had tried sleeping top-and-tail to make best use of the space. There was a technique for negotiating the narrow corridors of the moving train without becoming black and blue and by day two we had got the hang of it. I would like to be able to say I mastered the art of putting on mascara at 30 miles an hour, but the photos suggest otherwise.

At night, dramatic whooshing and sluicing sounds rumbled through the carriages. Light sleepers, we often found ourselves peering blearily at deserted stations and sleeping towns as the bathroom symphony played on. We kept on even terms, despite the challenge of our diddy cabin.

The school bell goes at 8 a.m. on our last full day on the Transcantábrico. A station mistress in a red cap waves her flag and toot-

toots us off to Ribadeo. Birdsong trickles in and out of the open windows as we roll along. 'Too many tunnels!' I scribble on the breakfast menu. We drift around the old centre of Ribadeo with its ornate turn-of-the-twentieth-century houses, but not for very long. A seafood lunch is calling. On the final burst by train, to the pleasant, hilly little town of Viviero, we relax into the delightful passivity of locomotion through sunlit countryside. A Mexican gynaecologist is making jokes of a professional nature that we don't quite understand. The staff are getting the public carriages ready for a knees-up later in the evening.

We could perhaps have done without the final Butlins-style party, culminating in a competition to find Mr and Miss Transcantábrico, the Nicest Person on the trip and the Sexiest Person. As the Spaniards turn the carriage into a dancing frenzy, we slip away to pack. Next morning, we are woken at 6.45 by the movement of the train as it dips and climbs towards Ferrol, our destination. There, in the drizzle, the coach is waiting to take us to Santiago de Compostela.

Of the many fine sights Santiago has to offer, the most wonderful was a king-sized double bed.

STITCHING THE BALKANS BACK TOGETHER

ADRIAN BRIDGE TRAVELS FROM SARAJEVO TO BELGRADE, ON A TRAIN THAT IS ABOUT MOVING ON IN MORE WAYS THAN ONE

I was thinking of Jasmina as I boarded the 11.35 Sarajevo-to-Belgrade express. That laugh! You could hear it a mile off: a loud cackle that developed into an ear-splitting affirmation of all that is fun in life and which always brought a smile to the faces of even the most hardened of us in the offices of the *Daily Telegraph*. Jasmina – a member of our design team – learnt to laugh like that growing up in Sarajevo, an unbelievably beautiful city surrounded by green hills and lush pastures and replete with the richness (and sadness) of Balkan history. When she lived there in the Seventies and Eighties, Sarajevo was a melting pot of Muslims, Serbs and Croats, and there was a genuine sense of community (like many, she was the product of a mixed marriage).

She recalls it as a time of happiness: under the stewardship of Josip Tito, Yugoslavia had worked as a unified state and enjoyed a unique position somewhere between the feuding capitalist and communist worlds. It was a time of wellbeing – Yugoslavia may not have been the wealthiest country in the world but its people did not starve and they enjoyed far greater freedoms than those in neighbouring East European states. It was also a time of hope, symbolised by Sarajevo's successful staging of the 1984 Winter Olympics (remembered with particular fondness by the British for the performances of Torvill and Dean). The people of Sarajevo knew there was something special about their city and they treasured it. But that was before the war . . .

DEPARTURE FROM SARAJEVO

While most visitors to Sarajevo rightly marvel at the wonderful juxtaposition of Ottoman and Austro-Hungarian architecture in its centre, there can be no denying that the city has its fair share of socialist-era eyesores. A good example is the main railway station – a concrete monstrosity that hardly evokes the romance of travel. And yet there was something romantic – or at least uplifting – about arriving to board and sampling a service that for more than 18 years had been defunct.

When Jasmina was a girl, this particular route (known then as the 'Olympic' Express) was one of the most popular in the country. City-weary Belgraders would ride it to enjoy the exotic café-style culture of Sarajevo (and the ski slopes nearby), while those going the other way would head for the bright lights and shops of the big city or to visit family and friends in Croatia and Serbia. In those days there were 15 carriages and there was frequently a party atmosphere on board. 'The train used to be packed; often someone would be playing guitar,' Jasmina recalled. 'We were Bosnians, Serbians and Croats on board, but the atmosphere was great. When I was growing up this felt like the perfect country; but then the fanatics drove us apart. I lost the best years of my life.' In 1995, aged 18, Jasmina left to seek asylum in London – just one of the thousands who fled.

After all the years of disuse (several bridges were blown up), the railway link between Sarajevo and Belgrade reopened late last year. There was no great fanfare – as tomorrow's election in Bosnia will no doubt show, political divisions remain intense – but it was hailed by some as evidence that the wounds were at last beginning to heal; that the peoples of the former Yugoslavia were getting their lives back on track.

There is no denying that trains do enable us to move on. As we pulled out of Sarajevo station, I noted that two railway staff in peaked caps and uniform saluted, grateful perhaps for the restoration of some semblance of normality. I noted, too, that the waiter in the buffet car had thick bushy sideburns reminiscent of those once sported by the last Habsburg emperor, Franz-Josef.

My immediate neighbours were two backpackers (one Scottish, one Irish) animatedly comparing notes on journeys to the more remote parts of the Balkans. In the carriages farther along (there were only three in total) were families, young men on their own, older couples. I couldn't tell whether they were Bosnian, Croat or Serb – but I was sure they would all have their own tales to tell.

Within minutes we were passing the distinctive yellow exterior of the Sarajevo Holiday Inn, the place of refuge for journalists covering the siege between 1992 and 1995. I thought of Martin Bell, the BBC correspondent in the city for much of that time, who, despite being shot there, has become one of Sarajevo's staunchest advocates.

The mosques and minarets of the city already seemed a distant memory as we passed through the drab housing estates and industrial sites that mar the outskirts, before crossing the line that for three years delineated the position of the Serb forces encircling the city. Soon the ugly apartment blocks had been replaced by green fields in which women toiled by hand. It was an image that had a timeless quality about it – such scenes were no doubt common before the war; they were no doubt common before the Great War (famously triggered by the shooting in Sarajevo of the Austrian Archduke Franz Ferdinand). And then we were into the beautiful hills and mountains of Bosnia-Herzegovina.

ELVIR'S STORY

The train journey from Sarajevo to Belgrade may have huge symbolic significance but, scenically, it cannot rank among the all-time greats. Even in this part of the world there are stronger contenders (Sarajevo to Mostar; Belgrade to Montenegro). With its utilitarian green carriages and electric locomotives, the train itself, unlike its illustrious predecessor, is also no beauty. That said, the early part of the ride, against a backdrop of mountains, fields and forests, is undeniably a feast for the eyes.

I left my backpacker friends discussing the relative merits of Skopje and Tirana ('There's a great little B&B there where you can do all your laundry') and wandered down the train to seek out a better vantage point. At an open corridor window I started chatting to Elvir, a 23-year-old Bosnian Muslim (Bosniak) with a cheery face and a welcoming smile. He had not been on a train journey in this part of the world since he had fled the country as a boy, heading north to Slovenia and on to Italy and then Germany. The emotion was palpable. 'Isn't this a beautiful country?' he said as we passed more rolling hills and fields full of haystacks.

Elvir's father had been killed in the war; the boy had escaped with his mother, who came from Srebrenica (site of a notorious massacre). For all the horrors of the war, Elvir had missed his homeland during the years in Germany. When he returned he found the map had been redrawn and his bit of the country (a village near Modrica) had become part of the would-be breakaway 'Serb Republic' within Bosnia-Herzegovina.

Wasn't it difficult being a Muslim in a Serb stronghold? 'Not always. How can you tell whether someone is Muslim or Serb? We all speak the same language!'

As we passed forests where signs gave warning of the continuing danger of mines, Elvir said he struggled to eke a living out of milking cows ('I get only 25 cents [10p] for a litre of milk') and that the holiday he had just had (visiting an aunt with an apartment in Dubrovnik) was his first since returning. He refused to be downbeat. At one of the numerous station stops, he eyed the passengers getting on and off before fixing on an attractive brunette. 'Ah, Bosnian girls . . . they are the prettiest in the world!'

DJURO'S STORY

In the old days, the journey between Sarajevo and Belgrade was a domestic one and took six hours; now it involves crossing two international borders (Bosnia/Croatia and Croatia/Serbia) – and a brief stretch in the 'Serb Republic' of Bosnia. It takes nine hours. At Doboj station, three hours into the trip, we entered the Serb-controlled part of Bosnia and waited as the locomotive was changed.

By now I had made my way to the buffet car where, alongside the man with the bushy sideburns, I ran into Djuro, the buffet car manager and a fluent English speaker. Djuro had sad eyes, a slender figure and a kindly demeanour. He brushed aside my request for a salad and said that, with six hours to go until we reached Belgrade, goulash was in order.

Although it came from a cardboard packet, it was surprisingly tasty. As I ate, he told me his story: of how before the war he had run a successful restaurant on the Croatian coast and that when hostilities broke out he didn't know which side he was supposed to be on (although Serb himself, he had a Croatian daughter through marriage) ('I was told to go back to Serbia'); of how when he was growing up it had never mattered to him whether someone was Serb, Croat or Bosniak ('It still doesn't matter; people are good or bad and that is it'); of how, although people liked to blame the Americans for everything, 'we all know we made a big mistake'.

The scenery had become flatter, less diverting. There were many more bullet-scarred and derelict houses. We passed cornfields that had recently been flooded. 'We have natural catastrophes every 15 years and wars every 50,' Djuro remarked. Where there had been the occasional minaret, there were now the bulbous forms of Orthodox churches. Not for long, though. On crossing into Croatia (and being scrutinised by its somewhat severe border guards) we moved briefly into Roman Catholic territory and another form of ecclesiastical/architectural demarcation. Here, too, the land was flat, betraying few secrets of what so recently had transpired.

Back among the backpackers, the talk had moved on to why one should spend time on extended trips such as this. For the Scottish lad it was the last chance before taking up a position with a law firm: 'When asked what did you do this summer, it would be nice to say I went to a folk festival in Macedonia.' For the Irish lass, it had all come about due to her going through a 'mid-twenties crisis' (oh, for one of those!). She had seen many wonderful things and places; she was thinking of taking the train from Varna to Istanbul. She had snogged a younger Dutch man. She had also loved Sarajevo. 'I grew up with images of the city as a burnt-out shell and was amazed to see how modern it is. I also couldn't believe those Muslim girls with their eyeliner and fashionable matching headscarves.' Both were looking forward to Belgrade, a place where, word had it, there was a 'neat buzz'.

NATASA'S STORY

Natasa, too, revealed herself to be a huge fan of Sarajevo, although it had been years since she last visited. A striking blonde woman with green eyes and a passion for biology, she had boarded the train at Sid where, seven hours into the journey, we had finally entered Serbia proper – or rather Vojvodina (another name with resonance, another complication: Vojvodina is a large region in the north of Serbia that has considerable autonomy . . . though not as much as Kosovo in the south). The train had been barely a quarter full, but the arrival of a few more passengers for the final leg into Belgrade gave it a busier feel.

'With all my heart I want to go to Sarajevo,' Natasa said. 'It was such a beautiful place before; there were always so many people of different religions.' She still didn't feel the time was quite right for her (very clearly a Serb) to return to Sarajevo. But she did feel that the fact that one could now get there again by train was a very positive one. 'We have been held back 20 years, but I think we will be together again,' she said, displaying more optimism than most. 'There are many of us who still have friends from each of the former republics. I think one day it will be like the war never happened. We are not aggressive; we are normal like you.'

As the sun set over the cornfields and plains of Vojvodina, Natasa waxed lyrical about her homeland. Sid, of course, was the best place in the world. Then there was Novi Sad –'too beautiful'. She was excited at the prospect of the cafés of the Terazije in Belgrade the next day . . .

ARRIVAL IN BELGRADE

As I was subsequently to discover, Belgrade certainly does have its attractions (not least the lovely fortress and park of Kalemegdanska). But I wouldn't say that the concrete blocks that line the route to the city's main station are among them. By then, however, it no longer mattered: for those of us who had started this journey that morning in Sarajevo, there was a definite sense of elation at having finished it where the Danube meets the Sava.

The train ride had provided a series of moving snapshots – of the region's geography and history; of its cultural and ethnic complexity; of the haunting legacy of the terrible years of civil war; of its hopes. Beyond the physical territory covered, through the stories of the characters on board, it had been a journey that had reached into all six republics of the former Yugoslavia – Serbia, Croatia, Bosnia, Montenegro, Macedonia and Slovenia – and had provided a real sense of the scale of the human dramas and tragedies that had unfolded (and continue to unfold) in this part of the world. The Yugoslavia of Jasmina's youth will never return (now 33 and settled in London, nor will she). But while the wounds of war still run deep, there are encouraging signs of a desire to build anew.

As the train pulled in, Djuro made a final inspection of the by-now spotless buffet car. He looked happy to be home. 'Yes, I lost a lot in the war; I used to be a rich man and now I work on the railways,' he said. 'But at least I am alive. I have a lovely wife and a five-year-old daughter. I am a lucky man.'

SURREAL TRIP TO THE WRONG COUNTRY

'Wake up to a new skyline' is the slogan of the Ellipsos train hotel, a joint venture of French and Spanish railway companies. Passengers travelling from Barcelona to Milan certainly did, but it wasn't the one they were expecting: they ended up nearly 200 miles away from their destination, in Zurich.

Two Ellipsos trains left Barcelona on Sunday night, one bound for Zurich, the other for Milan. They travelled coupled together to Lyon, where, in the early hours, railway staff were to split them and send them on their separate ways. The 135 passengers on the Salvador Dalí, which does the thrice-weekly run from Barcelona to Milan, were sent towards Zurich. Meanwhile, the 105 people on board the Pau Casals, bound for Zurich, were sent towards Milan. Staff on the latter realised the mistake at the Italian border and the train was sent back, finally arriving at its destination three hours late. But the Salvador Dalí went all the way to Zurich before the error was spotted.

'Signallers made a mistake during the points switch in Lyon,' a source at Renfe, the Spanish company, said. 'The drivers of the two locomotives went the right way, but they left Lyon with the wrong set of carriages. It must have been a bit of a shock for the people expecting to wake up in Italy. They were put on another train to Milan when they got to Zurich, and apologies have been made.'

PEAK PERFORMERS

A TRIP ON THE BERGEN LINE, THE HIGHEST MAINLINE
RAILWAY IN NORTHERN EUROPE, LEAVES
JOLYON ATTWOOLL FULL OF ADMIRATION FOR
NORWAY'S RAILWAY ENGINEERS – AND ITS HIKERS

They were a curious trio, the men awaiting the 17.30 to Oslo. I noticed the most garrulous first, sprawled over the armchair facing me. Clad in shorts and hiking shoes, he had his left leg flung over the armrest in a pose that might have been struck by Kevin the Teenager, the Harry Enfield character. In the same cluster of chairs, his friend was noticeably more upright; a lean, high-cheeked man whose bearing you might have called noble in a different era – were it not for a large plaster that covered a nasty gash on his upper right arm. The third member of their party was more elusive, choosing to shuffle around the lobby of the venerable station hotel rather than perspire in the sunlight that trapped the one remaining seat, his white hair bobbing into view at irregular intervals.

'It is my fault we must catch the train,' the 'teenager' told me, abruptly. 'We should continue hiking tomorrow, but now we must go home because I have hurt my back.' He acknowledged his unusual posture with a gesture. 'And I am the baby of the group, too,' he chuckled.

A decade separated him from his companions, it transpired, but his youth was relative – they turned out to be 80 and 81. Both were former employees of the Norwegian state railway – a station master, and an administrator – and lifelong walkers, who had agreed to let their younger friend, a less experienced hiker, join their annual trip to the mountains. A fall had sliced the upper arm of the dignified 80 year-old, but it hadn't hampered their progress. This was their third day on the trails and they had just hiked a dozen miles over a mountain pass to

Finse, the road-free hamlet at the pinnacle (at 1,222 metres, or 4,009 feet) of the Bergen Line, the highest mainline railway in northern Europe.

Their gamble on youth, however, had backfired. The 'baby' of their party was convinced that two plunges into glacial streams en route had put his back out – although he had no regrets: 'You feel like you rule the world when you come out of the water.' So they whiled away a long wait for their train home, cheerfully engaging complete strangers in conversation in a foreign language. We would have lingered, were it not for a sharpening guilt at our own inactivity in the presence of these elderly adventurers.

'Spend lots of money – you must help pay for our pensions,' the group's youngest member shouted as we left the hotel to cross the railway tracks and hike part of the trail they had just descended. When we returned they were gone, having caught the train down the mountain while we eased our consciences roaming the expansive, stark beauty of the plateau above.

Life is like that at Finse: it ebbs and flows to the rhythm of the railway. I imagine it has always been that way. The settlement was founded more than a century ago as a base for railway construction workers building a crucial high-altitude link between Oslo and Bergen, Norway's two main cities. More than 30 years separated its inception and completion, with the railway finally opening to much fanfare in 1909. Today, the latest train arrivals and departures are announced in the station hotel – and, tellingly, the only permanent resident of 'Finse City', as locals jokingly refer to it, is the station master.

Our own journey there began more than 150 miles southeast, and three quarters of a mile down, on the 10.39 from Oslo. We were drawn to travel to the rugged, mountainous interior on a railway journey billed by Norway's tourist board as 'the world's best train ride'. That ours was a carriage of sightseers was apparent even before we left the platform. A French mother and son argued about who had the tickets as we approached our seats toward the front of the train, while a young woman posed by the electric locomotive (adapted from Swiss engines used for similar, high-altitude, twisting sections of track) as her companion took photographs.

As we pulled out of the station, a sense of quiet anticipation settled upon the carriage, despite the spoilsport clouds over the Norwegian capital. The train stuttered along the busier urban tracks, hesitating its way beyond the giant Holmenkollen ski jump towering over central Oslo, before threading between the bright clapboard houses of suburbia. Our ears popped as we gathered momentum and altitude and the city outskirts opened into fields of wheat, and lily-strewn ponds, one with a delightful wooden swimming platform.

Long, uninterrupted rows of pine occasionally blocked the window-seat panorama, leaving us to speculate idly about fellow passengers. There were the newly wedded teenage Americans in front, the mother of the bride in tow somewhere behind; lots of outdoor types; the now calm French mother and son; and rows of amateur photographers poised. The man sitting in the opposite aisle – ruddy-cheeked, in his mid to late sixties – was somehow different, we decided, after spotting him eating smørbrød (Scandinavian open sandwiches).

As the train climbed, the first of the great fjords opened up on the Hallingdal River side to the west, and the photographers swooped on empty seats for a better vantage point. I did, too, trying to do justice to the monochrome grey and green of sky and foliage mirrored in the fjord's still waters with a smartphone camera lens. In between snapshots, I heard deep breathing, alerting me that not everyone was so captivated by the scene – our smørbrød-eating neighbour was asleep. That confirmed it for us – he was an old hand, a native.

When we adjourned to the train cafe, we passed through other similarly composed carriages. Guidebooks to Norvège, Noruega and Norway nestled on laps, amid unfolded walking maps and brochures from Hurtigruten, the cruise company. Taking our seats, we wondered what slice of Norwegian life we might encounter. At the next table a woman called towards a man at the counter: 'Dick, can you get me a napkin?'

More Norwegian was the *lefse*, the delicious cinnamon-sprinkled flatbread we nibbled while supping an instant coffee. We eavesdropped as the passengers behind debated the merits of the slogan of the beer they were sipping ('Well, they do only say probably'), while the alpine scene filled the larger dining car windows. Beyond the winter resort of Geilo, where the railway is at its steepest, the pines and birch began to stunt, then thin out. Soon they disappeared, replaced by the scrub, moss and rocks of the high mountain plains. The biggest stir in our carriage came on the approach to Finse. As we rounded a curve in the track, there was a hushed gasp as the Hardangerjøkulen glacier came into view, its fingers of pale blue ice stretching down the mountains.

During our hiatus in Finse, we often saw that moment replicated from the outside looking in – on the station platform, or the rail-side path – as incoming passengers stared over our heads, their gaze fixed on the glacial middle distance. People have reacted that way for at least a century. Captain Robert Scott was also struck by its rawness and used the location as a final training base before his ill-fated expedition to the Antarctic. Hollywood too; the glacier doubled as the Ice Planet Hoth in *The Empire Strikes Back*. The shoot was in the winter of 1979, Harrison Ford arriving in a blizzard on a snow-plough train.

The elements were kinder to us on our departure – but only just, as driving rain forced us to huddle under the hotel portico as we waited. On leaving, the train entered a tunnel hewn through the mountain west of Finse in the 1990s. This lowered the Bergen Line's pinnacle by more than 100 metres, reducing its vulnerability to snow drifts (the Rallarvegen, a wonderful, if demanding, bike route, climbs the old rail-worker road to the former summit, before descending to the west). When we re-emerged, snow sheds punctuated the view, another reminder of the railway's annual battle with winter.

The scenery opened up, flitting from rapids to aquamarine water-falls, improbably steep forest banks with dark green pine branches stacked neatly amid chaotic birches, sheer gorges, then fjords. In between our hushed whispers of admiration, the conductor, a short cheerful man with glasses, brought welcome news for our arrival in Bergen: 'They said it would be good weather. We'll cross our fingers.'

The train wound its way down past the adventure-tourism town of Voss. Freshly evaporated wisps of cloud were snagging amid the pine as it skirted another exhilarating run of rapids. As we drew near to Bergen, the outlook on to the lower fjords was frequently swapped for the tunnels chiselled through the peaks rising eastwards of the port city. There is little getting away from tunnels in Norway; the Lærdal on the route from Oslo to Bergen is the world's longest road tunnel, and this sequence, which was forged in the 1960s to shorten the Bergen

Line's journey time, is just one among many. Norway's railway engineers, you come to realise, are an unyielding bunch, undaunted by fierce topographical odds – just like its octogenarian hikers.

RUSSIAN PRIESTS SAVE SOULS ON THE TRAIN TO ARCHANGEL

BY **KEVIN O'FLYNN** IN MOSCOW

Senior Russian Orthodox clergymen are deploying a 'church on wheels' to counter poaching by foreign missionaries who have won many converts since the Soviet ban on religious freedom ended. A lavishly gilded Orthodox train, complete with stained-glass windows, is heading for the frozen Far North, where most villages and communities have not seen a religious minister for decades.

It set off for Archangel, in northwest Russia, last week. As it prepared to leave platform two of Kievsky station in Moscow, Patriarch Alexei II, the Orthodox leader, sprinkled holy water on its two carriages while a choir sang. He said: 'We bless this church to help people to return to their faith.'

One of the carriages has been converted from its former drab and sombre brown decor to a chapel decorated with icons of the Virgin Mary and Child. A golden altar serves as the focal point of worship. Bells hang from the ceiling. Destination signs have been replaced by prayers written in large letters along both sides of the carriage.

The second coach provides accommodation for the priests, students and railway workers who will travel on missionary journeys to remote regions. A typical journey will consist of one day in a village, starting with Mass and a series of weddings, baptisms and other religious ceremonies, before an overnight journey to the next destination.

Alexei II said the mobile church would carry the faith to the many small and remote places in Russia that did not have access to a conventional church or priest. Archpriest Georgy Studyonov, who accompanied Alexei II during the blessing ceremony, said that everything was as it would be in a real church. 'Even better than some churches. I was astounded. It was all done with love.'

The Orthodox Church in recent years has been making greater efforts to reach out to remote communities. It already has a number of boat churches, which sail the rivers of the Volga in southern Russia and the Ob in Siberia, bringing services to the riverbanks where churches are uncommon.

The Far North is a vast area with few churches and an especially large influx of foreign missionary sects, such as the Jehovah's Witnesses and Mormons, whose activities are resented by Orthodox leaders.

As part of efforts to restore the nation's spiritual life after 70 years of communism, about 12,000 churches have been built or renovated over the past decade.

The new train is reminiscent of a revival movement that began during the era of Tsar Nicholas II, who ordered a church on wheels to be built in 1896 to take the Orthodox Mass to the farthest reaches of Siberia. The idea for a modern version was proposed by a priest three years ago at the All Russia Convention for Railway Workers, said Viktor Skorik, the deputy general director of the Moscow Carriage Building Factory, which carried out the project. It was paid for by Russia's Railways Ministry. 'There was a carriage at the start of the century, then there was a break, and now there is again,' said Mr Skorik. 'Today is a return of the memories of the last century.'

THE WORLD'S BEST TRAIN SET

JAMES BEDDING, IN SWITZERLAND, TAKES A TRIP THROUGH A CENTURY AND A HALF OF RAILWAY HISTORY

If you stand in the middle of what will be the longest and deepest railway tunnel in the world – the new Gotthard Base Tunnel under the Swiss Alps – you can feel a current of air on your cheek and a hum in your ears. Peer down the dimly lit hole into the distant future, and for a moment you think a train is coming. But the thought does not last long; after all, with trains scheduled to rocket through here at 150mph, how could it?

In fact, you won't be able to catch a train through the tunnel for another five years or so. 'That sound is the air conditioning,' my guide, Maurus, said. 'Swiss law says that the temperature must not exceed 28 degrees [82F], for the sake of the workers. Without the air con, it would be as hot as 45 degrees [113F] down here.'

Once work on the 35-mile tunnel is complete, however, you will be able to hurtle in air-conditioned comfort from Zürich to Milan in just two hours 50 minutes – a saving of 50 minutes on the current travel time. Along the way, you can enjoy the novelty of burrowing up to 8,000 feet, or one-and-a-half vertical miles, below the surface of the earth – at double motorway speed limits.

For now, though, you can join a group tour of the tunnels, organised by one of the visitor centres, on which you can learn all about the gargantuan project. The railway line will pass through two single-track tunnels, located about 130ft apart. Engineers excavated five stretches simultaneously to speed progress; this, in turn, required the construction of additional access shafts and passageways, bringing the total distance tunnelled to 94 miles.

You can see a model of the machine that did most of the work: a mechanical mole nearly 500 yards long, weighing more than 300 tons, and guzzling as much electricity as more than 4,000 family homes. When conditions are good, it can chew through more than 125ft of rock a day. By the time the metal monster has moved on, it has secured the walls with steel anchors, nets and hoops to prevent the tunnel collapsing under the mighty pressure of the rock above, and encased the walls in a smooth concrete lining.

The tunnelling machines finished their work in March 2011, but engineers still have to install the track along with the power supply, and assorted electrical and telecommunications equipment. The first trains are expected to thunder through towards the end of 2016 – 20 years after engineers dug the first shafts. That's a year ahead of schedule – a source of pride in a land that places punctuality next to godliness.

The logistics involved in completing the scheme are impressive enough, but more remarkable still is the effect the project will have on the emotional map of the continent. The new railway route will be 25 miles shorter than the existing one, as well as much faster. Not only will the Alps shrink in significance as a barrier, but the Latin and Teutonic realms will find themselves within commuting distance of each other. Europe is about to be redefined.

Which is why I had embarked on my journey. I wanted to explore a mountain massif that has been a gateway between north and south – as well as a strategic obstacle – for nearly a millennium. Starting deep underground and a decade in the future, I wanted to travel up and over this mass of rock as well as through the various tunnels that pierce it, threading backwards and forwards through a century and a half of railway history, describing a four-dimensional doodle in space and time.

The Gotthard massif has an additional resonance for me. When I was a child, we would cross it every summer holiday on our way to visit family on the palm-lined shores of Lake Maggiore in the Italian-speaking south of Switzerland, where my mother grew up. We would drive over from Sussex in our 1961 split-windscreen Volkswagen Caravette, and the climax of the journey would be the grinding climb over the St Gotthard Pass – where, more often than not, the clouds of the Germanic north would give way to Latin sunshine, my mother's mood would lighten by ten degrees, and we all knew the holidays proper had begun.

If, to my brother and me, the mountains were a portal to the lighter side of family life, they also felt like a giant playground: as we drove from the north up towards the pass, I often had the sensation that our Caravette had been shrunk, and that we were exploring an oversized train set.

I had the same feeling as I set off from the visitor centre at Erstfeld at the northern end of the Gotthard Base Tunnel, and headed south on the existing rail route. At first the line climbs gently along the banks of the River Reuss. Soon the valley steepens, and in order to gain sufficient height, the train throws a couple of balletic tricks. Beyond Gurtnellen, it disappears into the mountain to perform a dainty underground pirouette before re-emerging higher up; and near Wassen, it spirals into the mountain, and re-emerges pointing in exactly the opposite direction, back down the valley – before repeating the move, effectively tracing a big, elegant zig-zag up the mountainside.

From our family Caravette, I would watch the trains' antics: they seemed to be playing hide-and-seek with us as we chased them up the valley. Now, from the vantage point of my train seat, I felt as though the whole outdoor train set were laying on a show. Three times the whitewashed, onion-domed church of Wassen glided past on its craggy outcrop: once high above, then level with us, heading in the opposite direction, and a third time far below. It was as if the scenery were performing an encore – including once backwards, purely to show off. Everything – from the geraniums in the window boxes on the wooden chalets to the manicured meadows full of plump cows, their neck bells a-clanking – appeared to be fresh from the toy-shop box.

The train finished its climb at Göschenen, where I alighted, before watching it vanish into the funereal gloom of the first Gotthard railway tunnel. This, too, was a pioneering feat of engineering in its time: drilled, dynamited and dug between 1872 and 1882, the nine-mile tunnel provided the first modern link between northern and southern Europe, transformed long-distance railway travel – and cost the lives of 199 labourers.

To continue my climb on to the massif, I switched platform and boarded a train of the Matterhorn Gotthard Railway. The narrow-gauge cog train grinds up a narrow-gauge steep-walled and barren ravine known as the Schöllenen Gorge, eventually passing the giddying stone 'Devil's Bridge' atmospherically painted by JMW Turner 200 years ago. It was the construction of the first bridge here about eight centuries ago that first made the Gotthard into an important Alpine crossing.

The train crawls farther up along the banks of the foaming Reuss until suddenly the walls of the gorge recede, and you emerge in a long, wide valley lined with high peaks, popular with hikers and cross-country skiers: the Urseren valley. Seconds later you pull into a small station, Andermatt, at the junction with another line running east-west.

This is a good place to pull out a map to get your bearings. Leading away from Andermatt are four great river valleys, echoing the cross on the Swiss flag. Follow the Rhône to the west, and you would ultimately reach Marseille and the Med; head downstream from the source of the Rhine just to the east, and eventually you would get to Rotterdam. Leading north is the valley of the Reuss, which empties into the Rhine; flowing south is the Ticino, which gives its name to Switzerland's only Italian-speaking canton, before flowing into the Po and ultimately the Adriatic.

In each valley, a different language predominates. The Swiss to the west speak French, those to the south, Italian, and those to the north, German; while to the east live the 35,000-odd souls for whom Romansh, Switzerland's fourth national language, is their first.

The Gotthard massif is not just a barrier and a junction, then, but a watershed, physical and linguistic, at the heart of Europe: a manifestation in rock of the divisions that lie at the core of this continent, as well as a meeting-point of peoples, and the centre of gravity of this curious little country of four languages and cultures.

It is also an intriguingly three-dimensional crossroads. Lowest of all is the new railway tunnel, at an altitude of about 1,800ft above sea level. The existing rail link is about 2,000ft higher – roughly level with the 10.5-mile motorway tunnel which, when it opened in 1980, was the longest road tunnel in the world. Another 1,000ft up floats the town of Andermatt, while the original road over the St. Gotthard Pass lies another 2,000ft higher still: a millennium of transport routes, laid under, through and over roughly a vertical mile of mountain that is as perforated as an Emmental cheese.

On our family holidays we would drive through Andermatt, and along its main street lined with shingled houses and converted coaching inns, on our slow climb in the Caravette to the Gotthard Pass – before a stomach-churning descent of the Tremola, the switchback road down the other side to Ticino. You can still ride the route, as a passenger in a scheduled PostBus – but perhaps the most atmospheric way to travel it is on board a historic mail coach, pulled by a team of five horses. The service runs throughout the summer – and this being Switzerland, the website even gives you details of connecting train services.

Indeed, one of the great joys of travelling by public transport in this country is the way that the various services interlock. Look up the official timetable (www.cff.ch), key in your departure point and destination, whether in a city or on a mountaintop, and the site will give you full details of all your connections en route – including stretches by train, cog train, funicular, gondola, cable car, postal bus or boat.

So, while many visitors to Switzerland end up travelling on one of the various 'scenic routes' that transport operators have devised – such as the Glacier Express, which negotiates 91 tunnels and 291 bridges on its seven-hour journey from Zermatt via Andermatt to St. Moritz, or the Wilhelm Tell Express, which links Lake Lucerne and Ticino via the Gotthard, by paddle steamer and train – you can very easily devise your own journey. Even language isn't a problem: the timetable is quadrilingual – with English as language number four.

One stop that you cannot find on the timetable is a station that many snow-sports fans, myself included, pray will one day appear there: the Porta Alpina. The resort of Sedrun just east of Andermatt – a small ski area known for its fine powder and freeriding – also happens to be the location for one of the access shafts used for the construction of the Gotthard Base Tunnel. Backers of the Porta Alpina suggested building a station deep underground, and using the shaft to bring skiers and snowboarders up to the surface. It would certainly make for the quirkiest transfer to any ski resort in the Alps: at 150mph by high-speed train to the world's deepest underground station, followed by a ride to the surface in the world's highest and fastest lift, rocketing 2,600 vertical feet up in just 70 seconds.

At nearby Andermatt, I asked one of the railway staff if any trains would be stopping at the Porta Alpina in the foreseeable future. He shook his head. There would be the technical challenges, he said, such as the steep temperature gradient: from a tropical 105F in the tunnel to an Arctic 15F or lower at the surface. Plus the logistical and safety issues, too: 'Why build a tunnel to carry trains at 250kph, and then stop a few of them half-way along?' With cost estimates rising sharply, the project was put on ice in 2007. The cavity that could house a station is already in place, however, deep under the resort, and we snow-sports enthusiasts will continue to hope that one day it will open to welcome us.

You can easily reach Sedrun from Andermatt, though, by taking the narrow-gauge cog train from Andermatt over the Oberalp Pass and into the valley of the young Rhine. And before long you will be able to travel from one resort to the other and back on skis – if a billionaire Egyptian investor has his way. Samih Sawiris claims that his Andermatt Swiss Alps project will result in the 'largest integrated holiday resort in the Alps'. The bulldozers have already begun turning the floor of the Urseren Valley into an 18-hole golf course, while in August 2010 work began on a 'five-star-superior' hotel to be run by Chedi – perhaps best known for its ultra-luxurious hotel in Muscat, Oman – and due to open in time for the winter of 2013/14.

All in all, the project foresees the construction of six new hotels with more than 800 rooms, 500 apartments in more than 40 blocks as well as 25 villas to be put up for sale, nearly 2,000 underground parking spaces, plus a concert hall, and a sports-and-leisure complex. He also intends to link the existing resorts of Andermatt and Sedrun to create a single ski area with 80 miles of piste.

Walkers, cross-country skiers and others who love the tranquillity of this wide, high valley have fought the plans, but locals are backing the scheme. Understandably, perhaps. The reason so much land is available for development is that it was recently vacated by the Swiss army – which ran its principal alpine training base here. 'The town was going to die,' one resident told me. 'First we lost all the tourist traffic when they built the motorway tunnel; now we have lost our biggest employer. But young people are making plans to build a life here, and that has to be good.'

If locals are looking to the future, I set my sights on the past for the remainder of my journey. From Andermatt I headed west up the Urseren Valley, following the route of the Glacier Express as far as Realp. A tunnel leading from there under the Furka Pass to the Rhone valley opened in 1981, providing the first year-round link between the two valleys. However, its opening spelt the death of the Furka line that from June to October every year carried passengers over the pass, 2,000 vertical feet higher up.

Just two years after the new tunnel opened, railway enthusiasts clubbed together to form an association dedicated to the resurrection of the summit line. Nine years later they reopened their first stretch of line, and 18 years after that – in August 2010 – they completed the final link, and were able to run trains on the full 11-mile route for the first time in a quarter of a century.

At Realp I met one of the thousands of volunteers who have helped restore the line: Paul Güdel, the retired owner of an electrical goods business in Lucerne, now an evangelical convert to steam. He showed me the railway's workshops, and the line's two prize steam locos, built in 1913 and sold to Vietnam in 1947 after the line was electrified. Enthusiasts traced them to a jungle depot where they had stood rusting since 1975, and in 1990 shipped them home and restored them – along with a couple of other steam locos, and a variety of period carriages.

We boarded one of them, each of whose wooden seats was taken – mostly by Swiss, it seemed, folk mature enough to have travelled the line in its previous incarnation. We pulled out of the station, and within seconds were puffing laboriously up towards the pass. As we climbed the mountainside, over little bridges across mountain streams and past fat cows grazing in the flower-strewn pastures, Paul told me about some of the challenges the restoration team had faced. We soon reached one of them: the Steffenbach Bridge, which spans a ravine scoured every winter by avalanches powerful enough to sweep away any structures in their path.

The solution devised by the engineers who created the line was ingenious, and remains unique worldwide: a folding bridge that can be dismantled every autumn, taken out of harm's way, and reassembled every spring. The restorers retained the original design – but whereas in former days a team of 20 men needed eight hours to erect or fold away the 32-ton bridge, now a team of ten can do the job in six hours, with the help of hydraulic winches. Still, reopening the line every spring is a mammoth task, requiring thousands of hours of volunteer labour – not least to clear a path through the snow, which can lie up to 60 feet deep.

After about 45 minutes of climbing through the thin Alpine air, the wheezing loco had reached the highest point of the line: the Furka station, 7,100ft above sea level. We shut the windows for the short glide through the one-mile summit tunnel, to stop the smoke billowing into the carriages, before beginning our long glide down into the Rhone valley – starting with a glimpse of the glacier that is the river's source.

At the village of Gletsch we embarked on the last sector to be reopened. This, too, presented special challenges, said Paul: not least the renovation of a spiral tunnel – designed to help trains negotiate a drop of 1,300ft over a distance of just three miles – which leads out of the mountainside and straight on to a 40-ft-high viaduct over the young Rhone.

As we glided down the final stretch, through fragrant glades of pine, Paul explained how the railway was installing a sprinkler system along the line to fight any fires that might be started by its steam engines. Just before we pulled in to the little station of Oberwald, where the old and new lines rejoin, he pointed out one final feature: 'We're especially proud of this one,' he said, with a glint in his eye. It was a level crossing. In former days, motorists crossing a mountain railway line would know to slow right down in order not to wreck their tyres on the toothed rack between the rails. 'We came up with a better system,' said Paul: and showed me how, as soon as the train had passed over, the entire track disappeared, automatically, back under the surface of the tarmac.

Once again I had the impression, as I had had many times on this journey, that there's nothing the Swiss like better than solving a challenge – especially if it involves mountains and trains. Throw in clocks and timetables, and they are happier still. This seems equally true whether they are working with steam locos designed to crawl up mountains at 15mph, or their electrically driven descendants hurtling underneath the Alps ten times faster.

I wondered what my great-grandfather would have made of all this. He, too, was a railway man, who helped build a branch running from the main Gotthard line to Locarno. He used to tell how the construction workers, when they were laying track through the marshes north of Lake Maggiore, would receive a daily tot of rum to ward off malaria.

Three generations on, his successors are once again redefining the way the country sees itself. But by tunnelling under the great physical barrier at the heart of Europe and thereby shrinking its demographic and cultural importance, are they not undermining Switzerland's raison d'être? After all, without the Alps, this quirky little country would not make sense.

Perhaps. But I am more than happy for businesspeople and other busy folk to rocket underneath the mountains, well clear of the spectacular scenery that is the best reason for lingering in this part of the world. And I am delighted that the line will divert much of the freight that currently crosses the Alps at higher altitude, and so reduce pollution: after all, this was the main reason for building the line in the first place.

The mountains will be that much fresher and quieter as a result. I shall continue to catch the clanky old trains to get there, travelling at speeds with which my great-grandfather would have been familiar. And I like to think that, however far I travel from the childhood in which I first fell in love with this part of the world, I will never tire of playing with the world's best train set.

CHAPTER 2
THE AMERICAS

---

8 JANUARY 2011

RIDING ON TWO TRAINS

ON THE COAST STARLIGHT, AMTRAK'S FLAGSHIP TRAIN
BETWEEN SEATTLE AND LOS ANGELES, **PAMELA PETRO** IS
HAUNTED BY A MEMORY OF AN EARLIER JOURNEY

> You can't shut off the risk and the pain
> Without losing the love that remains
> We're all riders on this train
> (*Human Touch* by Bruce Springsteen)

It's been dark for two hours now. A suspicious darkness for the 21st century, almost medieval in its depth. Not a single watt of electricity interrupts the night.

We're in rural Oregon, but as late as dusk there was evidence of human habitation: lumber and railway yards, small towns where cars sat at flashing level crossings, waiting for us to pass. Bungalows with front porches facing the tracks, and hardscrabble farms along the coastal plain. I begin to wonder if there's been a power cut.

Then the vision. We're in a curve deep enough for the train to snake on itself, showing me the engine from my window in the fifth car. In the headlights I see a forest of giant conifers heavily weighted with snow. Flakes gust, swirl, and sparkle with frantic blizzard force in the beams, and snow banks up against the tracks. The trees look prehistoric, they're so big, so feral, so far from all humans but us. Their self-contained dignity makes me almost ashamed to call them beautiful.

Then they're gone. The tracks straighten out and the forest disappears. Blackness again, making a mirror of the window and showing me only myself, startled and blinking. The last time I'd been able to see past my own face we'd been travelling alongside a green embankment, with the sea, flat and grey, in the distance.

The train had curved to the left just now, but my brain flips the image, and in a memory it curls to the right. I'm looking at the back of the train instead of the front, and the forest has thinned out. It's a straggly thicket of young oaks and maples, and there's enough space between the trees to see snow on the ground.

The train has stopped with no station in sight. Doors open and people step out, carrying suitcases and making their way between the trees. The extreme clarity of the image turns it into a Brueghel scene set in present day. I don't remember whether I look in the other direction.

At dinner I meet Pat, who smells of cough drops and is about to turn 94, and Michael, her son. They take the train often; they know the darkness. 'There aren't any lights because we're in the Cascade Mountains,' Pat explains. 'There's a little station at Kalmath Falls, but that's about it. Right, dear?' She leans against Michael and squeezes his arm. 'That's right.' Michael's tone vibrates between irritation and pride. He adds that there's usually snow in the Cascades by early November. It is, in fact, November 9th.

Michael, Pat, and I are aboard the Coast Starlight, the flagship Amtrak train that runs from Seattle to Los Angeles (or vice versa) over 36 varied hours. The price of my sleeping car 'roomette' includes dinner in the dining or parlour car. And so I'm drinking peppery Columbia Crest Shiraz from Washington State and raving about my manicotti stuffed with portobello mushrooms. We all agree that we've never tasted better lime sorbet.

Dinner is pleasant – I wouldn't mind another glass of wine, and Michael seems like a dark horse, letting his mom do the talking while uttering occasional asides that suggest an eventful life – which is why after dessert I excuse myself and head back to my roomette. I can have fun on this train, but not too much. A gauge in my head flips a warning switch if I veer close to attracting the attention of a minor but jealous god.

My roomette is essentially a walk-in closet, but I'm happy inside it. Because I'm usually in coach, its flip-down seats and sliding door along the corridor strike me as the pinnacle of ingenious luxury. When I return from dinner I find that Robin, my personal attendant, has folded the seats into a bed that she's made with crisp, white sheets.

There's an elemental thrill in making yourself vulnerable – stripping off your clothes, closing your eyes, letting yourself succumb to comfort and warmth – while hurtling into the unknown, inhospitable night at high speed. It's such a great pleasure, I think, because it's counterintuitive to every brain-stem response we've learned as a species about safety. It shouldn't be safe, but it is. That's reason enough to revel in it. And I do, guardedly. As I lie in my bunk, rocking pleasurably from side to side, images and scenes from the day flicker across my mind like film trailers.

Late afternoon sun breaking through clouds and beaming on a Canadian Pacific Railway freight car, its hue flaring suddenly from dull rust to crimson.

The neatly ponytailed dreadlocks of William, the parlour-car attendant. A man so convinced I'd been wounded by his wit – when I asked him what was in the fruit tart he replied, 'fruit' – that he spent the journey in a paroxysm of apology.

King Street Station in Seattle, a hundred years old, cavernous and archaeological. It looked like a dig stalled at midpoint. Some elements – the San Marco look-alike clock tower – were fully restored, while others – the dusty, entombed interior – were still awaiting their share of $50 million in renovation money. I see myself in the station, trotting at a professional clip toward a set of handsome oak benches, carved and polished and clearly original to the 1906 decor, but then veering off at the last second and settling into a row of commonplace, black vinyl seats instead. What was that about?

My eyes snap open. The oak benches were nearly identical to benches in Baltimore's train station, where I'd sat nearly 24 years ago, waiting for Amtrak's Colonial to take me to Newark, New Jersey.

Another image arrives, now. I let it try to form on the screen of my mind, but it has trouble resolving into focus. The train car appears to retain its shape – it's still a horizontal lozenge – but everything inside has come loose. People, seats, luggage jumble together at odd angles, as if they had been stuffed in without any logic. For the most part the seats have wound up on top, cresting like whitecaps, the people who had been sitting in them somewhere below. I'm lucky, though: I'm on top, too, riding the seats, arms draped over their backs. A boy in a bright blue sweater bobs nearby. He looks at me and screams.

The sea of luggage and humans beneath us starts very, very slowly to writhe and churn. At first there is no sound – it's a film, I think, with the volume down – but now I'm becoming aware of distant moaning and weeping and weak shouts for help. No screaming except from the little boy. It doesn't occur to me to make any noise.

Eventually I become aware of a human touch. A man has broken a window from the outside and is scrambling toward me over the whitecaps, asking if I can move. I nod that yes, I can – it seems like a silly question – and he tries to help me forward, but I'm stuck. That's when I realise I've been in flesh-on-flesh contact with someone all along.

A woman's hand is clenched around my ankle. That's all I can see of her, just a hand. I know now it's been there for several minutes, warm and tight, a good feeling, since everything else is cold, and I'm shivering. I look down and see red – blood or nail polish, I don't bother to discern – and yank my leg away as hard as I can. She loses her grip and I scramble toward the window. I don't tell the man who has come to help me that she is there. I think about telling him. I want to tell him. But it takes so much energy just to think, my thoughts seem to have sinkers attached, that speaking seems out of the question.

The Coast Starlight conductor blows the whistle as if on cue – he's been trying to blow it less during sleeping hours, which I appreciate, but I can tell it's a struggle; this man loves his whistle – and I shove the memory off my mind's screen, turning on my side to burrow under the Starlight's warm blue blanket. Back in the '80s Amtrak went in for warm tones – the seats, if I remember right, were maroon. I'm glad they've changed the colour scheme.

On my first afternoon on the train, William, the parlour-car attendant, announces a wine tasting. What a good idea. When I arrive, two cars down, two leaps through the cold, interstitial spaces where

Amtrak cars join together, he sets into apologising again for the fruit-tart crack. One more time and I will hit him.

The parlour car is the best place on the Coast Starlight to channel the glamorous ghosts of trains past. Amtrak owns five vintage parlour cars, built for the Santa Fe Railroad in 1956, and they all ride the Coast Starlight route. (Two head north from Los Angeles 24 hours apart, two head south from Seattle, and one is reserved as a spare.) With its banquette seating and cocktail tables, its swivel chairs, its white tablecloths, real silverware, and tie-back curtains, the parlour car is Amtrak's nod to the fact that train travel has a cultural history separate from transport.

Aircraft don't have enough physical space to generate the kind of human interaction that draws an environment, almost a proto-society, from the small talk of strangers. In the air there's no room to mingle or seek, stalk or snub. Nor is there as much room to play out the social hierarchies that 1930s movies revelled in, and which Amtrak happily perpetuates.

After William's announcement for the wine tasting, he added, italics in his voice, 'For sleeping-car passengers only.' I feel a little guilty participating in the caste system – only sleeping-car people are allowed in the parlour car – but as we're travelling through vineyards, it seems almost a duty.

Someone at Amtrak has prepared notes. The Whistle Stop Red, a blend of cabernet and merlot, yields 'currant and blackberry flavours.' The Rogue Rive Bleu, one of the three cheeses we try, is 'Roquefort-like but made from cow's milk,' and has been cave-aged 90 days. All represent the train's *terroir*: the wines are from Washington State, and the cheeses from California, Oregon and Washington. We're eating the scenery.

No one cares. The caravan park owner from Florida – Central Casting apparently called and told him to wear a Hawaiian shirt – knows an opportunity to score three glasses for $5 when he sees it. He gives me his card, unasked for. Leaving it on the table is rude, so I hand it to the woman next to me.

Her name is Rene. She and her mother have crisscrossed the country on trains, and firmly believe this is the best route. She lets me eat her blue cheese – small cubes, like the free samples they put out in supermarkets – which I find delicious. I give her the remainder of my Chardonnay, not caring to detect 'vanilla and plum on the palate.'

Farmland rolls by. Twilight catches tractor ruts full of rainwater and they gleam quicksilver, like mercury.

'Hey ladies! What's your favourite football teams?' This comes from the Floridian in the Hawaiian shirt.

'San Diego,' says Rene.

'The New England Patriots,' I say.

Everyone in the car, including William – no longer sorry, now, for his quip – stares at me in disbelief bordering on horror. I've betrayed that I'm not only from the opposite coast, but that I support a team that regularly beats theirs.

Jokes are made. Rene turns her shoulder to the caravan park owner (See? You couldn't do that on a plane), and we abandon sports to form a group that discusses why our country doesn't appreciate train travel.

'How about you?' Rene asks me. 'Do you ride trains much back East? Any good stories?'

My brain screeches to a standstill. Her question is fraught, and it echoes something from long ago. My search engine flips files at top speed. I find it: '*Tell you a story? But I don't know any. Well, yes, after all, here is something I might tell.*'

That's how Thomas Mann begins his 1936 anecdote 'Railway Accident.' I feel like a character being set up by a hostile author. My heart quickens as I consider the options. But as in the case of Mann's narrator, it takes only a moment's reflection for me to find a safe answer.

'I've ridden more trains in Europe,' I reply, truthfully. And I tell them about a journey I made before the Iron Curtain came down, on a workaday train temporarily lent the name 'Orient Express.' I got on in Vienna and shared a six-seater compartment – bench seats, facing – with two other passengers: a man opposite who seemed stern and spoke neither French nor English, and an Asian man next to me to whom I chatted in poor French. Toward the beginning of the trip my neighbour noted that I was holding my backpack on my lap, and suggested I put it beneath the seat. I tried to shove it under but it refused to go. Curious, I put a hand down to see what the obstruction was. And grabbed another hand.

After a near-eternity the gentleman across the way left the compartment, and I grabbed the Asian guy by the arm.

'There's someone beneath us!' I might have said there's someone above us – I often confuse French adverbs – because he refused to understand. Finally I got up, pulled him to his feet, and lifted the seat. A man in a brown corduroy coat and a ski hat, lying in an elongated foetal position, put a finger to his lips. We shook our heads: we wouldn't tell anyone. He also spoke French (better than either of us), and said he was a Hungarian journalist escaping to Paris. We offered him food and coffee, which he declined. How could we help? Just knock on the bench, he said, when we get to Gare de l'Est, and then leave. The rest of the ride was nerve-wracking, especially when the conductor appeared to check our passports. Nonetheless, we arrived without incident and knocked on the bench. Then we left.

The story I don't tell Rene and the others, of course, is the Wreck of the Colonial.

The train crashed on 4 January 1987, 18 miles north of Baltimore at a place called Gunpow Interlocking, an intersection of tracks a quarter of a mile from the railroad bridge at Gunpowder River, in Maryland. (There's a thought that invites midnight heebie-jeebies. 'What if we'd been on the bridge . . . ?') A Conrail freighter travelling at about 40mph passed through a stop sign and chugged into the path of the Colonial passenger train, travelling at 118mph. The Conrail engineer and his mates were watching a football game – the playoffs had just begun – and smoking pot. They saw the passenger train approaching and jumped. None of them died.

Here's *Baltimore Magazine* on what happened next:

A CRUMPLED MASS. Alone in the cab, Jerry Evans scans ahead for Gunpow Interlocking as he rounds a curve . . . Suddenly he sees a 'stop' signal, then a patch of Conrail blue occupying the place 2,700 feet ahead. He throws the Colonial into emergency. The braking will last eight seconds.

Evans does not jump from the locomotive. The physical pain is gone in milliseconds. He will be eulogised as 'the best darn engineer.'

A fireball mushrooms at the point of impact. The Colonial has slammed into the rearmost Conrail engine. The lead Amtrak engine is crushed back to its rear cab, and the Conrail locomotive explodes in countless pieces, the largest a chunk of scorched metal the size of a motorcycle . . .

Almost a quarter-mile south of the switch, the Colonial's rear cars continue forward, shoving those ahead off the tracks in a zig-zag chain reaction . . . The empty food-service car behind the Amtrak engines telescopes as it is crushed by cars behind it. The next car . . . flips on its right side. Luggage and people fly everywhere.

Not really suitable for parlour-car chit-chat. As I ride the Coast Starlight, walk the corridors and mingle, I feel I have to protect the other passengers from this dark memory inside me. I don't want to ruin anyone's trip or make anyone anxious. (Who knows how people will react as they career along at 75mph?) The memory of the crash isn't in the forefront of my mind, but it lurks near the brain stem. As I walked down the platform in Seattle looking for my car, I caught myself counting how many others were between it and the engine. (That's how I knew I was in the fifth.)

I was in the third car of the Colonial. I had tried to get on at the rear, but a conductor informed me it was crowded and I needed to find a spot towards the front. I believe everyone in the second card died, and many people in my car as well. There were no fatalities from the fourth car back.

I say that this memory is inside me, but the passage I have just quoted from *Baltimore Magazine* is no memory of mine. In fact, the story of the wreck isn't really mine to tell, and I believe that by dramatising the crash *Baltimore Magazine* betrays what it's like to be in one. It's a distinction I find important.

I didn't know Jerry Evans; I didn't know a Conrail train had missed a stop sign; I didn't know that the braking lasted eight seconds; I didn't see the mushroom cloud of fire.

With omniscient perspective shielding them like a force field, *BM* readers are free to indulge in an attack of the shudders. Knowledge is safety. To know these things, to see the fireball erupt, is to be outside the event. Whereas the truth of the crash, from my interior perspective, was ignorance followed by confusion, culminating in boredom.

I had been staring through the window, making plans for the New Year, arranging the months in tidy bundles, when the train abruptly lost its rhythm. The comforting clackity-clack of wheels on tracks accelerated suddenly and astoundingly fast in a mechanical equivalent of panic. Clack — beat — clack became clack-beat-clack became clack-clack became CLACKCLACK. There was no sudden stop. No time for fear. More like an instantaneous and chaotic loss of control. I kept trying to understand the situation, but it flew ahead of me, out of my grasp.

I hit something — the floor? — and then my thoughts tumbled with my body. I was conscious and my eyes were open, but I have no images to share. Maybe it's not possible to see pure chaos when you're a piece of it. What I do remember is pleading with God: if you make this stop now, I'll have lived. How many seconds I repeated that mantra, over and over, I don't know. But God finally got the word, and I got my wish.

That Brueghel image, of people getting off the train, carrying their suitcases in snow? That's what I saw after I jumped from the window. My car had landed atop the second car, so it was a long way down. A man caught me around the middle, which is probably when my broken ribs sliced into my left lung and spleen. But no one knew that then.

Once I was outside — it was 14 degrees F, and I was in shirtsleeves; a life-saving combination that slowed interior bleeding, I learned later — the wreck became an almost bureaucratic affair. Lots of waiting around, doing nothing. You would never guess that from the reactions of my family and friends. Within an hour of impact scenes of the wreckage were interrupting the football game on television. My car was filmed astride the second one like two great, silver animals having sex. It looked obscene and deadly, and let loose emotions that matched the images' violence.

If I saw any of this I didn't take it in. Like the woman under my seat, I had a worm's-eye view of the wreck. No signs of tragedy tugged at my emotions. Which is why the so-called literature of disaster betrays the actual experience of it. Accounts like the one in *Baltimore Magazine* bring together an assemblage of viewpoints and time-frames and offer up the completed puzzle. Readers are with Jerry Evans inside the cab the moment before he dies, very much in the present tense. In the next sentence we skip to the future — 'the breaking will last eight seconds' — offering readers an opportunity for some gruesome, imaginative voyeurism. Then we're outside the train — unlike Jerry, still alive — watching the fireball erupt.

In just three sentences the deconstruction — surely a train crash is the ultimate deconstruction of the simplest narrative sequence, the linear progression of cars on a track — is reconstructed. Filling the gaps and making the crash comprehensible also makes it dramatic. The language, in fact, reads like stage directions. And that lets readers enjoy a good scare. But by telling us everything these stories really tell us nothing. The completed picture is not a train wreck. It's the story of one. So I suppose I needn't have worried. I didn't have a personal tale to tell Rene and the others after all. Just an increasingly truncated angle of vision on an event that became news. A memory of confusion, chaos and lost control.

I fling back the curtains at dawn, and the world outside the Coast Starlight is radically different again. My vision of trees and snow seems delightfully, tantalisingly suspect — did I imagine it? Was magic involved? — in the light of California's big, bright landscapes, its busy skies, hard-edged buildings and palm trees. We roll past flat farmland bordered by bald and furrowed hills so furry-brown I want to stroke them. By the time I finish my breakfast tea and eggs I'm peering at Alcatraz Island and the Golden Gate Bridge, the ships of San Francisco Bay. At lunchtime we streak through Elkhorn Slough, a salt-marsh reserve near Monterey, where egrets preen and massive, whiskered sea lions loll in mud.

We spend the bulk of the day bisecting vast agricultural valleys where California grows the lion's share of the world's fruits, vegetables, and berries — veritable inland seas of geometrically planted, irrigated crops, penned by parched hills and dusty, dun-coloured pastures. Cows run from the train as we rumble past.

One of the best things about following a north-south route is that the sun bounds over the tracks in a triumphal arch. By 3 p.m., however, as we crawl through the empty Diablo Mountains, so worn they seemed to wear prehistory on their slopes, I'm not feeling so triumphant.

'Hey, Robin!' I grab her as she passes my roomette. 'When do we reach the coast?'

'At San Luis Obispo,' she says, checking her watch. 'Don't worry, we should make it before sunset.'

We do, but just barely. I'm travelling three days after daylight saving time ended, and an hour's less light means I just catch the sun sinking into the Pacific beyond the rugged, sand-and-rock-strewn shore at Vandenberg Air Force Base. Oil rigs glint in the last rays, far offshore.

At dinner, in darkness again, I meet a handsome glass-blower and motorcycle-restorer, coming home from helping a friend carry a life-size glass man across the country in a caravan. I momentarily wish I'd held on to the Floridian's card – here's someone to give it to! – though I guess I wouldn't saddle him with it, he's too nice. He tells me how he'd taken a wrong turn in New Jersey and wound up in Hoboken, thinking it was Manhattan. He was so disappointed that New York City wasn't all it was cracked up to be. The buildings were so much smaller than he'd imagined.

I laugh so long I forget to eat, and my dinner gets cold. Here's someone, I think, I could tell about the wreck. But lately I no longer trust myself to talk about it. In less high-minded moments I used to crib from *Baltimore Magazine* and give eager listeners the reconstructed blow-by-blow account; but now, more often than not, I cry. It's embarrassing.

A friend suggested that it's because as I age, and become more conscious of my mortality, I grow more sensitive to my long-ago, near-death experience. But I think it's just simple sadness. A week, a month, even a year after the crash, the 16 people who died – many of them students, returning to university after Christmas – hadn't been gone very long. They hadn't missed much of their lives yet. But now they have lost out on 24 years: nearly a quarter of a century, doing nothing but being dead.

I almost died. I remember a nurse at the hospital stopping to take my pulse – my trolley was lined up with others in a corridor – and yelling to someone, 'We're going to lose this one!' Oddly, it didn't faze me. Maybe I was in shock.

After I jumped off the train I wandered into the snowy trees. We had crashed alongside the straggly backyards of a rural neighbourhood:

one-family wood-frame houses, white and green. A black woman and a white woman rushed toward me with ice and a towel. 'Put it around your head,' they said in unison. When my head and eyes were covered one of them took me by the hand and led me to a place where I could sit. It smelled of fire and metal and damp earth.

Eventually a paramedic made me lie on a stretcher and covered me with his jacket. He asked who was President of the United States. I wanted to say something snarky, but couldn't muster more than 'Ronald Reagan, unfortunately.' Then he asked my name. I said 'Pam.' Pamela seemed too much for the circumstances.

And then I waited. And waited and waited. Again, maybe it was shock, but I was bored. I did fret about the people I loved who wouldn't know if I were dead or alive, but eventually I lost track of both my fears and the surrounding distractions – helicopters and sirens, mainly – and my thoughts dispersed, evaporating as soon as they formed. The only external perception that penetrated my cocoon of vagueness was the life-saving cold. I never took the trouble to cry.

(I waited so long because I had been misdiagnosed at triage. No one checked for internal injuries because my head grabbed their exclusive attention. It was spectacularly grotesque, swollen to twice its size by impact with something very hard. When I asked to remove my contacts before surgery, I found my eye where my ear normally is. It turns out my jaw joint had petrified, it had been hit so hard.)

That's it for the Wreck of the Colonial. I have some scars. A zipper seam down my front and some faded brown gashes here and there. Because my jaw had to be reconstructed my mouth doesn't open all the way, but that only poses a problem with large apples.

I'm not afraid of riding trains. But the wreck's legacy – its real scar – is wearying, ever-present, wary self-consciousness. I may be in the moment but I'm also in the next one, and the next, because I never want to be caught unawares again just having a good time. On some subaltern level, my mind long ago decided to purchase a weird kind of insurance policy that it pays for by expecting the worst. It feels it must keep a constant eye on fate's ironic hand, lest it trip me up again.

The god of irony has become my constant companion and arch enemy. I wasn't paying attention that day of the crash. I was naively planning the future. Try as I will – and I do try, I hate living in thrall to superstition — I can't do that on the Coast Starlight. Faced with 36 hours of extremely rare free time, I'm able to gaze out the window at the edges of other people's lives, but I can't dwell on my own. To plan my future while in motion is just begging not to have one. That's how the god of irony thinks, and my job — particularly exhausting when I fly — is to outsmart the bugger.

The night I leave the Coast Starlight I wind up with a motion echo, as Rene dubbed it. My body keeps anticipating the rhythmic rock it no longer experiences. I try to walk from bed to bathroom at my hotel, and miss the doorway. After 24 years, my mind is still in the throes of something similar: anticipating an impact it no longer needs to navigate (cross fingers, knock on wood; don't read that, god of irony). I guess I'll call it a crash echo.

JOURNEY OF MANY MOONS

Hundreds of people bared their bottoms at every train passing through Laguna Niguel, California. The annual 'Mooning Amtrak' ritual is said to have begun in 1979 when someone in a bar offered to buy a drink for anyone who would run outside and moon the next train.

WAIT FOR IT . . . WAIT FOR IT . . .

MICHAEL DEACON TAKES CANADA'S SKEENA FROM JASPER TO PRINCE RUPERT – A 20-HOUR TRIP IN WHICH THE HIGHLIGHTS COME RIGHT AT THE END

If you come from a poky little shoebox like Britain it's difficult to grasp how big Canada is. Then again, Canadians don't seem to grasp how big Canada is either. After a sleepless nine-hour flight from London I landed at Edmonton, in the south-western province of Alberta, where I had a cab waiting to drive me to my hotel in Jasper. Woozy and jangling, my mind was still set to British time: a quarter to one in the morning. 'Jasper far?' I mumbled to the driver. 'Oh, no,' he beamed, squinting in the late afternoon sun. 'Shouldn't take more than four hours.' A few evenings later a publicist for Tourism Vancouver told me that Hollywood producers love to film in her city because it's 'so close to LA'. The two are over a thousand miles apart. Vancouver is close to LA in the way that London is close to Belgrade.

Were Canadians to take the Skeena train (which they wouldn't, because trains in Canada are for tourists or freight), they'd probably look on the journey as we'd look on a stroll to the post office. To me, though, it might as well have been a trip to the moon. Travelling from Jasper in Alberta to sparkling Prince Rupert on the Pacific coast – where humpback whales can be seen lunging out of a sea that is otherwise as smooth and blue as a pool table – you're on the train for two long days. All the same, I was keen to try it, having read about the beauty of the route's views and pictured a Narnia of pines and firs and snow-draped mountains. A woman on the TripAdvisor website wrote that she'd glanced out of her carriage window to find bears loping to keep up with the train. I was desperate to have the same experience. Provided the bears didn't board at the next stop.

Although the route takes its name from the language of the native

Gitxsan tribe (Skeena means 'River of the Clouds'), the man behind its construction was from the US: Charles Melville Hays, president of the Grand Trunk Pacific Railway. The track was completed in 1914, but sadly Hays never got to see it. Having visited England to secure financing for the railway, he set sail for home, pink with excitement. His ship was the Titanic.

I had a week to spend in Canada, but the purpose of my visit was the Skeena. I boarded the train on a warm Sunday lunchtime in early September, after a morning in Jasper. The national park in which it sits is magnificent – glowering Rockies, bellowing elk, air fresh as a mountain spring – but Jasper itself is not so much a small town as a large souvenir shop. If the goal of your holiday is a humorous sign saying DO NOT FEED THE MOOSE or a jar of maple syrup in the shape of a maple leaf, I can't recommend it highly enough.

My appetite for idly fingering souvenir tea towels sated, I strolled down to the station early to admire the train. Silver, snub-nosed and built in the Fifties, it looked curiously like a Thunderbirds toy, not least because of its 'panorama dome car', a carriage with a curved, transparent ceiling. Like any avant-garde design, it had an innocent quality: a self-conscious stab at the future that, now the future was here, seemed endearingly antiquated.

I climbed aboard. A quick warning: even if you've paid extra to travel 'touring class' rather than economy, don't expect the interior to be fancy. It's fine – crimson cushions, laptop sockets, enough leg room to seat a giraffe – but you will be eating your meals off a tiny beige plastic table that unfolds from your armrest. The cutlery will be tiny, beige and plastic, too.

Don't expect the meals themselves to be fancy, either. As the train wheezed out of Jasper we were served lunch. It consisted of a super-market-standard cold beef sandwich, a tub of rubbery pasta in a squirmingly sweet sauce, and a biscuit from Subway. All the same, I did feel taken care of. In the lavatory was a helpful eight-step guide, with pictures, to 'effective handwashing'. '1) Wet hands,' it read. '2) Soap.' And so on until '8) Open door to leave cubicle.'

The dozen of us dotted around touring class (there were about twice as many in economy) were in good spirits. This was in part thanks to the train staff, the booming Tracy and the deadpan Steven, who strode up and down the carriage, telling us about the route and what to look out for, and doing jokey little routines. Tracy: 'Steven, can you blow those clouds away from Mt Robson? These people have paid a lodda money to see it.' Steven: 'Oh, just show 'em the postcard.'

What we saw, apart from Mt Robson smothered in cloud, was the Scottish Highlands. Or rather, a version of the Scottish Highlands stretched in every direction: higher mountains, thicker forests, broader rivers. Our first great river was the Fraser, which Tracy said was the world's most important for salmon: in 2010, 25 million of them returned to it to spawn. How the authorities counted them she didn't let on – perhaps the salmon had to sign a register at the river's mouth.

I'd be impressed if they could count the number of trees. My guidebook told me that 50 per cent of Canada – the world's largest country after Russia – is forest. This struck me as a severe underestimate. Drop Britain from a helicopter into a Canadian forest and it would be lost as irretrievably as a pine cone. Much of the Skeena route, I soon found, was a 40ft-high corridor of trees. Very similar trees, at that. Past the windows they went: fir, pine, spruce, larch, hemlock. Spruce, hemlock, fir, larch, pine. Pine, spruce, larch, hemlock, fir. Within 20 minutes I sensed that I'd already seen every possible sequence of these five trees. Still, the view wasn't monotonously green: a plague of pine beetles had thoughtfully added variety by infesting British Columbia's forests, causing many trees to turn a fiery red.

As we chugged on down the corridor, I had three things on my mind. First: what a feat of stamina it had been to lay such a length of track through this mute, prickly wilderness. Second: imagine living out here. Because people do, or did. Not many – whole half-hours heaved by during which the only evidence that man had ever passed this way was the track itself – but now and again we'd spot a clearing with a shell of a shack, long deserted, and beside it a neat, lonely stockpile of logs. Or, more remarkably, surviving communities, such as Dunster, with its all-in-one general store, gas station and post office, but no houses I could see to serve, and McBride, which even had a hotel. I wondered what kind of guests it could possibly attract: honeymooning chipmunks, perhaps, or philandering moose.

Which brought me to my third thought: where were the animals? Until a coyote at 5.25pm on day one, I saw no creature more exotic than a crow. The forests of British Columbia, Unesco says, are home to more life per square yard than anywhere else on Earth: wolves, hawks, deer, bears, eagles, raccoons . . . Yet there was barely a bird in the trees. Perhaps it was just my bad luck, or the weather that day: drizzly gloom. Steven told me you often see bears feeding trackside on grain spilled by freight cars. Once, a heap of grain had been rained on before any bears got to it — so by the time they waddled out of the woods it had fermented and was giving off boozy fumes. He gazed as the bears tumbled and lurched as drunkenly as students.

'Happy hour!' shouted Tracy, with expert timing, and poured out white plastic cups of wine. These were very welcome, as local laws forbid you from bringing your own booze on to the train — although they do allow you to buy it on board. Tracy's wine, cheeringly, was free of charge. Another warning, though: if you want to buy beer, remember that it'll be Canadian and will therefore, irrespective of brand, taste like chilled bath water. Canadian beer cans are half the size of British ones, which, coupled with the foulness of their contents, creates an intriguing optical illusion: at first your can looks insultingly small, but after a couple of sips it looks dauntingly large.

On we trundled. One reason that British commuters in particular should feel at home on the Skeena train is that progress is slow and punctuated by long delays. These are caused by freight trains. On Canadian railways, freight (grain, lumber and coal) takes priority over people, which means that a couple of times a day your train stops for about three quarters of an hour until, finally, a 150-carriage freight train clatters by, allowing you to bumble back on your way again. I suppose I could have devoted these fatiguingly idle spells to polishing off a book; instead I spent them in the lounge car consuming my own weight in complimentary muffins.

With day one nearing its end, I couldn't decide what I thought of the journey so far. On the whole it put me in mind of a Booker Prize novel: beautiful, but uneventful. And, as happens whenever I force myself through a Booker Prize novel, I felt guilty for not enjoying it as much as I felt I should. Frankly, I blamed the bears. There was still no sign of the shiftless brutes. They plainly failed to appreciate their responsibilities to the Canadian tourist industry. For C\$525 (£323) a ticket, touring class, I expected to see them performing cartwheels and card tricks.

Perhaps I was just being grumpy. That made me feel guilty too, because Canadians are the world's friendliest people. In fact, their friendliness verges on the oppressive. They speak almost exclusively in merry exclamations. Visiting a Canadian restaurant, hotel, bar or shop is very different from visiting a British one. In Britain, most staff give the impression that their business would be infinitely more profitable if only they didn't have to put up with all these customers. In Canada, by contrast, they welcome you as though you were a visiting dignitary from some higher civilisation.

I learnt this on the first morning of my stay, when ordering breakfast at my hotel in Jasper. The waitress, who wore a smile that appeared to be marginally wider than her face, was so pleasant and cheerful I could barely look her in the eye.

Everything I did was perfect. She asked if I'd like a newspaper. I ordered the *Edmonton Journal*. 'Perfect!'

She asked what I'd like to eat. I ordered scrambled eggs. 'Perfect'!

She asked what I'd like to drink. I ordered coffee. 'Perfect!'

I tried to imagine what an imperfect order would have been. 'I'd like to set fire to the tablecloth then somersault naked across the carpet while bawling the hits of Cyndi Lauper, please.' 'I'm sorry, sir. Not in the lakeside restaurant. Please try the main lounge.'

After finishing my breakfast I inspected the bill. 'Thank you!' it read at the bottom. 'Have an outstanding day!' In Canada, even pieces of paper are friendly. With the bill — or as North Americans call it, the check — came a diners' survey, inviting me to rate my experience. Alongside each entry in a list of categories (among them 'menu selection', 'cleanliness', 'ambience') was a range of adjectives for me to tick. As I sat pondering whether the 'delivery of your check' had been 'outstanding' or merely 'excellent' (it certainly hadn't been 'poor'), the waitress returned to remove the monumental coffee pot I'd finally drained, and to replace it, unsolicited, with a fresh one of the same size. So sunnily did she smile at me that I felt bad for not wanting the coffee, and so dutifully began to slog my way through it. It was the same wherever I went in Canada, from flash hotel to dingy bar: people acted as though paying them money for their goods and services entitled me to courtesy and respect.

To a man raised in Britain, all this friendliness was most perplexing. My face ached from having to smile back at everyone. Still, it did make travelling alone much nicer. I was by myself, yet at no point did I feel isolated or alienated. Aboard the Skeena train, where, aged 29, I was the youngest passenger by at least a generation, there was a lovely, good-humoured, all-in-this-together spirit, of the sort you might find when a crowd of strangers huddle together in a bus shelter during a sudden hailstorm. There was a married couple from Britain, a group of old friends from Switzerland, a pair of unfailingly jovial women from Seattle. Most passengers come from Britain, Western Europe, the US and Australia. They tend to be older couples who have a fair amount of money tucked away, and have wisely decided to spend it on lengthy, expensive holidays before their grown-up children innocently mention they're trying to scrape together the deposit on a flat.

Everyone, I'm slightly ashamed to admit, seemed to be more forbearing than I was. I asked a beaming little old lady from Oregon whether she was disappointed not to have seen any exciting wildlife.

'Oh, no,' she said sweetly, 'I don't really like animals to be exciting. I met a bear once. It was in my back yard.'

Goodness, I said. What did it do? Did it try to attack you?

'Oh, no,' she said. 'I was fine. I had a big pot of honey.'

You had a big pot of honey? How on earth did you pluck up the courage to feed a bear?

'Oh, no,' she said. 'I didn't feed it. I threw the pot at its head.'

I wasn't sure I believed this, but it would have felt impertinent to query a little old lady. Especially since she seemed to be enjoying the free wine so much.

As dusk crept over the treetops we pulled into Prince George for the night. The train had no sleeper car, so you had to have booked a hotel. Prince George, unlike the communities we'd seen earlier, was a proper town; a fur-trading post in the 19th century, it's home today to more than 80,000 people. A publicist for local tourism took me to dinner and tried valiantly to persuade me of the town's merits. Unfortunately for her, the next morning I saw the place in daylight. An endless succession of concrete rectangles (the streets all gridded, the buildings all blocks), it appeared to have been designed by some bug-eyed fundamentalist intent on proving, by the proximity of so much verdant, mountainous splendour, the superiority of God's creative powers to man's. Trudging towards the station I looked up to see a colossal yellow sign saying LIQUIDATION WORLD. It sounded like the planet's bleakest museum, but instead turned out, no less bleakly, to be a discount chain store, flogging goods from shops that had gone out of business. Dangling from electricity wires near the station was a pair of grubby white trainers. A friend later told me that they would have been placed there by a drug dealer to mark out his patch. This may be an urban myth, but even if it is, it doesn't suggest there's much to do for fun in Prince George. If the most exciting way its younger inhabitants can find to spend an evening is to clamber an electricity pole and tie a pair of old trainers to the wires, you couldn't blame them if they did get into hard drugs.

By 8.00am we were back on board. Tracy and Steven had already been up for two and a half hours, preparing our breakfasts, tidying the train. Their working day had a further 13 hours to go. This, mind you, was nothing to Tracy. 'My first job on the trains?' she boomed proudly. '1981. Dishwasher, 18 hours a day, six days a week, five months straight.'

I have never declared war on a sovereign nation, but if I ever do, I'm appointing Tracy my general. She's one of those formidable North American middle-aged women before whom, even when they're smiling or serving you coffee, your first impulse is to salute. I could see, now, why so many of Canada's next-door neighbours were prepared to countenance voting for Sarah Palin. It's nothing to do with policies or pledges or ideology. It's the overpowering matronly bustle.

Never mind her round-the-clock dishwashing of the early Eighties – even Tracy's work today, as the train's service manager, storming up and down the carriages with drinks and snacks and information, struck me as drainingly relentless. She'd also devoted a lot of time to writing and printing a minutely detailed brochure, as thick as a Bible, containing everything she knew about the train and the journey, and which she handed out to passengers. (Thanks to Tracy's brochure I can tell you that the Skeena train's engines are GM 3000hp, two-stroke unit injection, water-cooled, turbo-charged V-16s, otherwise known as F40PH-2Ds. I hope I copied that out correctly.)

All the same, she said, if you average it out she works much less than someone doing nine to five in an office – she'd been on the trains for only 142 days the year before, which meant plenty of time off to spend at home. She said she lives 'four hours' drive' north of Vancouver. There they go again – these Canadians, with their nonchalant four-hour drives, their insouciant, think-nothing-of-it odysseys. Anyway, she seems to have sold the joys of the job to her grown-up stepson – he works for Canadian National Railway (Tracy pulled strings).

She plainly loves what she does, but she did confess, quite candidly, to a few worries. Since the beginning of the global recession two years earlier, she said, the number of passengers on the Skeena train had declined. Previously, they'd had ovens on board, better meals, proper cutlery, but the drop-off in ticket sales meant they'd had to make cutbacks. She thought, or hoped, that it was only a blip, and that once the recession ended, service would return to the way it was in the good old days.

The train panted on. I slouched in the dome car, scanning the glum marshes, the khaki rivers, the lakes discoloured an alien turquoise by glacier silt. At intervals stood fishermen in waders, an abandoned tractor rotting in a field, a pair of deer, a cluster of mobile homes, an ancient Indian village with totem poles hard to glimpse through the trees. (They're good at naming places, Indians – or, as Canadians call them, First Nations. One First Nations village we passed was named Kitwanga, which translates as 'The People of the Place of Plenty of Rabbits'. There was also Telkwa, or 'Where the Rivers Meet', and Kwinitsa, or 'Place of the Beaver'. The non-Indian village names, by contrast, tended to sound dumpy and dowdy: Terrace, Smithers, Doreen, Vanderhoof.)

We passed Lorne Creek, where gaggles of mad-haired prospectors would pan for gold in the late 1800s. In fact, Tracy said, there's still a prospector who goes there today: 'We carry a passenger regularly to his spot, and he sets off into the wilderness for weeks on end, staking claims.' Whether he ever actually finds gold, she didn't say, but I suppose it's reasonable to presume that he doesn't, otherwise he'd surely be making these trips by personal helicopter rather than a trundling 1950s-built locomotive with grimy windows. 'I worry for his safety,' Tracy admitted. 'We are in bear country.' Perhaps that was where all the bears had got to. They were downstream in their most elegant evening wear, napkins spread across their furry laps, dining grandly on confit de prospector.

Disappointed though I was not to see any bears, I was grateful not to see something else: the freeway. Canada is home to the dullest roads anywhere in the civilised world outside the American Midwest. Even thinking about them makes me limp with boredom. Whoever designed them was an almost fascistic literalist. I say designed, but that seems an exaggeration, given that Canadian roads are no more than straight lines – straight lines that roll on and on and on for hours, and for all I know days and weeks (the country's big enough). Why Canadians bother having driving lessons, I've no idea – all you need to do to drive a car in Canada is to start it and stop it. There don't appear to be any bends or corners or T-junctions or winding rural lanes to negotiate. I can't think how Canadian drivers cope with the tedium. Perhaps they read a book or watch a DVD or pootle about on their laptops – after all, it's not as if they need to keep their eye on the road.

But back to the train. This stretch of the country, as we toiled westward, was no more populous than that of the day before. Mind you, it's even less populous to the north. Ninety per cent of Canadians live within 100 miles of the US border. In Canada, averaged out, there are just under nine people per square mile. (In Britain, it's 660.) You become so used to this desolate spaciousness that when you visit a big, humming city like Vancouver you feel as though you've landed by accident in another country. Look, they have buildings over two storeys high! And shopping malls! And motor vehicles! And look, over there – human beings!

Vancouver, which I visited after my Skeena train trip – it's a two-hour flight south of Prince Rupert – felt to me more like an American city than a Canadian one. Of course it's Canadian in some ways (the beaming politeness of its inhabitants and serving staff, for one; being in Canada, for another), but it's American in its bunched and dizzying skyscrapers, its whooshing freeways, its abundance of restaurants from lavish to tacky, its buzzing malls and its opulent hotels (the Fairmont even offers guests a pillow menu, in case the almost decadently plump pillows that are already on the beds fail to meet Sir's or Madam's exacting standards). Perhaps most American of all, though, is Vancouver's thriving begging industry. All right, it isn't that bad, but every now and again in the city's heart I would notice a blotchy, bearded shape hunching cross-legged on the pavement, and propped before him a cardboard sign of his own devising (I was about to call it 'home-made' but that possibly isn't the right word). Still, this was Canada, where even the beggars have exemplary manners. On my walk to the subway on the final morning of my stay, I passed a beggar who was repeating, 'Small change, anybody?' in a tone so gentle and courteous it suggested that he was offering coins rather than requesting them. I just about fought off the temptation to say, 'Sure, I'll take two quarters and a dime.'

I've been trying hard to think of something, anything, that's irritating about Canadians. At last I think I've hit on it. Languages. Canadians insist on having two. Now, there's nothing wrong with being bilingual. It's embarrassing that most of us in Britain can't manage a foreign language; to go by most internet messageboards, we can barely manage our own. But the trouble with Canadians is not that the people are bilingual, but that everything in their country is. Every label you read and every sign you see, in the street, on the freeway, in the mall, is written both in English and in French – even in cases when the similarity of the two languages makes translation superfluous, such as, at Jasper station, 'baggage/bagage'. They're as bad as the Welsh. On the Skeena train I flicked through the railway company's complimentary magazine and found that every article was printed twice: on the left-hand page in English, and on the right-hand page in French. Pity the poor editors.

Well, I say pity them. For all I know they're deliriously happy in their work. Canadian magazines are much jollier than British ones. British magazines specialise in celebrity sniping, true-life shockers ('My DAD Wanted Me as His WIFE') and pull-outs of babes with boobs like footballs. Nothing wrong with that, of course: cynical prurience is one of the few fields in which we can claim to lead the world. I did feel wistful, though, gazing at the simple, wholesome innocence beaming from Canadian news-stands. Such titles. Such coverlines. There was

Country's Best Log Homes (sample feature: 'Best Floor Plans: Our Annual Contest Winners'). There was *Woodsmith* ('Discover How to Get More from Your Table Saw'). There was *Traditional Bowhunter* ('Hog Linguistics – How to Call Them In'). What peculiar people they must be, the Canadians, filling their free time not with prattle and porn but hobbies and interests.

A corollary of this type of innocence is earnestness. Not a po-faced, finger-wagging earnestness, but a trusting, unsmirking earnestness. Canadians don't automatically look for the joke in everything; they lack our snigger reflex. Take their television ads. In Britain, television ads are remorselessly jocular, as if their producers consider the punchline more important than the product. In Canada, by contrast, they're remorselessly straight-faced. They simply tell you, over and over again, at impressive length, that this product is good and you should buy this product because this product is good so be sure to buy this good product. On my first morning in Canada, in my hotel room in Jasper, I spent three whole minutes watching a television ad for a chainsaw. Shot after shot after shot of this life-changing, revolutionary chainsaw: one moment cutting wood, the next moment cutting a different piece of wood, the next, cutting a third piece of wood. 'It knows how to do one thing,' gurgled the voice-over – 'and that's cut!'

In Britain, most ads are over in less than 30 seconds. In Canada, they can last as long as documentaries. They call them 'paid presentations'. Paid presentations generally feature a microscopically minor celebrity or tangerine-skinned businessman lecturing the camera about the product or service in question, and are interspersed with testimonials from ecstatic customers – while, at the bottom of the screen, infinitesimally small print contradicts every word these ecstatic customers are saying. 'I lost 50lbs in 10 days on the SupaSlimmoKwik Diet!' (Small print: 'Results not typical.') 'I made $250,000 in a week thanks to Donald H Beaver Jr's Easy-as-Pie Cash Flow Scheme!' (Small print: 'Results blatant fiction.')

Still, I thought, 48 hours later, as the Skeena train shouldered onward, that's one comfort: I may be hundreds of miles away from civilisation, but I'm also hundreds of miles away from a Canadian television.

We were now well into day two. The sky was still a tin roof of grey. Lunch had been a flaccid wrap filled with ham and cheese, a bag of small damp carrots and a brick of chocolate something-or-other. I watched as a village slid by, its houses silent, its streets empty. On a patch of grass stood two swings, motionless and alone in the wan afternoon light. I turned, as I had done several times during the journey, to my iPod.

But enough. By this point you may be under the impression that a lot of the Skeena route is hypnotically repetitive, and that therefore it isn't worth doing. In the first case you'd be right, and in the second you'd be wrong. The Skeena route is a test. A test of your resilience, your patience, your ability to hunker down and sit tight till something wonderful turns up.

And it does. Over the two days, you'll be on the train for a total of 21 hours. And all the most spectacular sights will come in the final two.

Suddenly the corridor of forest is gone. In its place is sheer disorientation. Mountains, each with a halo of white mist. Between them, a golden sunset draining down the horizon. The river, sharp as a mirror. You lean out of the window and feel the cold bright air whistling past your face. It's a rush.

The photos you take will not do it justice. This won't be your fault; the landscape is mischievous. You aim at some astonishing peak or a swerve of the Skeena, then examine the screen on the back of your digital camera. A rogue, blurring tree has dived across like a goalkeeper to block your shot.

The sky seems bigger than you've ever seen it. Almost unnoticed, night descends. The train rattles on through the gathering black. Tracy, doling out dinner, leads the carriage in a chorus of 'If You're Happy and You Know It, Clap Your Hands'. Wind whooshing through your hair, you stand at the window, as stupidly euphoric as a dog sticking its head out of a car. You've forgotten the dearth of bears, the monotony, the punishingly long hours in your seat. All that matters is this vast, peerless panorama. It streaks by, as dizzying as a dream, for two extraordinary hours.

Eventually, your senses overloaded, you feel the train slow as you rumble towards your destination, the port of Prince Rupert, a looming silhouette of cranes tacked with red lights. As you clamber down on to the platform, you stumble as clumsily as a calf. 'You feel like you're swaying?' barks Tracy cheerfully. You nod. 'Same here, every time,' she says. 'Even in my hotel room after, I stand there and I feel like I'm swaying.' Still, she's used to it. She's done this trip 180 times in the past six years.

You might not manage to match her. But you will want to do it again.

TO THE SOUTH

IN A CLASSIC RITES-OF-PASSAGE JOURNEY,
CHRIS MOSS TAKES A BIG DIESEL AND
A SMALL STEAM TRAIN TO PATAGONIA

There is no anticipation like that stirred by a long railway journey. For years I had been driving – oh, the humdrum motor car – past Constitución station, wondering when my time would come to wander on to the concourse and find my platform for the great journey south. 'Sur' is a beautiful tango, and in Argentina, which is already pretty far south, you just want to keep going down and down, all the way to Antarctica.

Sadly, there's never been a train to the ice continent; but in 1997, towards the end of my 10-year sojourn in Buenos Aires (I had gone there to teach and stayed on to work at the *Buenos Aires Herald*), the government, on what seemed a generous whim, reopened a long-distance railway service between Buenos Aires and the ersatz Swiss Alpine resort of San Carlos de Bariloche, 1,060 miles away in the foothills of the Andes.

Local newspapers announced that the big 'new' diesel train had been imported from Spain; in fact it was just new-looking compared with the rusty old 1950s Japanese Toshiba trains used by the Argentine commuter networks; it was actually old rolling stock that the Spanish national railway firm, RENFE, no longer used. But the exciting thing for me was that you could get off the train just short of Bariloche, at Ingeniero Jacobacci, there to board the Trochita Angosta steam train, which Argentines affectionately call La Trochita: the Little Gauge.

My anticipation was particularly keen as I was travelling with an old school friend, Mike, who had flown over to join me for the adventure. He was getting fed up with living in a box of a flat in north London, a city he hated, and his girlfriend, Sharon, had just left him for an accountant. He needed some space. Mike and I had both been born in the Lancashire village of Burtonwood, and had grown up only half an hour's walk from the oldest railway track in the world, the Rainhill-Manchester line. For us, trains always meant freedom, or the idea of it.

For our journey south, we had four weeks free, a wad of pesos in our pockets, a carton of cigarettes, a bottle of bourbon, two full rucksacks and – yes, I know it's sounding very Blues Brothers – we were wearing huge smiles. We knew the journey would be epic and memorable even as we were buying our *pebete*-bread ham-and-cheese sandwiches at Constitución and ensuring we had enough water, beer and loo roll.

The first leg was in a six-man compartment, and we had four friendly, intelligent young Argentine men for company. Despite Mike's poor Spanish (he knew only the words for water, beer and whisky, and one expression: '¿Donde está el toilet?') we hit it off as a group right away. We talked about politics, the Falkland Islands, music, girls and football: the five pillars of Anglo-Argentine macho intercourse. As the diesel train crawled across the dead-flat pampas, we drank beer, played *truco* – the card game all Argentines love – and shed the angst and accelerated pace of the big city.

You have to get used to slowness on Argentine trains. Look in an old *South American Handbook* (from, say, the early 1940s) and you will see how Argentina once boasted one of the most extensive networks in the world. The Gran Ferrocarril Sud – or Great Southern Railway – was built in phases from 1862 onwards by British companies and largely managed by British expatriates. It was one of four major lines radiating out from Buenos Aires, and played a key part in populating the interior of north and central Argentina. But in 1948, President Juan Perón, in a moment of nationalistic fervour, bought the entire network. Investment dried up, lines were closed, and those that remained open were left to moulder and rust. By the late 1990s, the network was minuscule relative to the size of the country and all the lines were in poor repair.

Our train shuddered through stations with names I knew only as fortresses or generals from the 19th-century campaigns against the indigenous tribes: Las Flores, Azúl, Laprida. Sometimes we were no faster than the half-wild horses that cantered alongside the line.

Sometimes we stopped altogether in the middle of the undulating pampas for ten or fifteen minutes, and the cows got tired looking up at the long chain of carriages and went back to chewing grass. But I was in no hurry. On a good train journey, you secretly wish that you will never arrive.

It was late afternoon when we stopped at a station close to the Ventana mountains. The range isn't well known outside Argentina, though it is popular with hikers and an important geological landmark: where the Andes are 100 million years old, the Sierra de la Ventana sits on a precambrian base perhaps two billion years old. But the mountains were merely a blip on the horizon; they petered out into a few scraggy hills and soon we were back on the grassy plains.

Approaching the port city of Bahía Blanca, however, we could see that something about the landscape had changed. Even by the weak light of dusk, the green of the humid pampas had given way to a yellowish hue. During the night, this would turn ash-grey. The air was growing noticeably colder, too. Ñandues or, in English, rheas – the larger of the two South American emu-like flightless birds – could be seen alongside the line, and occasionally the perfume of the pampas skunk would drift though the window to mix with the black tobacco being smoked.

From here onwards, we were on the fringes of Patagonia, travelling through three smallish towns – Carmen de Patagones, Viedma and San Antonio Oeste – making a huge curve to point the train towards the Andes. The Spanish founded Carmen in 1779 with the intention of colonising Patagonia, but attacks by the Brazilian fleet, aided by British privateers, in 1827 put paid to that plan. Viedma, too, had a brief moment of near-glory. After democracy was restored in 1983, following seven years of oppressive, even murderous, military dictatorship, the incoming president, Raúl Alfonsín, announced that Argentina would create a new capital in the south. Viedma was the chosen site. The *provincianos* were euphoric; at last power and wealth would be spread around the nation. Blueprints for a model city were drawn up. I have even seen maps produced with '*capital federal proyectada*' written beneath Viedma's name). As with Carmen, the idea was to colonise and develop the empty hinterland, to fill it with cows and people, roads and football pitches, taxis and tax officers. But the Buenos Aires-adoring bureaucrats and politicos weren't going anywhere, and soon the plan was shelved. I didn't see much of the town as we passed through it that night, but if the number of streetlamps – and what they illuminated – was anything to go by, Viedma remained small and nondescript.

Patagonia might be doomed as a social and political project, and yet the name retains a mythical potency for travellers. I had read Darwin's accounts of exploring the coastline in search of fossils. I had with me a borrowed copy of *In Patagonia*, the 1977 travelogue in which Bruce Chatwin unearths, and makes up, some wonderful tales about its people. But the land we were traversing was best described by William Hudson, the great ornithologist born in Argentina and raised in Quilmes, just south of Buenos Aires. He travelled to the Rio Negro – the river that marks the northernmost limit of Patagonia – in December 1870. Unfortunately for him – but luckily for us – he accidentally shot himself in the knee and was forced to convalesce for several months. He lay back and observed, and wrote down his thoughts, which would later be published as *Idle Days in Patagonia*. That he wrote the book later, in London, is not incidental: it is imbued with longing from afar, and with a sentimental, but also mystical, notion of northern Patagonia. Hudson quotes a memorable passage from *The Voyage of the Beagle* in which Darwin wonders why he can't get out of his mind the 'arid wastes' of Patagonia and decides that it is because their emptiness gives 'free scope to the imagination'. But Hudson challenges this theory of landscape as a *tabula rasa*, arguing that Patagonia is affecting because the absence of noise and movement, of animals and plants induces a 'state of intense watchfulness' and also wakes up the primal and animal in us.

I'm not sure that my journey across the same region woke up quite the same aspects of my nature. We all got drunk together on the second night as we sensed the diesel train was nearing its destination. Our last supper was a debauched bout of competitive drinking. When the bourbon ran out, the Argentines passed around a bottle of Old Smuggler, an Argentine variation on whisky that smells a bit like peat but tastes like turps. With only a bag of peanuts for food, to share among six of us, the results were predictable, and the compartment had a prison-cell atmosphere by the time we pulled into Ingeniero Jacobacci.

At the station I saw a flyposter advertising 'El Viejo Expreso Patagónico'. It was Paul Theroux who had branded the railway line between Ingeniero Jacobacci and Esquel – which he rode at the end of an epic journey that began in Boston – the Old Patagonian Express. I found it somewhat depressing that some Argentines had even translated and adopted that nickname. I far preferred the diminutive 'Trochita'; a small train, but with enough power to get you all the way across the fearsome Patagonian steppe, come rain or shine, blizzard or tornado. When I made a later trip to Bariloche, in 2004, I would see black-and-white photographs taken in the 1950s, when railway workers had kept the line open even though the snow was higher than the running board; they shovelled loads away, and managed to get the train over the highest stretch at Ojo de Agua, 3,630 feet above sea level, where the snow lay deepest. But that was in the days when Argentines nurtured an ideal – a fantasy, maybe – that infrastructure would one day lead to development and a vast population in the remotest provinces. On the platform now, in late January 1997, we were mainly tourists, hippies, university students and the odd steam enthusiast. It was summer, and we didn't need to get anywhere.

The Trochita was leaving in three hours – it seemed our arrival was more a coincidence than a connection – so we had plenty of time to look it over. At the front was a Henschel steam-powered engine shipped from Germany in 1922. The pistons and valves were already making quite a bit of noise, but for the moment only small commas of black were rising from the great smokestack at the front. As always with old trains – and especially perhaps in underemployed Argentina – there seemed to be far too many people shouting and advising and watching for the surely quite straightforward job of getting some water boiled. '¡Dale!' shouted one working below the cow-catcher. 'La puta que te parió,' complained another, burning his fingers on some greasy old metal joint. The first expression is Argentina's catch-all expression for 'Do it man!' or 'Come on!' The second is too offensive to translate but relates to prostitutes and their offspring.

Finally, the driver, helped by his co-workers, had mustered enough coal, fire and faith for him to be able to commit himself and the little engine to embarking on a 250-mile journey across a barren no-man's land. With a whistle and a whoosh of steam, we said goodbye to no one at all – I didn't even register whether Jacobacci was a hamlet as well as a station – and we were off. Well, I say 'off', but if the diesel had moved at the pace of a horse we were now on an ailing *burro*.

We were in basic class. Some seats had cushions, but we had only wooden slats. I spent most of the time sitting at a doorway at the very back of the train, with Mike and a few others – our four compartment friends were still with us – just looking backwards along the line. Flocks of the smaller Patagonian rheas called *choiques* were around us now; the train's whistle would startle them and it wouldn't be unusual to see one run off in rapid meanders, hopping across the line, one wing opened out like a sail to capture the Patagonian wind. I spotted a *guanaco*, too, high up on a hill. Smaller and less hairy than its cousins, the llamas and alpacas of the north, the *guanaco* is a quite beautiful red-haired camelid that has delicate toes adapted to the scrubland.

Northern Patagonia is mainly desert. Not the archetypal desert of sand and dunes, but a barren, stony desert occasionally punctured by thorny bushes and spiky tufts of grass known as *coirón*. Scraggy-looking lambs could be spotted walking among these bushes on the lookout for a juicy-ish bite; there are more sheep than people in Patagonia, but so scarce is the food that each animal needs several acres.

But the land was less level now. We were close to the foothills of the Andes, and already rocky formations and low bluffs were cracking through the arid crust. The tone of the land was brownish, dead-looking. A low sierra – or mountain range – rose on the left side of the line. Vultures, hawks and maybe condors – I couldn't make out the Shakespearean ruff they wear – wheeled in gyres above the peaks.

When we steamed around the long bends past hills and tabletops, I looked down from the back to the front of the train. Dozens of heads hung out of windows, all gawping at the landscape. There comes a moment on any long journey when everybody just shuts up. It's the best time, perhaps, and, in near-silent, unpeopled Patagonia, is utterly fitting. This was my first really long journey – I had been on the tracks for three days by now – and the first time I realised how a train functions like a movie camera. Where Hudson and Darwin, walking or on horseback, had been fully conscious of the stillness of Patagonia, for me it was a constantly changing place. Though one of the flattest, most featureless, greyest places on earth, it remained alive because it flickered past my eyes like celluloid. In the early 2000s a new generation of Argentine filmmakers would use cars and road trips in precisely this way to bring Patagonia to life in films such as *Historias Mínimas* and *Bombón: El Perro.* A long black smoke trail chuffed out of the train all the time; steam adds its own spectacle to a train journey. When I went back inside I was covered in dust from this and from the steppe.

At Aguada Troncoso, we were told the train would be pausing for half an hour, so everyone got off and went to the toilet. Or rather, waited for the toilet. There was no platform as such, just a bamboo-walled kiosk-type building standing in the middle of a field. You could almost see through the bamboo and observe the solitary user doing his or her business. There were perhaps thirty of us in the line. For those who like a peaceful trip to the throne, it was a minor crisis. After fifteen minutes, I gave up and went in search of a bush.

Every few hours, the train stopped in the middle of nowhere. No one got on or off. It was as if the driver were imagining a populated land – just as so many dreamer-colonists had done before in Patagonia. The names of the stations were sometimes not Spanish but Tehuelche, or a mixture of both: Futa Ruin, Manuel Choique, Fitalancao. It was hard to imagine any indigenous peoples prospering in such barren terrain. There were no trees for shade, hardly any rivers for water – the only significant one we crossed was the Chubut, marking the border with its namesake province – only the hardest materials for building shelter. But I had seen photographs of Tehuelche tribes-people. They looked rather like the land they ruled over: tough, leather-skinned Indians, who dwelt in rudimentary huts made from *guanaco* skin, and carried spears and lassos. They had no horses until the Spaniards arrived. They never seemed to be smiling in the old photographs.

As dusk arrived a wind whipped up. Dust devils raced across the track and the low bushes bent their heads. When it stopped, the Milky Way glowed and the temperature fell to below freezing.

That night we didn't sleep, but sat huddled close on our wooden benches, hugging cups of tea. Each carriage had a samovar – I would later see this in Russia, but it was a surprise in Patagonia, not known for its char-drinking culture. Our four Argentine companions were now proper amigos, so we could sit in silence and still be at ease. They had also brought yerba mate, the green tea all Argentines drink communally, and we were soon incorporated into their constant rounds of sipping, refilling and passing along.

In Esquel we were greeted by a frosty orange dawn. We said our goodbyes to the Argentines and Mike and I set off into town. There were Italian coffee shops, Spanish bars, Welsh flags. But we wanted to keep on moving.

In the 18th century, Spanish explorers came to this region searching for a local Eldorado that they had been told was called Trapalanda. Perhaps it was the absence of anything remotely like a city that made long-suffering, well-travelled men conjure mythical golden cities. Or perhaps the nomads were just having some fun and pointing the lost Europeans towards the Andes to get shot of them. Mike and I decided we wouldn't rest till we got to the Pacific. As there were no more railway lines, we took a bus to Lago Puelo and set out on foot across the low passes of the Andes that connect a string of small lakes on the Argentina/Chile border.

We walked for five days, camped wild, bought bread from local farmers, drank water from Andean streams, and, once we'd drunk our two cartons of cheap Resero red wine, we detoxed. Finally, deep inside the clefts of the mountains, far away from new acquaintances and towns and trains, we were able to do our catching up. We talked a lot as we walked and shared silences during the evenings, watching the stars come out at night and rising with the early summer dawn. We took it easy, and walked slowly. As with all the best journeys, we didn't want this one to end – when you travel with friends, it always feels like a rite of passage, whatever your age, and you secretly wonder if it won't be your last such trip. When we finally made it to the Chilean coast our minds were as mystically Patagonian as Hudson's and our skin as leathery as any Tehuelche's. I had not read any of the Chatwin, though; we were far too busy telling, and living, our own stories.

A RUM KIND OF RAILWAY

DERVLA MURPHY, STILL TRAVELLING ROUGH IN
HER LATE SEVENTIES, SET OUT TO GET TO GRIPS
WITH CUBA – A PLACE OF IMPULSIVE FRIENDSHIP
AND IMPENETRABLE BUREAUCRACY. ALONG THE
WAY, SHE HAD A HARD TIME ON THE TRAINS . . .

In 1837 Cuba acquired Latin America's first railway, originally laid to serve certain cane plantations, then gradually expanded to its present 3,030 miles. Yet Havana's imposing station is almost tourist free, for reasons which soon become apparent. At 'Information', a chatty, elderly woman told me that the only service to Santa Clara was the thrice-weekly *especial* to Santiago; it would depart next day at 2.15 p.m., arriving in Santa Clara four hours later, leaving me time to find my friends' house before sunset – new English-speaking friends, met on the Malecón [Havana's promenade] and impulsively hospitable.

Whether you're running a democracy, a dictatorship or an international institution, bureaucracy constipates efficiency. For years Fidel has been condemning the Cuban variety, to no effect; even during the Special Period [after September 1990, when trade with the Eastern Bloc collapsed], with its particular urgent needs, the Faceless Ones resisted most reforming efforts.

Cubans are of course the main victims. Tourists usually escape this net, woven of illogicality, but free-range travellers are soon enmeshed. For instance, Havana's railway ticket office is a brisk 10-minute walk away from the station – why? Moreover, there are two offices in separate buildings, one for Cubans, one for foreigners – why? Arriving at 12.50 p.m., I was told to return at 1.15; one's ticket must be bought within the hour of departure – why? Then, having queued twice in that office, one has to queue again, within the station, for the ticket to be 'confirmed'.

In the spacious concourse, high and wide, the seating seemed like a planning error: long rows of black metal chairs were welded to the floor and packed close together à la cut-price airlines, leaving open expanses between blocks. A six-foot barrier and locked gates allowed no access to the four deserted platforms.

A tall, slim young woman wearing a smart sky-blue uniform labelled 'Security Service (Private)' guesstimated that the Santiago *especial* might leave at five-ish. She and her three colleagues appeared to be in lieu of a police presence. Watching them, I again noted the cold, almost disdainful persona assumed by many Cuban petty officials when dealing with the public. Is this attitude, so unlike the average Cuban's relaxed friendliness, a result of Soviet training? Or is it a symptom of the tension that has come to exist between frustrated citizens and agencies now often despised as corrupt?

Obviously nobody expected this *especial* to depart at 2.15. My many fellow-passengers looked settled and resigned; most families were lunching, sharing saucepans or bowls of rice and black beans and pork fat. Some men played chess or dominoes while their wives dozed, others read *Granma* with close attention – surprising to me because Cuba's only daily newspaper is the Party's voice. Small extrovert children romped around the open spaces, making new friends as they went.

As the overhead clock registered 2.30, 3.30, no one seemed disgruntled. Beside two of the platforms long trains stretched away into the distance, looking as though they had been stationary for months if not years. And maybe they had.

At 4.10 the *especial* arrived from Santiago and hundreds disembarked; many carried a musical instrument, some wheeled bicycles. When our departure was announced, queues formed at four gates, each line confined between metal bars as in a cattle-crush.

Then came a delay, caused by several pairs of porters pushing long handcarts piled with cargo for Santiago. Shouting and laughing, they raced each other along the broad hundred-yard expanse between barrier and buffers, their loads wobbling precariously. Unsmiling young women eventually unlocked the gates and closely scrutinised each ticket and ID document. They wore the railway uniform of purple shorts and tunics with black tights and absurdly high-heeled shoes.

Although foreigners must travel first-class, I had trouble finding my allotted place; all the coaches had gone unpainted for decades. Excitedly chattering groups were being guided to their seats by other uniformed women, one of whom led me to a carriage with torn upholstery and mud-coated windows. My only companion was Raimundo, tall, lean, distinguished-looking and very black. A history professor, specialising in colonial Africa, he spoke fluent English.

At 5.15 our engine hooted hoarsely and as we moved, almost imperceptibly, I remarked that we should reach Santa Clara by 9.30. Raimundo looked sceptical and said, 'Maybe'. Then we stopped, still under the station roof. Raimundo, sorting through papers in his briefcase, glanced at me and chuckled. For 20 minutes nothing happened. After we had backed to our starting position nothing continued to happen. Again all the platforms were deserted, apart from one jovial railway official engaged in private enterprise, selling delicious sausage rolls, more sausage than bread.

At 5.50 we moved again, very slowly. At 6.10 we stopped again. Raimundo closed his briefcase, took off his spectacles and made inquiries. Our engine had broken down, decisively, and must be replaced. As this news spread, other passengers laughed uproariously, tuned up their guitars and began a sing-song. Standing in the corridor, watching our engine being detached, I was joined by an effervescent teenager who offered me a swig from her half-bottle of rum. 'Have a drink! Cuba transport bad for tourists, Cuba rum good!' Accepting her offer, I was conscious of Raimundo's disapproving stare. As the defunct engine passed us, on the next track, passengers crowded to the windows, leaning out to cheer and clap ironically. Raimundo smiled at me and said, 'That's how we survived the Special Period.'

Our replacement engine got going at 6.55, groaning reluctantly as we left the station. Beyond the suburbs shanty homes huddled close to the track — as shanty as any I've seen in the Majority World, yet the residents look better nourished than their equivalents elsewhere. For years past many Cubans have had to struggle to supplement their rations, but for most it's possible to do so, by being persistently ingenious and/or devious.

Beyond flat scrubland the sun was sinking, and when Raimundo calculated that we were unlikely to reach Santa Clara (170 miles from Havana) before midnight I decided to sleep in the waiting-room until dawn. Soon the only glimmers of light came from the stars and our engine's weak beam; even in the first-class coaches no one had a torch. 'This train years ago lost its illuminations,' Raimundo resignedly remarked.

I closed our door, to reduce the salsa decibels, and we stretched out, giving thanks for an uncrowded compartment, and discussed Ché's Congolese débâcle – an almost forgotten fragment of history that Raimundo had closely studied. Then he told me about Santa Clara's origins. For all Cuba's sparse population and distance from the motherland, Spain's Inquisition didn't spare the colony. In 1682, in the prosperous little town of Remedios, when a priest detected demons by the dozen he summoned Inquisitors from Havana to organise the 'trial' and incineration of 'the possessed' and the torching of their homes and property. This operation prompted many terrorised residents to flee 30 miles inland and found Santa Clara.

At 12.20am my escort handed me on to a long platform, lit by one feeble bulb, and we were about to seek the waiting-room when my friend Tania came hurrying towards us, arms outstretched, apologising for the unreliability of Cuban trains. Raimundo looked immensely relieved; he hadn't approved of my plan – not for security reasons, but because he refused to believe an 'abuela' [granny] could sleep soundly on a floor.

* * *

Undaunted by experience, I booked a seat on the twice-weekly Havana-Bayamo train service (alleged dep. 7.25 p.m.). The only alternatives were hitchhiking, which could take several days, or a Viazul coach. At 8.50 p.m. we passengers were loosed on to the ill-lit platform and confusion immediately set in; even by daylight the faint print on my ticket, giving coach, compartment and seat numbers, was well-nigh illegible. When I opened a coach door at random its inner panel fell off, blocking my way. Clambering over it, I groped down a corridor by a glimmer of platform light and found an empty compartment where I was still alone at 9.45. The engine then made eerie noises, setting it apart from any other engine I've heard, and moved off at a slow walking speed. All this seemed too good to be true; silence and darkness blessed my coach: I could stretch out and sleep, at least until the first stop.

Some time later three chain-smoking adults and a fretful toddler woke me. I sat up, eyelids drooping. Soon the adults (two male, one female) were furiously quarrelling and exhaling rum fumes. Cubans tend to shout even when not arguing, possibly because conversations must often compete with insanely amplified music coming from several different directions. This row, inexplicably, quietened the toddler.

An hour or so later, when the last cigarettes had been stamped on the floor and everyone except me was asleep, all hell broke loose nearby. A conductor was on the prowl, checking everyone's seating. In Havana, where conflicting views were held about the numbering of 12 unmarked coaches, many passengers had settled wherever they could find space and now resented being moved. Oddly enough, my companions were correctly placed – very clever of them, I thought. Now the combination of her own dying torch and my faintly inked ticket challenged our conductor. Only when one of the men lent his cigarette-lighter could she see that mine was seat three in compartment B in coach six – three coaches away. She then recruited this same man to lead me through total darkness. He wore my rucksack, I carried my shoulder-bag and used my umbrella to steady myself: hereabouts the train was behaving like a small boat on a stormy sea.

One is accustomed to the bits between coaches moving beneath one's feet. In this case, however, there were no bits: one had to leap from coach to coach. As we moved slowly along the corridor of the second coach I felt the floor giving beneath my feet and momentarily I panicked. (But the sinking floor was just another of the Bayamo service's idiosyncrasies and not immediately threatening – though one day those rotting boards may well claim victims.) In coach six my guide used his cigarette-lighter to peer at labels, then roused a man comfortably curled up on two seats – his and mine, apparently. Without complaint, he shifted his position as I thanked my guide; until then, he and I had exchanged not a word.

With rucksack on lap, because I couldn't see where to store it, I leant back in my seat and received a small but painful scalp wound; it oozed enough blood to matt my hair. Where a headrest had been three sharp metal spikes protruded. My bag contained one tin of Bucanero [beer], for emergencies. I now felt its time had come and quickly drank it – a mistake . . . In due course those 355ml sought the exit and by the light of a full moon, newly emerged from dispersing clouds, I located the 'baño' – seemingly occupied. Having waited a reasonable time I tried the door again, pushing hard. It swung open to reveal a vacuum: below was Mother Earth.

At a certain point one ceases to believe in the reality of what's happening – it must all be an illusion – yet somehow one has to go along with it. But for the moon, I would have stepped forward to my death – not exactly a premature death but an unpleasant and rather silly way to go. The door bore a prominent notice – DANGER! DO NOT OPEN! – but some more drastic deterrent is required in an unlit train that habitually travels by night. Opposite the 'baño' was the coach exit, its steps conveniently missing so that one could pee, more or less accurately, on to the track. But only more or less: such situations provoke penis envy. The 'baño' at the other end of the coach, visited during the day, had no door – or loo or washbasin, though their sites were obvious. Here one had to relieve one's bladder and bowels in full view of passers-by. The latter activity was performed as close as possible to the walls – a much used space, halfway through our 20-hour journey.

We covered the first 250 miles in 11½ hours, including a long stop in Santa Clara, while a passenger train and two freight trains passed on their way to Havana. Then, speeding up, we achieved 50 miles in an hour and a half. After that I lost interest in our progress and concentrated on my awakening companions. All five were going to a conference at Bayamo University and their company made the travail of moving to coach six seem worthwhile. Four spoke English – 'necessary for our research'. Academic salaries left them with no choice but to take this unbelievable train, one third the price of the cheapest bus. My tourist ticket cost about £36; they paid about £2.15.

Moribund sugar mills, their stacks visible from afar, punctuated these hundreds of miles of flatness. My commenting on the job losses brought a sharp response from Aleida, leader of the academics. All those workers had been retrained, given new jobs. When I asked what sort of jobs my tone perhaps suggested scepticism and the professor snapped, 'In factories and municipalities'. It would have been too provocative to wonder how those institutions suddenly came to need thousands of extra workers. Aleida seemed to distrust the foreign writer. Her colleagues would, I intuited, have talked more freely but she, their senior in age and status, retained firm control of our exchanges. Sometimes my companions spoke English for my benefit, sometimes they argued in Spanish about Bush, Guantánamo Bay, tourism – and then one sensed the men's hesitancy when disagreements arose. Rather than assert themselves, they exchanged furtively supportive glances.

From Bayamo's station, a 10-minute walk took me to my friend Miranda's rather luxurious 'casa particular', where my hostess exclaimed, 'Desde Havana en el tren! Muy difícil.' 'Sí,' I agreed, 'pero muy interesante.'

Later, writing my diary, I recalled a stimulating debate at a literary seminar I had recently attended in Florida: to what (if any) extent is it permissible for travel writers to embellish or exaggerate incidents – even to enhance narratives with fiction if that makes for a 'better read'? Our divergence of opinion was decisively age-related. The oldies – Peter Matthiessen, Barry Lopez and myself – were adamantly opposed to any element of fiction and only grudgingly tolerant of embellishments and exaggerations. I think it was Barry Lopez who noted that travel writers have a duty of accuracy. By being strictly factual they can make a small contribution to future generations' knowledge of how things were in countries A, B or C when they went that way.

Someone mentioned Afghanistan as an example. The version of that country's culture and history currently being promoted is counterbalanced or contradicted by such travel writers as Mountstuart Elphinstone, Robert Warburton, George Robertson, Robert Byron, Ella Maillart, Peter Mayne, Eric Newby, Peter Levi (and myself). Incidentally, Peter Levi's perception seems even more painfully keen now than it was when he wrote in 1971: 'As a political entity Afghanistan is nothing but a chewed bone left over on the plate between Imperial Russia and British India.'

All of which leads up to a solemn declaration. I can assure my readers that the foregoing pages give a true and faithful account of the condition of Cuba's Havana-Bayamo rail service in the year 2006 AD.

Extracted from *The Island That Dared: Journeys in Cuba* by Dervla Murphy (Eland Books).

CHAPTER 3
AFRICA AND THE MIDDLE EAST

---

4 SEPTEMBER 2010

A LINE IN THE SAND

GAVIN BELL CROSSES NAMIBIA
ON THE DESERT EXPRESS

At first I think it is a mirage. A lone figure, shimmering in the heat, loping steadily through the emptiness of the Namib Desert. In the distance it is a dark spectre, feet barely touching the ground, diminishing as it jogs towards a towering sand dune on the horizon.

I rub my eyes. I have just woken from sleep on the overnight Desert Express train from Windhoek. Is it an illusion, a trick of heat and dust, or the spirit of a long-dead San Bushman returned to his hunting grounds?

Neither. It is Cedric. He is a steward on the train, and a keen footballer with Gibeon United of Namibia's 2nd Division. It turns out he ran up the 100-foot sand dune for fun, and to make sure it was safe for passengers to trek up after him and view a wild expanse of the southern Atlantic Ocean from its summit. Journeys on the Desert Express tend to be a bit out of the ordinary.

Like most sightseeing trains designed for tourists, it is far from being an express service. On weekends it trundles leisurely between the Namibian capital and the old German colonial seaside resort of Swakopmund, stopping along the way for game drives, dune excursions and lion-feeding. Then a few times a year it continues north, on seven-day trips to the Etosha National Park.

Travelling by train through unfamiliar landscapes is like being in a moving cinema. The windows are screens depicting images that flicker, leave a fleeting impression, and then are gone. From the comfort of an armchair, the traveller gazes with interest at a changing world – in this case an ancient wilderness punctuated improbably by small towns and the occasional giraffe.

On the face of it, the Namib is not the most inviting place in which to build a railway. The San hunter-gatherers who once roamed its bone-dry gravel plains and shifting sands called it 'the land God made in anger'. Early Portuguese mariners wrecked on its aptly-named Skeleton Coast dubbed its hinterland 'the sands of hell'. Later, Charles Andersson, a 19th-century Swedish naturalist and explorer, recorded memorably his first impression of it: 'A shudder, amounting almost to fear, overcame me when its frightful desolation suddenly broke upon my view. Death would be preferable to banishment in such a country.' In fact, lingering death was the fate of countless sailors and travellers who became lost in its trackless wastes.

Then along came German soldiers and settlers, who decided in 1897 it would be a good idea to lay a railway across it. In fact, they had little choice. At the time there were no roads worthy of the name anywhere in what was then German South-West Africa, and the only way of travelling through it was by ox wagon. Then an epidemic of rinderpest, an acute viral disease, wiped out 90 per cent of the oxen in the country, leaving communities isolated and short of supplies. With commendable efficiency and imported Prussian Army stock, engineers completed the 230-mile Staatsbahn between Windhoek and Swakopmund in five years, and promptly began running passenger and freight services in 1902.

The first time I saw Windhoek I was a foreign correspondent, reporting on Namibia's transition to independence from South Africa in the late 1980s. Then it was a sleepy town among scrubby hills that retained much of the flavour of its German colonial past. There is a stillness in the Namib, one of the world's oldest deserts, that seemed to pervade the little capital. Now, two decades later, it has changed almost beyond recognition. It is bigger and busier, with new residential districts and shopping malls, and the old stores on Independence

Avenue are dwarfed by glitzy concrete towers built by South African banks and insurance companies.

Happily, the railway station is a survivor from the old days. Tucked away in a cul-de-sac off Bahnhof Street, its ornate facade embellished with gables and a pillared balcony, it stands with quiet dignity among the graceless monoliths thrown up around it. A photograph of the building decorated for the coronation of George VI in 1937 shows it has hardly changed in the intervening years. It is an oasis of calm in the city, partly because few people travel by train in Namibia. The local Star Line runs overnight trains to Walvis Bay in the west and Keetmanshoop in the south, but they take 12 hours to get there and Walvis is only 240 miles away. Unlike the Desert Express they have no sleeper or restaurant cars, only reclining seats and vending machines, and passengers are advised to bring their own bedding. But a single fare to Walvis is only £6, and the longer journey to Keetmanshoop costs an extra £1. There used to be services to Gobabis in the east, and over the border to Upington in South Africa, but notices in the station said they had been cancelled until further notice 'as all options to run them on an economical [sic] viable basis have been exhausted'.

Star Line tickets are sold by a friendly clerk from behind an old wood-and-glass partition, while the Desert Express has its own small office where staff relieve passengers of their luggage and have it delivered to their compartments. Signs are in old-fashioned Gothic script, and on the platform one indicates the 'Ladies' Waiting Room'. Cue Celia Johnson and Trevor Howard for their fateful meeting in *Brief Encounter*. I half expect the lady in the Desert Express office to ask if I'd like a nice cuppa tea before the 5.40 to Churley arrives.

In fact I have an hour to spare before our departure for Swakopmund, so I wander farther into history by climbing a wooden staircase on the side of the station. This leads to the TransNamib Museum, a treasure trove of railway bits and bobs gathered over a century and displayed in a warren of rooms smelling of old wood. There are stamps, photographs, posters, typewriters, Morse code books, maps, tools and postcards. There is the authentic office of the Bahnhofs Betriebsleiter (station master), complete with desks and clocks, a sleeping car of the old Suidwester, which ran between Walvis

Bay and South Africa until the 1980s, and a large scale model of a 280 tank locomotive built more than a century ago.

When South African forces invaded the territory in 1914, German troops used the railway to retreat, dismantling and destroying it behind them. The South Africans promptly repaired it and formed a football team. A photograph of the Windhoek Railway FC, winners of Collison's 'Commando' Cup in 1919, shows chaps in dark football shirts and long white shorts assembled around Captain N.B. Hewitt, resplendent in full British Army uniform.

I notice a timetable for the journey I am about to undertake, dated August, 1902. Then the trip from Windhoek to Swakopmund took 36 hours, including a night in a hotel on the way. Nowadays it takes just under 24, including a night stop in a siding for a restful sleep. 'You have to remember that in those days it was a narrow-gauge line,' says Konrad Schüllenbach, the museum curator. 'But compared with the ox wagon it was an improvement already. With an ox wagon it took three weeks.' I briefly consider the hardships endured by people who trekked for 21 days over 230 miles of bone-jarring wasteland, and am deeply grateful to have been born after the advent of railways.

A commotion on the platform below signals the arrival of the Desert Express, nine coaches in a smart livery of blue, orange and white with large hexagonal windows. The design is reminiscent of the 1950s, though the train wasn't built until 40 years later. It looks like the kind of thing the star-crossed lovers of *Brief Encounter* might have taken on honeymoon.

Four of the coaches are sleeper cars accommodating up to 48 passengers, and the rest comprise a bar and lounge, restaurant, bistro, and conference and recreation facilities. The first impression is of light and space. Clean lines of polished wood and glass doors and panels engraved with desert motifs create an ambience of casual elegance. The lounge has comfortable leather armchairs, and the air-conditioned compartments are spacious and cosy with small but perfectly formed washrooms fitted with showers. This is not the Orient Express or the Blue Train, but simply the way all first-class sleeper travel ought to be. In contrast to the contrived refinement of more luxurious trains, it offers an informal holiday atmosphere, with friendly and attentive staff. With 35 passengers on this trip, the public coaches are never crowded, and a troop of high-spirited but well behaved Afrikaner children adds to the sense of fun.

My only regret is that steam locomotives in Namibia puffed their last in 1960, and were replaced by diesel-electric engines. Herr Schüllenbach says people have been talking about bringing back the old locos ever since, 'but we don't have anybody who knows how to run these engines any more'. There is, however, a bell that clangs to announce our departure, and soon we are out of Windhoek and chugging through the low green hills of the central highlands. As if glad to be out of the city, the train slackens speed and proceeds at a leisurely pace an arthritic giraffe could match. I notice a yellow butterfly fluttering by, faster than us.

An hour into the journey, we spot a troop of baboons preening each other on a hillock. Then a flock of vultures, wheeling in the sky like scraps of burnt paper, above a carcass in the bush. Next there are springbok and kudu, then wildebeest and zebra, grazing in a private game reserve. The highlight is a giraffe, barely 20 yards from the train, regarding us with polite interest.

Okahandja, a country town of dusty roads and weatherbeaten stores, appears suddenly and is quickly left behind, like another mirage. The hills recede into the distance, and now we are in vast, empty grasslands dotted with termite mounds, skyscraper sandcastles of the insect world. The semi-arid savannah seems to go on forever, beneath huge blue skies. It is late afternoon when the train halts in the middle of nowhere. I wonder idly whether the engine has broken down, but it seems this is a scheduled stop. Beside the tracks there are two safari trucks waiting to take us on a game drive, and we all pile in and bounce along dirt roads for a couple of hours.

This is a disappointment. Supposedly there are white rhino and giraffe in the bush, but it must be their siesta because all we see are a few buck, two ostrich and a family of donkeys. The latter serve as guard dogs against hungry leopards – apparently their braying scares the daylights out of the big cats and keeps them from preying on game on the reserve.

The bushland looks more interesting from the Oropoko Lodge, where we end up for sundowners and snacks. From its hilltop vantage point, we gaze over a panorama of green sea in which craggy hills loom on the horizon like dark tsunamis. A raptor is hovering above a thicket in the hope of a takeaway meal, which reminds us that dinner time is approaching.

Back on the train, we tuck into freshly prepared game of the kind we have been admiring. It seems a shame to cull graceful creatures like springbok, but as Africans have known for centuries their meat is lean, tender and delicious, especially when served with a berry sauce and accompanied by a fine South African merlot.

Sleeping on a moving train can be tricky, but in a quiet siding outside a desert town it isn't. Sometime during the night I become aware that we have begun to move, but by then I am in the arms of Morpheus and drift back to sleep. When I wake and drowsily draw back the curtains, we appear to have passed through a space-time continuum and landed on Mars in the early days of human settlement. The hills, the savannah, the camel thorns are gone. In their place is nothing, an endless flat nothingness of sand and rock, and in the grey half-light of dawn it has a reddish tinge. The eerie sense of an extra-terrestrial experience is heightened by a line of yellow lights twinkling on the horizon, like a lone settlement on a hostile planet.

This is the land the Nama people called Namib, meaning 'plain without end'. In fact it stretches for more than 500 miles from north to south, and 75 miles from the Skeleton Coast, littered with the bones of whales and shipwrecks, to the grasslands of the Kalahari. There is no shade because there are no trees, and no rivers because there is no rain to speak of. Giant dunes driven by wind march across the desert, swallowing settlements that become ghost towns choked to death by sand.

Beside the train, the monotony is broken by two lines of wooden telegraph poles marching into infinity that serve to deepen a sense of loneliness. This is where we stop for breakfast, and the dune sprinter appears, jogging across the desert. In days gone by, this terrain was a place of death for mariners, their ships impaled on reefs and their bones bleached by the sun. Now it is a tourist playground.

Led by train staff, we stroll in the footsteps of the long-distance runner and climb a massive sand dune. It is hard going, but everyone makes it to the top, including an infant piggy-backing on his dad. From the crest there is a view to the sea, three miles distant, shrouded in fog created by the convergence of desert heat and the icy Benguela current. Close to shore, a vessel hovers in the gloom like a ghost ship suspended in mid-air.

I imagine a shipwrecked sailor climbing this dune, seeking salvation. The prospect of boundless wasteland that met his eyes must have been a vista of despair. Now we look down at the Desert Express, reduced to a toy train by the scale of the wilderness. And since none of us appears to be in danger of imminent death in the 'plain without end', we can appreciate its haunting beauty. This is nature of primeval splendour, where the troubles of the modern world become utterly insignificant. From being a killing ground, the Namib has evolved for some into a sanctuary, a place of healing. It is also a place of fun. Running down a giant sand dune is easier than trekking up it, especially when you bound down it in great leaps and fly through the air. We return to the train for showers and coffee like a happy band of Bedouins.

The yellow lights in the distance turn out to have been the outskirts of Swakopmund. Sadly, the original station, built in 1901, is no longer in use and our journey ends at an unprepossessing platform in a light industrial area. The good news is that the old station has been refurbished as a smart hotel, with a palm court and pool where the German-built railway once ran.

There have been other changes in the town. Like Windhoek, it has grown with new suburbs and shopping precincts. The old Strand Hotel on the seafront where I used to stay has been demolished, and in its place there is a palm-lined walkway leading to cafes and restaurants around a swimming pool and museum. It is more populous and vibrant than it used to be, but some of its old-world charm has been lost in the process. A few German cafes and bakeries have survived, but the ghosts of the Schutztruppe, the cavalry soldiers who trotted through its streets on thoroughbred horses, are long gone. Peter's Antiques used to be a quirky landmark, a dusty little shop with an eclectic collection of bits and bobs – and SS daggers and other Nazi memorabilia kept discreetly under the counter. Now Peter has retired and returned to Germany, and his shop is a store bulging with souvenirs for tourists.

I find myself reminiscing about the Namibia I saw in the final days of South African rule. Then it had an amiably ramshackle air, a quiet backwater of colonialism baking in the sun, that few people knew or cared about. When I flew in from the hustle and bustle of Johannesburg, it felt like a never-never land, and human settlement outside Windhoek seemed minimal and transient.

The wake-up call of independence brought freedom and democracy – and foreign investment that revived a stagnant economy and drew in urban developers. Everywhere in and around coastal towns there are new housing and commercial estates, and bulldozers preparing the ground for more. But even here in Swakopmund, in the midst of a growing settlement, nature demonstrates the power to sweep all of it away. At one end of town there is a funky open-air bar that is protected by sandbags. This is because the sea is gradually clawing back the shore and has already claimed the bar's kitchen. The bar is fighting a losing battle, and eventually it will be forced to move, lock, stock and beer barrel, to a safer location.

Out in the desert, the express has begun its slow journey back to Windhoek. En route, its passengers will disembark to watch lions feeding at a private game reserve, and a few hours later they will rejoin the bustle of the capital. I find it hard to leave the quietness and solitude of the Namib, and I join a desert tour led by a remarkable man. Tommy Collard is an erstwhile snake charmer and grape farmer who has become a kind of Crocodile Dundee of the Namib. Instead of grappling with crocs, he unearths an array of sand vipers, huge scorpions and a blind mole that 'swims' through the dunes, to illustrate how a complex web of life survives against all the odds.

He calls the desert around the town his office, and within minutes of leaving the last dusty streets we cross a dry river bed into a patch of sand dunes he calls his 'reception area'. This is where he gives us a rundown on unseen life forms burrowing and slithering around us. They survive thanks to sea fogs that roll in at night from the icy Benguela current running off shore. 'The currency of life is water, and the fog is the heartbeat of the Namib,' he says. To illustrate the point, he rummages in a bush and produces a beetle that drinks forty per cent of its body weight every morning, the equivalent of 35 litres of water for a human.

During the day, surface sand temperatures can exceed 100C (165F), and every plant becomes a small town, a refuge for wildlife. Some creatures bury themselves in the sand and become lurking dangers, like two tiny, dark objects we are shown in a photograph. They are the eyes of a sidewinding snake, Peringuey's adder.

This does not deter Tommy from removing his trainers and tying them to the front of his safari truck, which began life as a British Army cannon tractor. San hunters never wore shoes, so our guide doesn't, either. 'I have to read the Bushman newspaper,' he says as we lurch off into the dunes. He means the fine print of tracks and trails in the sand. 'If you want to see the real Namib you must get out and go on your knees. Open your eyes for the small things.'

They include the world's fastest beetle: 'Because of this we also have the world's fastest chameleon, which eats anything that doesn't eat it first.' The difference between life and death among denizens of the Namib is measured in micro-seconds.

Instead of the 'big five' of game reserves, we are searching for the 'little five' of the Namib – a chameleon, a spider, a gecko, a lizard and the aforementioned serpent. There is also the possibility of finding a Parabuthus villosus, a particularly nasty scorpion with eight eyes that squirts a neurotoxin for which there is no known antidote.

While Tommy scans the sand for small stuff, we admire the wind-sculpted beauty of the dunes in their myriad shapes and shades, a restless masterpiece of nature. They rise and fall like a mountainous sea, and we wallow among them like a ship cresting huge waves. In the distance, a lake seems to shimmer in the heat haze. 'You'll walk a long way for that water,' Tommy says of the mirage.

Dunes driven by winds can migrate up to 50 feet a year, and occasionally sandstorms roar through them. The local joke is that Swakopmund is the only place in the world where you can buy a four-wheel-drive vacuum cleaner.

Abruptly we stop, Tommy scrabbles in the sand, and produces the first of the 'little five', a palmato gecko. It is a tiny, delicate creature with webbed feet and big luminous eyes that seems content to sit on Tommy's hand and be gently stroked. We are still marvelling at this little miracle of life when one of Tommy's colleagues gestures towards a nearby patch of sand. The two men walk towards it and stop. Then they walk faster, and stop again. We see nothing, until Tommy crouches forward with a long-handled implement fashioned from a golf club, digs in the sand, and snares a squirming Peringuey's adder. This noxious little bushwhacker is less appealing and definitely not for stroking. Tommy keeps it at arm's length as we inspect its spotted scales and dark eyes. A few of us back off with involuntary shudders.

This is as nothing to the experience of holding the scorpion with the mind-bending toxin in its tail. It is big, black, and looks unspeakably evil. When Tommy finds one he calmly lifts it by the tail, thereby rendering it impotent, and invites us to hold out our hands. Amazingly, some people do, and find themselves tentatively cradling the mini-monster. I am not among them. I like the gecko, and little birds called trac-tracs, and the chameleon that changes colour to confuse its prey, and bouncing down impossibly steep dunes for the fun of it. The sea fogs are one miracle of life here, and another is seeds that lie dormant under the sand for years, waiting for rainfall to bloom briefly into grasses that attract herds of gemsbok, springbok and even zebra.

It is easy to understand why our guide is drawn to this place. There are Precambrian granitic rocks in the Namib that are two billion years old, and they exert an almost spiritual influence on travellers who take the time to stand and stare. Plans are afoot to protect them by creating the biggest nature reserve in Africa, linking Namibia's coastal belt with national parks in Angola and South Africa. Then the 'plain without end' will be preserved for the next generation, as a living desert of mirages and miracles – with a railway running through it.

DERAILED IN THE DESERT

CON COUGHLIN HAS TROUBLE BEING A
TOURIST AT THE RAILWAY LINE MADE
FAMOUS BY LAWRENCE OF ARABIA

The Bedouin tribesmen could not understand what all the fuss was about. For them, the narrow-gauge railway that cut through the village was nothing but an inconvenience. The fact that the tracks snaking through the desert are all that remain of one of the world's most exotic railways has no significance for them.

The Hejaz railway from Damascus to Medina once served as a vital route across the desert and was a principal target for the Arabs and Lawrence of Arabia in the revolt against Turkish domination. No sooner had I made my way to the track than I was rudely interrupted by a Bedouin tribesman brandishing what looked suspiciously like a First World War service pistol. 'Mamnour, mamnour,' he shouted. The railway, it appeared, was forbidden, and judging by the way the other tribesmen nodded in agreement, there did not seem much point in arguing. As I was led away, I was relieved to count six brightly polished bullets still lodged in his holster.

The police station was new, but as we approached it I could see it was deserted. I was led instead to an outhouse with smoke pouring from the roof. On the floor lay a heap of carpets and cushions and in the corner, sucking extravagantly on a hookah, sat an elderly man dressed in a black cloak and displaying an impressive set of gold teeth.

I was invited to sit among the cushions, and almost immediately a servant appeared and poured me a cup of sweet tea. Nothing much happened for the next few minutes, except that more tea was poured and more tribesmen wandered in. Finally the interrogation began. Who was I? Where was I from? What was I doing? Where was my permission? Each question was asked with a smile and the offer of more tea. I explained as best I could that I was a journalist who had taken advantage of a rare opportunity to see the railway line made famous by Lawrence of Arabia. 'Railway?' demanded my inquisitor. 'What railway?' I pointed to the scene of my arrest. 'No train. Train finish,' my interrogator helpfully added.

The most difficult part of the dialogue was to explain how I had travelled there. I said that an aircraft had brought me to a nearby town. That made me an instant hit. Waving his arms in a bird-like fashion, the interrogator explained to the assembled crowd my means of transport. They responded by smacking their thighs and chuckling. These Bedouin are more than accustomed to the sight of RAF Tornados hurtling across the night sky on their way to bomb Iraq, but I had a strong feeling they did not really believe anyone was in them.

Eventually it dawned upon me. My interrogator was not a policeman but the local tribal chief. While I had broken no law in visiting the railway, I had offended time-honoured Bedouin custom by not asking his permission first. By this time, many cups of tea later, the chief had decided I meant no harm and could go on my way.

It will be 75 years this October since T E Lawrence arrived at Jedda, which was the capital of the Hejaz before the creation of modern Saudi Arabia. Several generations later, the forces of the West have returned, this time to tackle a tyrant who is challenging the structure the West imposed on the Middle East once Lawrence and his allies had freed the Arabs from Turkish rule.

At Hajj, the last stop before the Hejaz line enters Jordan, the only reminder of the Arab Revolt is the well-preserved wreckage of rolling stock embedded in the sand. The local inhabitants' apparent disregard for an important symbol of their political heritage contains lessons for Western troops in the region. The Bedouin are aware that a war is being fought, but it is of only passing importance.

One of the ideological tenets of the Iraqi Ba'athist party, which Saddam leads, is the removal of the neo-colonial boundaries and archaic systems of government imposed at the end of the Great War in defiance of the population's wishes. It was in part to avenge the unwitting role that King Hussein of the Hejaz played in the post-war settlement that the Saudi tribesmen overthrew the Hejaz dynasty and created the first truly independent Arab state in the peninsula.

As for Lawrence, the Arab view of him is different from that held in the West. For them he was a hopeless romantic who never fully understood them – the kind of man who, in another life, might have dreamt of taking a railway journey through the Hejaz.

CHAPTER 4
ASIA

13 AUGUST 2011

FROM SAR TO TAR

FIONNUALA MCHUGH, TRAVELLING FROM HONG KONG TO LHASA, HAS 'THE CONSTANT SENSE OF CHINA INSINUATING ITSELF FARTHER AND FARTHER INTO IMPROBABLE PLACES'

It takes two trains to get from Hong Kong to Lhasa – to go from China's 'Special Administrative Region' in the south to what the Chinese government likes to call the 'Tibetan Autonomous Region' in the far west. Of course you can fly – also two separate journeys – but the last time I had flown to Beijing, a month earlier, the front page of *China Daily* was reporting the previous evening's plane crash in Heilongjiang (42 dead). Inside the paper, there had been details of a nine-day traffic jam on the Beijing-Tibet Expressway: truck drivers sat on the road in the August heat, playing cards and eating instant noodles, exactly as if they had been on a Chinese train, except no one was going anywhere.

And so I took the T98 from Hong Kong to Beijing (1,547 miles in 23 hours and 30 minutes), in order to take the T27 from Beijing to Lhasa (2,540 miles in 45 hours and eight minutes). It was September, autumn in China's north, yet still so hot in Hong Kong that the mainlanders fanned themselves as they waited to board at Kowloon station, and in my four-berth soft sleeper a young woman produced a colourful box labelled Body Dampness Expelled Granules to counteract the humidity. 'The package looks nice,' she said.

Her name was Susie, from Beijing, and she had been staying with relatives in Hong Kong. 'Such a Western city,' she said. 'Different from China.'

But our fellow passengers – two Turkish women, a mother and grown-up daughter, who were stuffing bags and suitcases into every corner of the compartment as if arranging dumplings in a steamer – said, 'To us, Hong Kong is very Chinese.'

That's the lure of the Special Administrative Region: China, but not. Since the 1997 handover of the British colony back to the motherland, so many mainlanders have been travelling to, and settling in, the SAR that Hong Kong people have become twitchy about their identity, their job prospects, their housing, their language. It's disconcerting when 1.3 billion neighbours see you as just an R&R theme-park, an imitation of yourself.

'Hong Kong is like Chinatown!' cried Susie. And shortly afterwards, before the leaves had settled to the bottom of my first cup of green tea, as we crossed the Shenzhen River – official boundary between Hong Kong and the rest of China – she said, looking out of the window, 'Different atmosphere!'

It's true. Immediately, the giant neon words on the skyline shift shape (Hong Kong still uses the traditional characters that, after 1949, Mao simplified in the rest of China), the traffic jams are on the opposite side of the road, men squat along the platforms coddling cigarettes, and the sky turns a powdery grey. We were on a through-train, so there was no immigration-halt at the frontier; but the Chinese border had announced itself, as unmistakeable and emphatic as the young, uniformed train attendant who took our paper tickets, placed them carefully in his little attaché case and handed each of us a plastic card, with a berth number on it, for the trip.

Everyone changed into the railway's free slippers, and I shook out a map – printed by 1206 Factory of the People's Liberation Army – that I had bought in a Foreign Language bookstore years ago, and traced our route up through a thicket of unknown cities, each one containing millions of people. Examining maps of China can induce both eye-strain and claustrophobia, but over in the north-west, the place names breathe out in relative spaciousness. On mine, there was a long, red, dotted line running south through black dots (for desert) and blue dashes (for swamps), from Nanshankhou to Lhasa. Railway Under Construction, said the legend. You would look at that geological Morse code and think, it'll take forever. But the line had been finished in 2006.

I pointed to Lhasa and asked Susie if she would like to see it. She said, 'Oh yes. Because of the mist.' I had visited Tibet before in the autumn, and it had, indeed, been misty in places but I hadn't realised that this was part of its attraction for the Chinese. I must have looked puzzled because, after a while, she said, 'M. Y. T. H. Is this a word? In Tibet, there is special cultures, unique cultures.' It's the official party-line – the ethnic quaintness of mysterious, needy Tibet – but Susie added, less predictably, 'I think the monks are very respectable.'

The Turkish women smiled and nodded, earnestly. Tibet, however, was thousands of miles away, ungraspable; they were more interested to learn about Susie. What personal freedoms, for example, did she have? Could she email her friends on the Internet? Could she talk freely about human rights? Susie looked alarmed. It was possible that interrogation by three foreigners hadn't been what she had planned for her train-trip. 'I am just the home person!' she cried. 'I go to my work, in the evenings I am with my family, I don't know about these things.'

Then what, asked the Turkish mother (adroitly changing tack), did Chinese people think of the Turkish people? All four of us were speaking English but Susie and the women found it difficult to understand each other so they had begun to use me as an interpreter. Susie had already mentioned that she had studied business administration in Sydney. ('Hong Kong is like the Commonwealth country!') Now she leaned forward and said, in a confidential tone, 'I meet some Armenians in Australia, when they talk about Turkey they always use this word' – she hesitated, then said –'massacre? Is this a word? To do with killing?'

There was a short pause. The Turkish women looked at me expectantly. Now it was my turn to feel alarmed. There's nothing like a lengthy train journey to make you aware of the ramifications of conversational insensitivities, and we were still only in Guangdong province, with another 22 hours to go. I began, feebly, 'Well, you know the Armenians . . .' but Leyla, the daughter, had caught Susie's drift and she repeated it rapidly in Turkish. After that, her mother spoke for a long time, quivering a little, about statistics, research, proof – about the treacherous mists of historical truth – while China's 21st-century metropolises got on with slicing and thrusting their way past, in sunlit flashes of steel and glass.

By late afternoon, despite air-conditioning, that sun had toasted our compartment, and all four of us lolled sleepily on the two lower bunks. Unlike the upper bunks on Indian trains, the upper bunks on Chinese trains can't be folded away, so, if you want to relax at ground-floor level, you are reliant on the goodwill of your bottom-bunk neighbours. What with the net curtains and antimacassars and fake flowers, and the female attendants who accessorise their military look with big navy bows in their hair, inter-city train travel in China can resemble an unusual cross between the set of *Upstairs Downstairs* and a 1950s Sino-propaganda film; in the T98's dining-car, the uniformed waitresses marched indignantly to and fro in frilly aprons, like parlour-maids trained by the People's Liberation Army, with chopsticks peeping out of their pockets.

'How is gender equality in China?' asked Leyla, as she perused the photographs on the menu, trying to decide what looked least like pork (a pointless exercise – in China, even vegetable dishes contain pork). Her mother was sleeping back in the compartment and Susie had already dined on noodles from the cart that was intermittently wheeled up and down the train.

I said Mao had famously stated that women hold up half the sky and, although you have only to glance at official photographs of Chinese state-gatherings to realise that any female sky-holding is mostly being done off-stage, the gender gap feels narrower than in many other countries. Leyla agreed. She told several hair-raising stories about working with village women in the more remote parts of Turkey, and said her impression was that Chinese women weren't threatened in the same way by lustful men. 'Here, I don't feel I would be hassled.'

Her instincts were right; and that's one of the pleasures of Chinese trains, especially for a foreign woman travelling alone. On the whole, it feels as safe and as sociable as a sleepover with people whose names you just don't happen to know. By 9 p.m., the train had loosened its belt and became a small Chinese town winding down after the heat of a summer's day. The six-berth compartments (no doors, a permanent nicotine haze, people massaging each other's backs) were its public estates; the two-berth compartments (in which anything might have been happening, I never caught more than a quick glimpse inside) were its gated compounds; and our four-berth compartments, its mid-level housing.

I got into my pyjamas, in local fashion, and wandered up and down the corridor, listening to the pre-bedtime-chat in Cantonese and Mandarin. There was a six-day-old baby in the compartment next to ours, tightly wrapped in a pink blanket and laid out in the middle of the lower bunk like a delicious offering of dim sum; there was a ring of card-players two compartments along, laughing and groaning over piles of yuan; there was a line of teeth-brushers and hawkers and spitters in the washrooms (a sign above the basins said 'No sitting or lying'); there were early snorers and late snackers. On a Chinese train, if you look through any open door, someone inside will be eating, and if you grin wide enough and linger long enough — and especially if you're that object of curiosity, a lone foreign woman with a (shamefully) tiny amount of Mandarin — that someone will probably offer you a share of whatever's going.

After I had gingerly filled my thermos with boiling water at the end of the corridor (Beware of Scald, the notice said), I got into bed. The berth, firmly unyielding, was a marshmallow compared with the penitential rock that's my Hong Kong mattress. The pillowcase and quilt rustled in a way that suggested satisfactory laundering. The train ran on through the powerful dark outside. A film about Mao's Long March was being shown on a small screen at the end of the bunk. The scenes of heroic struggle — on foot, in terrible weather, across the harsher parts of China's landscape — added to a sense of well-being.

'Gu Yue,' remarked Susie, from the next berth, pointing to the actor who had made an entire career (84 films) out of playing Mao. We agreed that the resemblance was remarkable.

In the night, the train halted. Behind the net curtain, beneath a single feeble star, the sky was filled with glowing red characters and cranes, through which a large, paternalistic, blankly sinicised face, the benevolent provider for the nation, stared into the train: not Mao, or even Gu Yue, but Colonel Sanders, presiding over some vast sleeping city.

Leaning against the glass, I listened to my companions' breathing and wondered about a few wakeful lights in the housing blocks. A white cat leapt out of a bush; I could see its tail flicking under the dusty leaves. ('What does it matter if a cat is white or black as long as it catches mice?' said Deng Xiaoping when he decided that capitalism could, after all, co-exist with Communism.)

By dawn, in Henan province, there was fog lying on fields of harvested corn that looked as if they might have been painted by Monet, had Monet included gigantic pylons and the shadow of a pulsating horizon in his landscapes. It was the week before the Mid-Autumn Festival, season of pale mornings and dazzling afternoons. You forget about China's agriculture if you're zipping by plane in and out of its cities, but from the train I could see the curled eaves of village houses, and a man cycling towards a lane of exclamatory poplars, and there was often a cluster of straw hats bobbing up and down, picking or planting or poking at something that grew right up to the track. Every molecule of the good earth has to be utilised to feed this nation that presses itself upon you. After we crossed the Yellow River, into China's heartland, people sprouted so close to the railway that when a mother fanned a child vigorously on her doorstep I blinked.

'Small factories,' Susie remarked, at Cixian. They had been sprawling for mile after dusty mile along the line while we chatted on our bunks. Above us, Leyla and her mother were reading Turkish novels. Leyla's mother had already told me she was a fan of Maeve Binchy; on a trip to Ireland she had had one request – that her friends bring her to Dublin 4, the postcode made famous by Binchy's work.

'Making what?'

Susie shrugged: 'Things for construction.'

Since Hong Kong, she had been perusing, on and off, an Australian women's magazine she had bought there. She had enjoyed Sydney for a decade. But now she was once more living at home with her parents, with a daily commute of several hours by bus through Beijing's awful traffic. When I asked her why she had returned, Susie simply said, 'I don't want to be alone.'

We continued farther north; the sky, the temperature and, I suspected, Susie's spirits descended; and by early afternoon it was coolly raining. The guard came in to re-swap the plastic cards for our tickets.

'Very luxury cars,' said Susie, glancing down at the adjacent motorway. 'I think we are near Beijing.'

As she said it, her phone rang with her father telling her that the city's Friday-afternoon traffic was badly congested because of the downpour.

The T98, however, reached Beijing West station on the scheduled dot of 2.50 p.m. An American, carrying a suitcase and a birdcage as he left, wanted to know the time difference, but all of China – from Hong Kong to Lhasa – ticks on the same clock. There was the usual arrival kerfuffle – a Hong Kong Chinese woman asked Susie to write an address in simplified Chinese, the Turkish women needed directions to their hotel – and we crammed into Immigration with our luggage, waving at each other from different queues, scribbling contacts on pieces of paper. We had lived together for 24 hours; and within minutes of exiting, we had dispersed into our separate lives.

I went to a friend's place, showered, slept, and bought provisions in a diplomatic-compound shop with vivid social notices (4th Charity BBQ & Fancy Fair: For the benefit of children whose parents are in prison or have been executed). When I picked up my Tibetan permit from Wilson, of China Travel Services, he gave me a brief lecture about altitude sickness – no drinking alcohol, no smoking – then added, 'Tibet is not safety. For the foreigner, is maybe OK. For the Chinese, is not OK.'

He wasn't referring to national lung capacities. Ever since the Lhasa riots of March 2008, the quaint Tibetan compatriots have required an even firmer military hand to keep their special culture under control. At the time, the Chinese media focused on Han Chinese who had been attacked, and Chinese tourists are advised to be vigilant. But Wilson, having issued his warning, moved on to rhapsody-mode. 'I think Tibet gives you the best impression of China', he said and summoned up a little sigh of pleasure. 'I think it is the best environment in China – it has the blue skies, and you can buy the real souvenirs.'

I asked Wilson if he had been to Tibet and he said not yet, he would prefer to visit Hong Kong first.

At exactly 9.30 p.m., the Lhasa train left Beijing West station. In the compartment, three Chinese men lined up, politely, on one lower bunk and I smiled at them from the other. It's difficult to tell the age of Chinese people, who are often older than they look, but I guessed that two of them were in their twenties and the third in his forties. None of them spoke English and my Mandarin exhausted itself while we were still in the suburbs. ('Piaoliang,' said one of the young men, softly, gazing out of the window as the Beijing night slid past, and I knew what that meant, and it was beautiful – even the building sites were transformed into fantastic art installations of glittering Meccano.)

When the guard came round to enact the ticket-for-plastic-card ritual, I took out my Irish passport, proclaimed my nationality ('Wo shi Aierlan ren!') and showed the men the harp on the front. Then I produced my Hong Kong Permanent Resident ID card ('Wo shi Xianggang ren!'), which was of more interest: they recognised the bauhinia flower, Hong Kong's emblem, on the back. I liked the idea of being a double ethnic-minority, and I knew that Chinese people are reassured by official documents. But I also knew that it wasn't enough and what they would be puzzling over was: why is she travelling by herself?

Giving the four of us time to adjust, I went for a stroll along the train. 'It is famous!' Susie, like everyone I had spoken to, had said. Its very existence had been deemed impossible because of the terrain, the altitude and the climate, and I was on the lookout for interior manifestations of this spectacular feat. There were signs in three languages – Tibetan, simplified Chinese and English (although announcements were only in Mandarin); and there were a few Tibetan symbols (the endless knot, the double-fish) dangling from the ceiling of the dining-car; and there were the much-publicised oxygen outlets above each bed, which would offset the effects of altitude sickness from the second night onwards, when the train started its climb to 16,500 feet.

But apart from that, it was an ordinary Inter-city Chinese train with – half an hour after departure – no soap in the washroom dispensers, a blocked sink and half an inch of water slopping to and fro on the floor of the Western loo. Occasionally, during the next 45 hours, the water rose further and grew slimy and congested, and by the second day, anyone I had a conversation with was comparing notes about lavatories in other coaches on the train. But no one officially solved the problem. 'They can engineer rail-track across permafrost but they can't find a mop,' as one traveller put it.

When I got back to the compartment, having changed into my pyjamas in the marginally-cleaner squat loo (which, I can tell you, required much dexterity and careful use of the single hook on the wall), the men were in their berths watching the night's film: *Mr & Mrs Smith*. Angelina and Brad darted around their home, trying to assassinate one other. There had been a despairing line in a review in *The New Yorker* that I remembered ('When you see it, you understand why the rest of the world thinks Americans are crazy'), but my companions, bare-chested and in shorts, watched it stoically. Stalking one's spouse with rocket-launchers, travelling in China by oneself – this was how foreigners behaved.

In the morning, the Smiths were still at it. The film was running on a loop and I knew the feeling: once more, the view outside the window was of the mist and yellow earth of China's heart, as the train dipped south. At 8.40 a.m., we stopped briefly at Xian – across the platform I could see hundreds of tourists, foreign and Chinese, disembarking from other trains, off to visit the terracotta warriors – before heading along an artery to the west.

In the dining car, the attendants were having a high-spirited breakfast, teasing and thumping one another; a row of their peaked hats leaned against the window, severely looking the other way. For 30RMB (£2.80), I had a fried egg with ham, sweetened bread and tea. I talked to a German technician working in Shanghai. He said he was surprised that the train wasn't more modern. He had understood that there would be showers (there aren't). He had thought there would be two-berth compartments (there aren't). Three Canadians nearby were hoping there would be an observation-car to sit in (there isn't). A group of disconcerted Koreans who had booked a tour under the impression that smoking was banned because of the extra oxygen on board had found themselves in the chaotic fug of the six-berth compartments. When I went to visit them again, later, I fell into conversation with a Chinese woman who turned out to be the aunt of someone I knew in Hong Kong; she was wandering through the carriages looking for a relatively useable loo.

Yet people weren't exactly complaining; they were slowly adapting, the way you do to altitude, except in the reverse direction. The Lhasa train has had so much publicity that even expectations of it are gaspingly high, but it's no more luxurious than any other Chinese train (and of the two I took on this trip, the Hong Kong-to-Beijing one was the better maintained). You needed to adjust down to that fact; then the experience of where it was going and what you saw, both inside and outside, took over.

By late morning, according to the digital temperature reading in the dining-car, it was 32 degrees beyond the air-conditioned window. One of the men in my compartment had fetched in a group of friends from next door, including a young woman called Liu Ming who spoke some English. We crammed together on the bottom bunks, cracking watermelon seeds and using an iPhone to translate difficult words: traffic survey, red dates, potato starch. These latter characters had been written on a huge sign we had passed, encouraging productivity. When I remarked that the Irish were famous for eating potatoes, one of the men skittishly said, 'And for the dancing!' and made Riverdance leaping motions with his hands.

On this train, it was my turn for interrogation, with Liu Ming as interpreter. It ran along entirely familiar lines: how old was I, was I married, how many children did I have, where did my parents live. I answered truthfully. I said that my mother had died. I said that my father's mind had gone, and that he no longer knew who anyone was, including me, his eldest child. One of the men made screwing gestures over his eyes and asked a question. Liu Ming (exactly as I had done, I recognised the delicate hesitation) waited for a second but even before she translated — 'Do you cry about your father?' — I had guessed.

Yes, I said. Of course.

I wanted to add, Why wouldn't I? In the West, the Chinese are thought to be inscrutable but that perception works in both directions. Being single and childless and choosing to travel alone were all so inexplicably peculiar to the Chinese mindset that you couldn't take any normal response for granted; perhaps I was the sort of foreigner to whom familial sorrow meant nothing.

Liu Ming must have brooded on this. A little later, she asked with bright-eyed solicitude, 'Do you feel lonely? You are by yourself, Chinese people don't do this.'

I looked round – there were now seven of us on the two lower berths – and laughed and said no, I definitely wasn't feeling lonely.

In my turn, I asked a few crypto-political questions, which quickly withered in the sunlight. 'Mr Mao is very important,' said Liu Ming, looking grave, but, really, they were in light-hearted pre-Festival mode. I didn't bring up any massacres, Tibetan or Tiananmen, but as we were carving through the fragile terraces and long, soft tunnels of Gansu, I mentioned the provincial summer mudslides in which hundreds of people had just died. A Buddhist ceremony for the dead had been held in Hong Kong, and I had kept photographs of it in my camera. When I scrolled through the images of altars and statues, one of the men, peering over my shoulder, smiled and said, 'Idols'.

That made me wonder why they were going to Lhasa. Except they weren't: Liu Ming, and two others, were getting out in Xining, and the rest at Geermu (Golmud on my map), both in Qinghai province. They weren't tourists, they were living on China's frontier. On this train, itself proof of it, you had the constant sense of China insinuating itself farther and farther into improbable places. Out here, factories weren't small – they were vast, with odd tentacles as if a troupe of giant octopuses had beached themselves in a desert. And these were the Han interlopers: an affable presence on the bunks, chewing corn-on-the-cob (which we had just bought on Lanzhou platform), and inspecting the snack cart (cigarettes and spiced donkey) as it was wheeled past the door by the attendant.

'Maybe I come with you to Lhasa,' Liu Ming said, shyly, and her friends laughed.

But you didn't have to go to Lhasa to see Tibetans. They were in Hard Seat, at the back of the train. Getting there meant stepping over a Muslim man, asleep on a prayer-mat in a doorway, and into a hinterland where China's minorities had set up camp: the Muslims in white caps and veils, the Tibetans in turquoise knuckle-dusters and coral-beaded braids, ignoring each other across the rubbish-strewn aisles as they prayed and chanted.

I had already seen a quartet of young Tibetan men in the dining car at lunch. That was unusual because the menu (Flesh with beancurd 25RMB, Cook the Fish 35RMB) wasn't cheap; another Tibetan told me later that her student ticket, from Xian to Lhasa, cost 149RMB. But they weren't picturesquely costumed Tibetans, they were dudes, in jeans and pointy boots, and perhaps they were making a point. The first time I visited Hard Seat, they bawled a welcome above their music, which was competing with the train's; and after that when I went back, crunching over the seed-husks on the floor, older Tibetans shouted and shook hands and guffawed (and days later, standing outside the Potala Palace – another husk – I heard a joyful yell from those same pilgrims, irrepressibly smiling and waving, as they passed by).

Beneath that noise, however, what you heard was a silence. I spent a lot of time dandling babies, but when one Tibetan woman patted her seat and I sat alongside, our voices soon dropped and we finally spoke in whispers. We talked about Tibetan outposts in India; and when I murmured the Dalai Lama's name, she gave a tiny hiss of warning. Keep Quiet said one of the train's trilingual signs, under a child's image of a bed with a horizontal figure in it; and we did.

By nightfall, we were climbing. The railway attendant handed out leaflets entitled Plateau Travel Information, giving warning of the likely side-effects of altitude on health and which everyone had to sign. Shortly afterwards, the night's entertainment began: *The Cassandra Crossing*, a 1976 British thriller, starring Richard Harris, Sophia Loren and O J Simpson, in which a plague virus wreaks havoc on a train heading for an unstable bridge, amid spectacular mountain scenery. I stopped watching after the bit when the scientists in white Hazmat suits sealed up the train's doors and windows, ignoring the screaming passengers inside.

Maybe it was the film, but by 3.30 a.m., when we stopped at Geermu (9,335ft), my heart was already giving little Riverdance leaps. I got up, slightly breathless, and stood at the door of the compartment. The departing passengers had left a gleaming spoor of discarded slippers; you could track them up the twilit corridor. A clutch of shadows was crossing the windy platform outside, hunched under the swaying lights. A few wispy trees shivered. And that suddenly felt like a quintessential train-travel moment: the land's abrupt change, the cold, even the railway sign – Exit West – made me inexplicably happy.

And in the morning, a yak stood outside the window. Then another, then another. Tibet had taken over – with its grasslands, its marmots, its prayer-flags, its skeins of rain and distant ice-cone-mountains – during the night. Snow-fences lined the track. Beyond them were occasional stone clusters of dwellings, under frayed Chinese flags, so desolate even in early autumn that it seemed impossible anyone could survive the winter. It was seven degrees.

The liquids in my washbag had leaked, and the silver-foil packaging round the snacks I had bought in Beijing had puffed up into mini balloons. At breakfast, passengers compared levels of queasiness and by mid-morning, when we passed Tanggula (16,725ft), the highest railway station in the world, some people were on their bunks taking oxygen through nasal tubes or throwing up in the washrooms. When I went to check out Hard Seat, the Chinese had their heads in their hands while the Tibetans continued chatting, airily unconcerned. I felt light-headed but ecstatic, high in every sense (Need to calm down, I scribbled as a warning to myself in my notebook). I had had altitude sickness once in Tibet, after flying in, and this seemed the perfect way to acclimatise: lying flat, with a thermos of green tea, while the scenery did all the work.

There were no observation stops, though. That was another myth about the train. I had to make an effort to grab the names and altitudes of the stations as we whisked through. I knew about Tanggula because I had read about it in advance, and happened to notice the name: it came and went completely unheralded. The only time we halted, at Naqu (14,890ft), a guard stood in the doorway while passengers photographed round his arms and legs. Against the grey sky, the station's name was picked out in two enormous golden, simplified characters; the Tibetan script stood above them, smaller, definitely complicated. A couple of women sat on the track. One was knitting.

What are they building here? I wrote that down, too, in my notebook at Naqu, as the train passed a huge (empty) roundabout with lengthy strips of (empty) road petering out in grassland. Ugly, I wrote at Sang Xiang (15,420ft); and at Gu Lu the grim scrappiness of pylons and tarpaulin was only relieved by a child in a red jumper running along a stone wall. You had to lift your eyes from that in order to see the region's beauty: the variegated lakes and peaks, the massive caverns of weather systems that came and went. In any language, it felt like a guilty happiness: the simple pleasure of the train journey offset by the complicated fact that it existed.

I was in Hard Seat when I saw the first military trucks outside Lhasa. I was talking to one of the Tibetan women, who cupped her hand in front of her mouth as if she wanted to capture her words before they flew away into the thin air and betrayed her. She had just insisted I take her rosary beads; I was wrapping them round my wrist, and looking out of the window to distract myself from crying. The grasslands had given way to cultivated fields, and the trucks ran alongside the stooks drying in the sun.

After a while, the fields gave way to roads, then tiled buildings, then shops, then car showrooms – the classic Chinese sprawl. In the distance, on its hill, framed by a lattice of cranes, I could just see the Potala Palace. That, 4,090 miles later, marked journey's end. But soon the track curved, and it disappeared behind the newer buildings. 'Just like Hong Kong,' someone remarked, and I said, No. Not yet.

BOLLYWOOD ON RAILS

IT'S A RED-CARPET RIDE, WITH STOPS FOR ELEPHANT
POLO AND LUNCH WITH THE MAHARANA.
MICHAEL KERR BOARDS INDIA'S NEW
MAHARAJAS' EXPRESS

Something was missing when I stepped from the train, and it wasn't just a temperature reading in the early forties. Where were the turbaned musicians, the dancers balancing bowls on their skulls, the smiling women dabbing vermilion dots on foreheads and draping garlands over shoulders? And where was the red carpet? After a week on the Maharajas' Express, India's new luxury train, the 07.57 from Stoneleigh to Clapham Junction was a bit of a comedown.

At least I had an early reality check. My wife, who is not a daily commuter, found it much harder to adjust when she next went up to London on Southwest Trains. She will also get a bit of a shock if she ever returns to the subcontinent. I had been several times before, had travelled on some of the more workaday trains, but she was on her first visit. She may have got the idea that our passage from Bombay to Delhi, by way of palaces and princely estates, working off luncheon with the maharana and high tea with the maharaja with a few chukkas of elephant polo, is the only way to see India.

The people behind the train might be quite happy with that as a slogan. They are Royale Indian Rail Tours, a joint venture between Cox and Kings (founded 1758), which claims to be the oldest company in the travel business, and the Indian Railway Catering and Tourism Corporation, which is one of the biggest: its cooks serve a million meals a day; its website registers 5.5 million hits a month.

The idea behind the train is of a princely progress, a journey on which you see India in something of the style of the maharajas, and by means of a mode of transport with which they were besotted. It was about 1880 – half a century after the start of the first regular passenger service in Britain – that the princely states of India began laying their own railway lines. But the Maharaja of Jodhpur, impatiently steaming ahead, had his own miniature version of Network Northwest up and running on his estate a full year before: his Raika Bagh Palace was probably the first station in the country. The Maharaja of Gwalior had a silver model train, its carriages filled with brandy and cigars that he sent chugging round the dining table at the end of his banquets. Then there was Maharaja Pratapsinh Gaekwad, of the state of Vadodara: he instilled his own passion for the railways in his son by giving him, on his fifth birthday, his own 10-inch-gauge train to shuttle him between the palace and school. We saw that train, and took tea with the son – which is the kind of thing you get into the habit of doing when you board the Maharajas' Express.

Our journey began in Bombay (Mumbai), a city where memories of the terrorist attacks of 2008 – in which 163 people died – were being sharpened by the build-up to the reopening of the Oberoi Hotel. We stayed in the Trident, the Oberoi group's business hotel next door. The promenade in front was just as I remembered it from 2006, full of chatting couples, family groups, grannies with trainers below their saris, and young men hawking 'Indian air-conditioning' – peacock feathers as fans. But among the peremptory notices – 'Do Not Spit', 'Do Not Litter' – was one I hadn't seen before: 'Do Not Touch Unidentified Objects. Let Us Fight Terrorism Together.'

On a brief tour of the city, we stopped at a place I hadn't had time for on my last visit: the house with tree-shaded balconies on Laburnum Road that was once home to Mahatma Gandhi. It's now a low-tech but highly affecting museum, where his story is told with pictures, possessions (his Boer War medal next to his prison mug and bowl) and captions that are a mixture of Old Testament and tabloid: 'The assassin of the ages came with unholy design and lodged hot death in the flesh of the man who had known no enemy.' Upstairs, housed in cabinets like Fifties TV sets, is a series of tableaux depicting scenes from his life, including one that was to prove formative: his eviction from a first-class railway carriage in Pietermaritzburg, South Africa, because of the colour of his skin.

Waiting impatiently that evening in the Trident to board our train

– departure time had been put back from 4.30 p.m. until late evening – we had time to reflect that the famously frugal Gandhi – who later made the most of India's trains on his cross-country campaigning – would have been horrified by the rates on the Maharajas' Express. They start at $800 a day per person for a deluxe cabin with twin beds and bathroom with shower, and rise to $2,500 per person per day for the Presidential Suite. The latter ('the only one of its kind in the world') has two bedrooms, one with twin beds and bathroom with shower, the other with double bed and bathroom with shower and bath, as well as a separate sitting room.

This being only the fifth run of the train's first season, our group of 35 or so was largely composed of journalists and testers from the travel trade. They included half a dozen Russians, among them the PR woman for the Indian group Taj Hotels in the Commonwealth of Independent States, and two male photojournalists, who turned up for the welcome dinner in dashing shalwar kameez – not because they were already entering into the spirit of the journey but because their luggage hadn't arrived from Moscow.

Other note-takers and critique-makers included tour operators from Britain, Egypt and Australia and the head of a Berlin-based company that sells wine tours. He would give his implicit verdict on the train's Indian wines (included in the package price; wines from elsewhere cost extra) by sticking to beer throughout. All of us were guests of the train operators, and had been asked to stump up no more than the cost of a partner's air fare – which made for some cagey conversations with the half a dozen paying customers from Britain. They were a honeymoon couple from Brighton who ran a training company, a teacher on a 60th birthday treat with her accountant husband, and a former food importer and his wife, who described his firm as 'the people who brought pasta to Britain'.

Having gathered at 9 p.m., we were first told we would be leaving at 11.15, then half an hour later. We did, sweeping away in a fleet of cars to the central Chhatrapati Shivaji – still better known as Victoria – Terminus. A red carpet led up steps. Staff, keen to avoid any further delay, sped us along it. We ducked through a security arch, had our foreheads daubed with the ritual tilak mark and then, with just time to glimpse the splendid red livery with its crowns and stripes and loping tigers, we were on board. Waiters in smart tunics and tailed turbans offered glasses of melon juice. We glimpsed leather chairs in the bar, a vivid mural of a tiger. Then our young valet, Himanshu, was leading us along the corridors to our suite, 'Navratna'.

He opened the door on a sitting room with sofa, coffee table, dining table for two and desk. Then he turned left to a room with twin beds, wardrobe and bathroom with loo and shower. 'Roomier than I expected,' my wife and I were both thinking. At which he said: 'And over here is your other bedroom . . .' He led us back through the sitting room, with its floral-patterned ceiling and chairs, and through another door. Our other bedroom had a double bed, starry-night ceiling above, and, beyond, a bathroom with not only a shower but a bath with hand-painted tiles.

My wife and I looked at each other. 'Is this the presidential suite?' I asked. Himanshu nodded nervously, as if mistaking the disbelief of a lottery winner for the disbelief of a potential complainant. When we had reassured him on that score he left, wishing us a pleasant night's sleep. And so it would have been, but for the noise. As the train picked up speed, it got louder. Imagine that Bond villain with the mouthful of metal getting so cold his teeth chatter and then sitting in front of a microphone. It was the snibs rattling in their doors. We got up, jammed a business card in each door frame, turned out the lights again, and slept until six.

We raised the blinds on the panoramic windows. Dawn over a dusty plain, startling flashes of pink blossom, families squatting under trees and men in a canal at their morning ablutions. Early morning, it would turn out, was the only time when we would see anything of the passing show, for – with the exception of the stretch between Agra and Delhi – the Maharajas' Express travels in the dark. We would open the blinds, prop ourselves up in bed, and look out on the slow life of suburban stations: policemen with bristling moustaches walking hand in hand; cleaners with palm leaves six feet long brushing dirt from one side of a platform to the other. They couldn't see us – or so we thought, until we wandered off the train and had a peep back in ourselves.

Our first stop, Vadodara (formerly Baroda), former capital of one of the most powerful dynasties, the Gaekwads, and now a growing industrial town, had not even featured on the first draft of the train's itinerary. It was included at the prompting of Karan Grover, an architect who has a practice there and a reputation throughout the world for his ecologically minded approach to building design. He has been credited with almost single-handedly securing the listing as a World Heritage Site of the nearby medieval ruins of Champaner-Pavagadh.

Our scheduled morning trip to Champaner had been shelved thanks to our late departure from Bombay, so there was time for a leisurely breakfast in Mayur Mahal, the more opulent of the train's two 42-seater restaurants, with its peacock-feather pattern on both high-backed chairs and window blinds and its ceiling of mirrored mosaic tiles. While the workaday world of container cars lumbered past, we settled down at a foxed-glass table to sweet lime juice, dhosas and scrambled eggs.

It was after one when we left the train, to be greeted by the sort of reception committee they never put on at Clapham Junction. Then we were sweeping away, in a fleet of cars and people carriers, bound for Jambughoda Palace, which bills itself on its website as 'a home for nature lovers', a place where, 'a brief get-away prepares you to be back to your city life with renewed vigour. Irrespective of whether you are a corporate head honcho, businessman, painter or a writer.'

Our getaway was briefer than most, for the round trip from the station was three hours, and we had a train to catch that evening. Greeted on arrival by Maharana Vikramsinhji and his family, and a shower of petals, we were invited to have drinks in a faded but imposing drawing room, its walls hung with portraits of princes and photographs of tiger shoots. Then we sat down to lunch in a marquee on the lawn – a traditional Gujarati thali of cereals, pulses, vegetables and rice, made with organically grown produce from the farms around the palace.

There was time only for a quick stroll round the immediate grounds, not to venture into the surrounding forests, which the Maharana has preserved from development as one of the few remaining green lungs of the state of Gujarat. They are said to be home to hyenas, sloths, four-horned antelope and even panthers. Karamveer, the maharana's son, began talking of his wedding. My wife and I, who would be paying soon for our elder daughter's, took a keen interest. Had the guests stayed here, someone asked. 'Oh, no,' he said. 'We have accommodation for only 38 and there were thousands.' The festivities, he added, had gone on for 10 days. We decided we were getting off lightly.

We paused briefly at Champaner on the way back for a wander round its magnificent Jama Masjid (Friday Mosque), where slanting light through the carved stone of window screens was painting patterns on the floor. Then it was back to Vadodara, to the school that a young maharaja used to arrive at on his own miniature train. The train, a scale model of the Flying Scotsman, is in a glass case outside. The school is now the Maharaja Fateh Singh Museum, Normal opening hours are 10.30 to 5.30 and we were being let in half an hour later. The museum has a prized collection of paintings by the 19th-century Indian artist Raja Ravi Verma, but most of our group were more taken with some wonderfully lifelike bronzes by an Italian, Augusto Felici, of a dancing girl and of cheetahs with their keepers. Our questions about the latter led to a fascinating account by the museum's curator of how cheetahs were trained – by being denied or rewarded a share in their kill – to hunt only male antelopes.

Drums beckoned us from the museum. We rounded a corner to find the drummers on a balcony of the Laxmi Vilas Palace, a yellow sandstone pile said to be the largest private dwelling built in the 19th century. It's 570 feet long, with towers 200 feet high, and has 170 rooms. Drinks were poured, and we were introduced to the current maharaja, Ranjitsinh Gaekwad, and his family. His memories of the train that took him to school are not so fond as you might expect. There were never more than three or four pupils in his class, so he had a tough time bunking off without being noticed. Life improved greatly, he recalls, when he learned to ride a bike and could go properly off the rails. He talked of plans for a hotel, while we gawped at his ancestral home, a building in the 'Indo-Saracenic' mode, combining oriental pattern with European design in an attempt to synthesise the best of East and West. Then we went in for high tea in its Durbar Hall, which included both curry and cucumber sandwiches.

That first day set the tone. The week that followed was a round of forts and palaces, learning of the style of those who lived in them, rubbing shoulders with their descendants and enjoying remnants of royal style. In Udaipur, having inspected a galleried museum of artefacts made of crystal, from a flywhisk holder to a bed, at the Fateh Prakash Palace, we sat under giant chandeliers in the Durbar Hall below it, to tuck into a lunch with a surprisingly Italian flavour: pancetta-wrapped scallops, provolone-stuffed chicken breast and chocolate pistachio mousse. In Bikaner, we opened our day in a fort where the showcases included both a 'Foe-Frightening Kettle Drum' and a pair of slippers for the temple made of ivory. We finished it in the desert, processing on canopied camel carts to our own torch-lit encampment for music, dancing and dinner. In Jaipur, our focus switched from museum cases to the workshops of modern craftsmen – and a diamond assessor's table where with one sneeze we might have blown away a maharaja's ransom. Then we went on to a camp in the foothills of the Aravali Range, stepping from our cars up steps to an elephant's back to play polo. We weren't sure which was more surreal, the summary of the rules (No 9: 'No elephant may lie down between the goalposts') or the post-match band, who came on in their kilts with a skirl of the bagpipes and a bass drum bearing the legend 'Jaipur Terriers'.

The elephant polo, it was generally agreed back on the train, over drinks in the clubby bar and in the restaurant, had been one of the highlights of the trip. And the lows? All the paying customers complained of the night-time noise. Rattling doors aside (fixed as soon as mentioned), my wife and I had had no trouble sleeping except on one other night. However, two couples, who had travelled respectively on the Orient-Express and by train in South Africa, said the Maharajas' Express – or at least India's track – had been a noisier experience than either; and Celia, the teacher marking her 60th, had had to resort to sleeping pills. I remembered the boast of the Indian railway executives when I had first heard of their new train, at a lunch in London in March 2009: its hi-tech suspension offered a ride so smooth, they said, that passengers might forget they were on a train at all. Clearly, there's no danger of that.

The Orient-Express veterans thought the food was inferior to that on the European train, and that too much of it was Indian. The latter seems an odd complaint about a vehicle called the Maharajas' Express. Food was a mixture of Indian and international cuisine: Mewari murg (braised chicken in a ginger-and-yogurt sauce) on one side of the menu, for example, with fried potato, zucchini, tomato and goat cheese terrine on the other. Execution was sometimes spot-on (creamy scrambled eggs at breakfast) and sometimes less assured: apple pie à la mode was served with ice cream on top, which didn't melt because the pie seemed to have come straight from the fridge.

As for service, it was clear that while staff were both warm and eager most of them were still under training. Passengers compared them with those they had encountered in Taj and Oberoi hotels and found them wanting. One tour operator, while acknowledging that in its 'hardware' the new train was far superior to the old Palace-on-Wheels, said the latter was streets ahead in service: 'They have people there,' he said, 'who can tell just by looking at your eyes what you want or are about to want.' On one evening, after our starter, what we wanted was our main course, and because of some mix-up it took nearly an hour to arrive. We were patient, because the staff compensated in enthusiasm for what they lacked in experience, but we might have been less so had we been paying $5,000 a day. Or maybe not, had we reflected on how pampered we were in comparison with the Bishnoi . . .

In Wes Anderson's 2007 film *The Darjeeling Limited*, three brothers from a dysfunctional family take a train journey through India on which the eldest is determined that they will 'find themselves.' They are shaken out of their self-absorption only once: when they see a raft carrying three children capsize on a river. They save two but the third drowns, his death confirmed by the local doctor, and the brothers are asked to stay on for the funeral. The latter scenes, although the film doesn't spell this out, were shot among the Bishnoi, a Rajasthani community of potters, weavers and camel herders who live in thatched huts made of cow dung and clay. They are so devoted to nature that they have sacrificed themselves in their efforts to stop tree felling and – as a photograph widely disseminated on the internet attests – saved orphaned deer from death by breast-feeding them. They defend flora and fauna aggressively – as a Bollywood star who was unwise enough to take potshots at antelope discovered about a dozen years ago – but they are welcoming and tolerant of tourists who come shooting with their cameras.

From the heritage hotel of Rohet Garh, where Anderson wrote his film and Madonna (though not at the same time) learned some Rajasthani folk-dance moves, we were taken by jeep to a Bishnoi village. The head of the family we visited, Sajjanji, had been an extra – the doctor – in *The Darjeeling Limited*. He stood silently watching us as our guide explained some of the principles by which his people live. They are unusual among Hindus, for example, in burying rather than cremating their dead, so as not to waste wood; and they share a part of every harvest with their 'children', from gazelles to peacocks and pigeons.

The Brahmins we encountered at a nearby village do not venerate animals in the same way, but they are indulgent of some of them. 'There's a bull that goes from house to house collecting chapattis', we were told. 'He stands at your door until you give him something to eat. A very big bull.' What the bull doesn't get is a share of the opium. In western Rajasthan, opium consumption is not only common but tolerated by the authorities. As with all drug taking, it is accompanied by elaborate justifications and elaborate ritual. We heard something of the former – how opium is deeply rooted in local tradition, having been used since ancient times as both analgesic and Dutch courage in battle – and were invited to observe and then join in the latter, which is considered indispensable to everything from the settling of a dispute to the sealing of a deal. If you're a man, that is. Poppy heads had already been boiled and mixed in a paste with molasses. We sat in a semi-circle watching as turbaned elders crushed a tiny piece of the resulting resin with a mortar, mixed it with water (bottled, in deference to tourist stomachs) and strained it several times. What opium was left, we were assured, was but a trace. A hand was proffered, and we were invited to slurp from it three times. Many of us did. But a few, mindful that in a couple of days they would be checking in at an airport, were wondering just how tiny a quantity of opium had to be to go undetected by a sniffer dog.

Our visit to the Bishnoi's huts of cow dung and thatch had followed a morning at the rather more solid fort Amber Fort in Jaipur. From its ramparts, our guide, Kundan, had pointed out local landmarks, including the Umaid Bhawan, part hotel, part home to the family of the maharaja. I had read that carriages of the previous maharaja's personal train were kept somewhere in its grounds. It would be interesting to see how they compared with ours. Was there any chance of having a look?

Kundan got on his phone, secured permission and, on completing our tour of the fort, we headed for the Umaid Bhawan. We were directed to the back entrance and car park, where a member of staff opened a garage and invited us to admire the bulbous lines of a '47 Buick and a '48 Packard (a vehicle one motoring writer of the time described as being fit for 'a dowager in a Queen Mary hat.'). Magnificent cars, we agreed, but what about the train carriages; those were what we really wanted to see.

The train? It was over there, half hidden by the bushes on the other side of the car park, but it was a long time since anyone had unlocked it, and he wasn't sure where the key was. He sent a fellow member of staff, a man in a smart tunic and beret, to go and have another look.

We strolled the length of the engineless train, peacocks fluttering at our feet. Monsoon rain had rotted its timbers, sun had blistered and peeled its paint. There were rust patches on the royal crest. On one carriage was an oval plate reading 'The Metropolitan Carriage, Wagon & Finance Co Ltd, 1927, Oldbury Works, England.'

Kundan had seen it in its prime, in the late 1980s and early 1990s, when tourism in Rajasthan was just taking off and the maharaja allowed companies – including Cox & Kings – to charter the train to take 20 holidaymakers at a time for two-night trips between Jodhpur and Jaisalmer. Passengers included the Prince of Wales, the actress Goldie Hawn, and Dominique Lapierre, the French author of *City of Joy*, that hymn to the unsung heroes of Calcutta's slums. When the railway authorities abandoned the metre gauge in favour of broad, the train became redundant. Its carriages were lifted by crane and taken one by one to where they are now. There has been talk of converting the train into a restaurant, but the talk has come to nothing.

The man in the beret returned, key in hand, rushing to a carriage door. It took both of them to prise it open even when the key had turned. Then they were rushing inside, like children showing off a playroom. 'Sir, Madam, come, please and see . . .' We followed them down the corridors – narrower than those on the Maharajas' Express

– and into bathrooms, sleeping compartments (much smaller than any on our train), a lounge, a pantry where staff used to make tea and chapattis, and a dining car with one long table. Everything was covered in a film of dust, but the beautiful carpentry, in Burma teak, was intact, and there was gorgeous detailing in cabinets, mirrors and lamps. When we thought we had presumed long enough on their time and patience, thanked them and made to leave, the two staff opened another carriage, and urged us to take more pictures. 'Sir, Madam, please . . .' They had enjoyed opening up this tomb as much as we had, and the nosing around had brought back memories for Kundan. 'When we were in there,' he said, after we had finally taken our leave, 'I could hear voices'.

Royale Indian Rail Tours seemed to be able to open all sorts of doors, but its greatest trick came on Day 7, when it proved that it could secure introductions by appointment not only to maharajas but to tigers. We entered Ranthambhore National Park at 6.30 a.m. 'Up to 7.30, 8 o'clock, this is the time for tiger,' our guide said. Barely half an hour later, he noticed that three jeeps were converging on the same patch of ground. We joined them, and saw a tiger – a female of four-and-a-half years old, he reckoned – emerging from long grass. She picked her way between the jeeps, went down an incline and came up again, no more than 25 yards away from the rear of our vehicle. For a few moments, as if declaring 'I shall now make myself available for photographs', she lay down on the track, close enough for my compact camera to register the glint in her eyes. The black tracking collar round her neck did not diminish by a jot her elemental power.

She turned her gaze on the lake below, sideways towards our camera lenses, then back on the lake. The deer grazing 100 yards away at the lake's edge were clearer the more compelling sight. She went down the incline into cover, settled again for a few moments, then rose. We saw her ears prick, the powerful shoulders rise, the stalk begin. As she tensed, so did we. A young deer was heading her way. The deer bounded forward. The tiger edged a few feet ahead, and waited. Then, spooked by something, the deer was off, back the way it had come. A peacock was still wandering dangerously close, but the tiger, it seemed, had decided that something more substantial was needed for breakfast. She moved off into longer grass to bide her time. A rufous treepie, a cinnamon-coloured, long-tailed member of the crow family, flapped down and perched on a bar of the jeep. 'Very friendly bird,' the guide said, and so it was, especially when it was offered some grain. 'Look at me, look at me,' it seemed to be saying as it whirred and pecked; and we did, but we were still seeing the tiger.

Though our journey ended in Delhi, the climax came in Agra, with an early-morning visit to the Taj Mahal and then breakfast on the lawn at the Taj Khema, a hotel that not only looks out on the mausoleum but was built on a mound formed from the digging of its foundations. Seeing the Taj for the second time, and with all the baggage of scepticism accumulated during another 15 years in journalism, I still found myself with a tear in my eye. Our guide, Yogesh, understood perfectly. 'I've been to the place 3,000 times, and I can still speak with the same zeal,' he said. In the inlay work depicting lotus leaves in the marble around the tombs, he drew our attention to a tiny detail I hadn't been shown during my first visit; a detail indicative of the lengths to which the craftsmen had gone in pursuit of perfection: 'Look – the lower part of the leaf is lighter green, the upper, darker, as it is in nature thanks to the chlorophyll effect.'

Timeless though the Taj itself is, there had been changes since my last visit in the tourist paraphernalia that surrounds it. Many visitors – we were among them – now wear disposable covers over their shoes rather than pace the hot marble of the inner areas in bare feet. Digital cameras, with their instantly displayable images, make for a lot of bunching and reshooting as couples and family groups strive for a shot that doesn't have a minaret growing out of Sanjiv's or Radhika's head. And the guides, when memory fails them, are more likely to power up a smartphone than flick through pages on a clipboard.

The evening before, as he took us round the Red Fort and my wife had her first glimpse of the Taj across the river, I had asked Yogesh whether there were any railway-related stories I should know about Agra. He couldn't think of any. The first telegraph in India, he knew, had been sent from Agra to Calcutta. He reckoned that the first train had reached Agra around the 1880s or '90s. He excused himself for a moment and then came back with his mobile phone in his hand. 'I have now become honest,' he said. 'Before, I would go in one of the corners and come out saying, "I have the answer." Now I admit I've been using Google.' He would check properly at home later, he said, because Google, designed to serve the interests of utility rather than of history, hadn't been very helpful. The answer it delivered when he keyed in the words 'Agra first train' was: 'First train leaves at 6.15 and is called the Shatabdi Express.'

THE LINE ENDS AT LEDO

STEPHEN McCLARENCE CROSSES THE BROADEST
PART OF INDIA FROM WEST TO EAST – FROM THE
EDGE OF PAKISTAN TO THE EDGE OF BURMA

The train judders to a halt and jolts me out of deep sleep. I peer out of the carriage window into the foggy night. On the final leg of a 2,300-mile rail journey across India, we have pulled up at a station somewhere in Assam, in the North Eastern States. It is 3.05 a.m. Under harsh overhead lights, dozens of people are sleeping on the platform, great lumpy bundles of bedding and shawls. I get up from my bunk bed, pad up the corridor of the sleeper carriage, a dark cave of snoring, and step down onto the platform.

The signs tell me that we're at Lumding, a small junction 40 miles or so south of the Brahmaputra river. Beyond the river are Bhutan and Tibet; to the west is Bangladesh; to the east, Burma. It's the far frontier of the Indian railway network. Half-asleep fellow passengers fill their plastic water bottles from platform taps or drink tea poured from huge chrome kettles by wide-awake 'chai-wallahs'. Stray dogs dart past, scavenging for food. A blast on the train's hooter warns us it's time to move on. Slowly the great caterpillar of carriages pulls off and we clamber back aboard. My wife, Clare, is still sleeping peacefully in the top bunk, unaware of Lumding, and I'm soon lulled back to sleep by the lumbering rhythm of train-on-track, train-on-track.

Clare and I have been trundling across India for 10 days. We started at the most westerly station on the regular passenger network – Okha in the state of Gujarat, 100 miles down the coast from Pakistan – and will soon be pulling into Ledo, the network's most easterly station, a tiny Assamese town of tea gardens and coal mines. We could have done the bulk of this journey on one train, the Dwarka Express, but it runs only on Fridays. It sets off from Okha at just before noon and, 2,000 miles later, pulls into Guwahati, the capital of Assam, on Monday morning. Sixty-seven hours at an average speed of 30mph. We love Indian trains, but not that much. So we have staggered the journey over five trains, four of them overnight, with brief stop-overs to draw breath. We're carrying the most luxurious British toilet roll we could find, two bottles of cough medicine, and a 1926 *Murray's Handbook for Travellers in India, Burma and Ceylon*. It's been a steady journey. But as Gandhi once remarked: 'There is more to life than increasing its speed.'

BEFORE THE JOURNEY BEGINS

Gandhi looms large in the early part of our trip. We fly from Mumbai into the nearest airport to Okha: in the small town of Porbandar, where he was born. *Murray's Handbook*, a useful perspective on the last century's changes in India, describes this port on the Arabian Sea as 'a very old-world corner'. It still is, offering a taste of everyday life at the extreme edge of the nation. We have come at the tail end of the monsoon. It's so hot and wet that clothes and bed sheets never throw off their clamminess. As we drive out of the airport, a Sikh soldier is huddled under a red umbrella dotted with pink rose designs. Old ladies and cows share trees for shelter; a man wears plastic bags on his feet in place of socks. Our young driver turns on a Bollywood soundtrack and honks the car horn in time to the music.

Porbandar looks less cheery than the soundtrack. The town is drenched, its buildings streaked with monsoon mould, as we set off in the drizzle for Gandhi's birthplace. 'Follow me,' says a man, beckoning us with a curling finger. 'You are from which country? UK? Ah, Leicester, Birmingham . . .' Past the marigold sellers, sitting cross-legged under their umbrellas, the birthplace lurks in the corner of a grand house. A sign asks us to take off our shoes, so we leave them at the entrance and skid and slide across the wet marble floor of the courtyard. And then a worrying thought hits me. If someone steals my shoes, I will be barefoot for our entire trip (Indian shoe shops rarely run to size 11). Clare gallantly skids and slides back to guard them.

The birthplace is mostly empty rooms, but minimalism has its pulling power. 'Seven hundred people come a day, all day,' says N.P. Mori, Monument Attendant, at a white desk with a green Formica top. 'All countries, foreign countries.' He pulls out the visitors' book –

France, California, Ilford, Canada, Luton. Up a staircase is a gallery of photographs of Gandhi with Nehru, Charlie Chaplin and Mountbatten, whose two-tone co-respondent shoes make a nice contrast to Gandhi's sandals. And my own shoes? 'No one has stolen them,' says Clare wryly.

Back at our hotel, the unexpectedly chic Kuber, I trace our forthcoming journey on a railway map. As they snake across the broadest part of the country, our five trains will take us to Ahmedabad, Jhansi, Varanasi and Guwahati before we reach Ledo, whose name no one seems to recognise. We shall be far from the 'metros', the great cities of Delhi, Mumbai, Chennai and Calcutta on which India's booming economy is being built. And (Varanasi apart) far away from the regular tourist trail and its prices. The Kuber charges just 20p to launder a shirt.

After dinner, we step out of the front door and get swept into the Janmashtami festival, celebrating Krishna's birth. The streets are teeming with people heading for a huge and muddy mela, a fair with helter-skelters and flying boats, dazzle and glitter and children blowing bubbles and eating popcorn and candyfloss. As possibly the only white-skinned westerners in Porbandar, we become a fairground attraction in ourselves, stared at with curiosity and amusement. Roll up, roll up to the freak show! See the Amazing English Walking Ghosts!

THE JOURNEY BEGINS

We discover much more in Porbandar, but there's no time to discuss it now, as our first railway journey beckons. We drive to Okha, past bullock carts and herds of goats, past peacocks, kingfishers and egrets. On the way, I study a table of Indian railway statistics. Okha is one of 7,030 stations linked by more than 40,000 miles of track and 130,000 bridges. Our train, the lunchtime Saurashtra Mail, is among 10,600 running daily, carrying 19 million passengers. Every day is like an exodus.

As the Saurashtra Mail starts at Okha, it's there waiting for us, so we have an hour to browse the town's single-street bazaar, with its watch repairers, its Opera Hair Art salon, and its tailors hunched over whirring 1920s sewing machines. There are stacks of plastic chairs, hosepipes, Kellogg's Special K, cricket bats, Hide & Seek Choc-Chip Cookies, lentils and Bournvita. We buy seven bananas for 20p ('Twenty pence?' says Clare. 'You could have got your shirt laundered for that!') and half a kilo of peanuts in case the train has no food for our 10-hour journey; the shopkeeper parcels them up in newspaper and ties it with string.

The station is the hub of this friendly little town. Painted pink, with a red pantile roof, it looks like an exotic take on an English country halt. The lines continue a few hundred yards past the platforms and come to a full-stop at buffers. Beyond here is only the Arabian Sea.

Dozens of people are standing on the platform and small, sharp-elbowed queues jostle at the reservation windows. The station master is sitting in his office, surrounded by assistants. 'You speak English?' I ask him. He shakes his head. 'You speak Hindi?' one of the assistants retorts with a smile. I trace our journey on a large wall map. The station master follows it with his index finger and comes to rest at Ledo. He shakes his head again.

Outside, a list of Passenger Amenities is painted on the wall. There are two columns: Minimum Facility and Actual Facility. Okha comes up trumps here. For 'Shelter', it need only offer five trees, but it actually offers 418 square metres (4,500 square feet) of shade. Someone will have spent months calculating that.

I check the reservation chart pasted to the side of the train. Reassuringly our names (and ages) are there, though Clare has transgendered into Clarke. I see we shall be sharing our compartment with Shankar B Patel (Male, 42) and Parag Vyas (Male, 30). It's a chance to build up a profile of your travelling companions before they arrive. Our carriage is Air-Conditioned Second Class ('Two-Tier'), the second-most expensive of Indian trains' half-dozen classes. The most expensive is Air-Conditioned First, which offers smart private compartments, but less opportunity to talk to fellow passengers. The classes ratchet down to basic unreserved Second Class: not recommended for the fastidious, but cheap. Tickets for the three-night 2,000-mile journey we didn't take on the Dwarka Express cost a little over £4.50.

'Two-Tier' carriages are split into curtained four-berth compartments with two-berth side-seats across the aisle (46 berths all told). Our carriage is obviously new, with plum-coloured padded rexine seats, spotlessly clean toilets and lightly tinted windows (on older trains, the windows can be the colour of orange barley water). Only one other couple is sitting here and there's no sign of Mr Patel or Mr Vyas.

I stand at the door, there's a piercing whistle from the engine, the guard waves a green flag, and we pull off at a stately pace. A man in a dhoti sprints past to reach his moving carriage and the station master waves to me from his desk. The crowds are still there on the platform. They have merely come to wave off friends and relatives and are now strolling home for lunch. And we are on our way across India, from the edge of Pakistan to the edge of Burma.

THE SAURASHTRA MAIL TO AHMEDABAD

The train crosses a flat landscape of palms and cactus and dazzling green fields. Camels amble past, water buffalo bask in rivers, shepherds in embroidered smocks and tight leggings keep watch over their flocks. Women in crimson saris carry huge bundles of branches on their heads. We stop in the middle of nowhere and on the next track a 'railway inspection trolley' trundles past us – a sort of park bench on a wheeled platform. The inspector sits on the bench and underlings push it.

Is tea available, we ask the Head Travelling Ticket Examiner, a busy man with sheaves of forms to complete in different coloured inks. No, he says, decisively. And then adds: 'You would like some?' Ten minutes later, one of his staff brings us tea in two thimble-sized plastic cups. The old days of railway tea served in simple clay pots have almost gone as India attempts to bury itself under slag-heaps of thrown-away plastic.

Three hours pass, the train pulls into Jamnagar station and some sort of revolution seems to be taking place on the platform. People are storming our train, surging aboard and strewing marigold garlands over the next compartment. Don't worry, says a young man in a designer T-shirt. Four senior army officers are retiring and a couple of regiments have turned out to wave them off. Their compartment looks like a shrine.

The young man is Parag Vyas. We feel we know him already from the reservation chart. He is taking boxes of confectionery to Mumbai from his 'spicy snacks' factory ('Seven storeys,' he explains. 'Eleven thousand square feet. Three hundred and sixty-five varieties.') For the next seven hours, our conversation ranges over recycling, the digestive benefits of sugar beet, arranged marriages versus love matches, the inequalities of India and his son's martial arts classes. 'I like going by train,' he says. 'You can sleep all the time, and when you reach your destination, you're fresh. Thirty-six hours is a very common journey for us. Go by flight and you are only three or four hours away from your work.'

He wants to know about Porbandar. We tell him about its bazaars, with their incense sticks and clay pipes and snuff and chilli stalls, and its processions of female pilgrims, heavy silver anklets on their legs. And about the boatyards on its wharves, where we saw great hulks of dhows, 6,000 of them with fluttering pennants, being repaired, a symphony of hammering and sawing. And we tell him about the sprawling Hazur Palace, where we turned up unannounced and the veteran caretaker, Natwar Sinhji, took us on a tour round some of the 175 dust-sheeted rooms awaiting the Maharajah's annual visit. Mr Sinhji, smiling in his natty cap, pointed out a framed photograph of a 1920s Conference of Princes in Delhi. Their titles read like verbal heraldry: the Nawab of Malerkotla, the Rao of Alipura, the Thakur Sahib of Limbdi. And from Britain, less sonorously: Major H. Wilberforce Bell. 'Porbandar was a 13-gun state,' said Mr Sinhji, and a slight sadness crept over him as he recalled: 'Mysore was 21 guns.' He rallied, however, as he proudly pointed out the Non-Splash Indian Sink in a bathroom.

Back on the train, at Wankaner Junction, the fourth passenger joins our compartment: Mr Patel. He spends silent hours totting up figures on his two pocket calculators. I spot the words 'Coal Cost Comparison' on one of his pads. We also have a few unanticipated travelling companions. A man perches on one side of Mr Vyas, with a young female paediatrician on the other. An older woman has sat down next to Clare and a mother and her son slump in silence on the side berth. Above them, on the top bunk, a fat man with three chunky gold rings sits cross-legged and stares down at us like a predatory eagle. Nine people in a space about 10 feet by six feet. We're in no danger of feeling lonely.

In the event, we don't need our peanuts and bananas. Thalis – trays of different curries – are brought round as evening settles in. We're the only takers in our cosy little group. The food is perfectly acceptable, if sloppy, but Indians generally bring their own, prepared at home. Mr Vyas offers us some spicy snacks. 'Made in your factory?' I ask. 'Made by my mother,' he says.

We are due to arrive in Ahmedabad at 10.30 p.m., but we're running late, and at 9.30 people start to bed down, generally in their day clothes. The main lights are switched off and the semi-darkness jingles with mobile ringtones. A thunderstorm rages outside.

At 11.15, we get off in Ahmedabad, great swarms of people get on and four porters, in their scarlet tunics, vie to be hired. We choose one and point out that both our suitcases are heavy, but can be wheeled along. He ignores the advice. It seems a point of honour for him to carry them on his head, so he hoists them up and bounds up the passenger bridge towards the exit, where we settle on a fee. Long gone are the days when Murray advised: 'The payment of coolies is best left to a servant.' We spend the night at the comfortable Gateway Hotel, which has an in-house yoga TV channel, yoga mats in the wardrobe and solicitous staff who ring a doctor when I accidentally take twice the regular dose of anti-malaria tablets. A little drowsiness may ensue, he says.

We're due to catch our next train the following night, so we hurry round Ahmedabad, described in the late 16th century, says Murray, as 'the handsomest town in Hindustan, perhaps in the world'. The big draw now is Gandhi's Ashram, a place whose calm neutralises the traffic noise all around it. At its centre is the studiously plain bungalow where Gandhi lived from 1917. An exhibition includes the spinning wheel and cushion with which he was often photographed. Nearby, an ashram worker squats on a similar cushion, mirroring Gandhi's usual posture. Except that he has a computer next to him, not a spinning wheel.

THE SABARMATI EXPRESS TO JHANSI

That night, we are back at the station in good time for the overnight Sabarmati Express. It goes to Varanasi, but we shall be breaking our journey at Jhansi to meet an old friend. We weave a way through the crowds sitting, sleeping, eating and reading in the concourse and I spot one of Wheeler's bookstalls, the WH Smith of Indian stations. I ask if they have *Trains at a Glance*, the railway's potted timetable and the Bible (or at any rate the Bradshaw) of train travellers. An assistant reaches one from under the counter, slaps it on his forearm to disperse the dust and hands it over. I stuff it in my bag to save for the 20-hour journey ahead.

The train is scruffy, with torn curtains and grungy toilets, but with a 'Laptop and Mobile Charging Point' in many compartments. With a hoot from the engine, which sounds half a mile away, it rumbles out of the station into the night. The bedding – pillow, two sheets and thick 'camel-shade' blanket – is waiting and most passengers immediately turn in.

A man with a clip-shut briefcase gets on at 1 a.m. and settles down on the opposite bunk. He lies on his side, propping himself on his arm and beaming like a businesslike Buddha. Around 3 a.m., his snores duet with those of a man across the aisle. People in the next compartment stay up chattering long into the night and everyone wakes at 4 a.m. when the tea-wallah makes his way through the carriage hollering 'Chai-chai-coffee-chai'.

The sun rises, accompanied by a chorus of hawking from down the carriage, and the businessman wakes, and immediately switches on his laptop to check emails. He shows me the BBC World News and offers some bad news of his own: 'There is no co-ordination of food on this train.' Which means we may have nothing to eat all day unless we dash off to buy vegetable cutlets or pakoras from platform food stalls during brief halts at stations (sometimes for just two minutes). If the train suddenly pulls off, you may have your vegetable cutlets but you will be stranded.

I wash in the toilet, juggling soap, towel, toothbrush, toothpaste and water bottle. I'm trying not to put anything down, never mind drop it on the floor. In the next carriage, a young woman cradling a baby pulls a box of matches from under her sari, takes one out and probes her ear with it.

The train, the businessman tells us, is notoriously slow. It crawls across India, stopping at places where only goats amble up the platform and clothes are draped over benches to dry. As the passing landscape gradually changes from broad, empty plains to something like wooded English countryside, a great snooziness settles on the carriage, Clare takes to the upper bunk, and I get out *Trains at a Glance*. What a delight it is with its timetables, fare charts, maps, advertisements for single-phase open-well submersible pumps and question-and-answer advice about refunds (Q: 'My little son tore my ticket. Can I get a duplicate ticket?' A: 'Refund is admissible on torn/mutilated ticket if its genuineness and authenticity are verified on the basis of particulars visible on the face of such a ticket.'). Nothing, though, beats the list of travel concessions. Fifty per cent off for 'either of parents accompanying the child recipients of National Bravery Award'. Twenty-five per cent off for members of the St John Ambulance Brigade travelling more than 200 miles to ambulance competitions. And all sorts of bargains for 'Artists – theatrical, musical concert, dancing, magician troupes'.

AN ANGLO-INDIAN INTERLUDE

I'm still mulling over magician troupes as we pull in to Jhansi, a busy junction 300 miles south of Delhi that Murray recommends for the views from its fort. We're meeting our friend Peggy Cantem, a doughty Anglo-Indian widow in her eighties who is the driving force behind the restoration of a once-overgrown cemetery with graves dating back to the Indian Mutiny (or First War of Independence, as Indians prefer). She hires a car from her regular 'taxi fellow' and takes us to see the cemetery's impressive spruceness. 'The peacocks are dancing and prancing all over the place,' she says.

On the way, she talks of Jhansi's golden days as a railway town, when it was, some say, the inspiration for John Masters' novel *Bhowani Junction*. 'I met John Masters when the film of the book with Ava Gardner was being made,' she says. 'He wanted to shoot some of it in my house, but the Indian government wouldn't give him permission.' The book explores tensions between the British and Anglo-Indian communities during Partition – a time that Peggy, whose husband was a train driver ('A-grade,' she says), remembers well. 'In those days, to work on the steam trains was hell-let-loose, what with shovelling the coal,' she says. 'The majority who worked on the trains were Anglo-Indian. Jobs would be handed down; the railway generally gave them to the sons of railway workers. It was a very strong community. We had the Institute, where we used to meet once a week. We had dancing, bingo, games for children, football and hockey. The dances were called "Pops", from eight to ten in the evening. The girls would wear very flouncy dresses – very pretty girls; our girls would win beauty contests. Some of them wore high-heeled stilettos. A little waltzing, a little foxtrotting, samba, rumba, valeta. Then the twist came in, disco-dancing. We really liked the British people. There was discipline. There was administration. There was punctuality.'

THE SABARMATI EXPRESS TO VARANASI

There isn't always such punctuality now. The following day, when we take up where we left off on the Sabarmati Express, it arrives on time, then stands for 15, then 30, then 60 minutes. It eventually sets off 90 minutes late, with no explanation. Will it make up time, I ask the conductor. He waggles his head in a way that may mean 'Yes' or 'No' or 'I waggle my head.' An old man across the aisle hears my English accent and leans over. 'Because you are from United Kingdom, I must treat you as a guest,' he says. Then he leans back and burps twice.

It's an uneventful night. At 6 a.m. I peer out of the window. In the pale morning light, people are walking and cycling through fields dotted with ponds of white water lilies. Around the edge of the fields, other people are defecating or brushing their teeth with tremendous intensity. We notice that the monsoon is not only making the countryside more luxuriant and vibrantly bright; it's also making our clothes smell musty. I stand at the carriage door as we speed along, and a sudden exhilaration hits me: we are travelling right across India by train!

We make up time, but then wait and wait outside Varanasi station. I read the notices on the carriage walls. On the left: 'Harrassing women passengers is a punishable offence. Obscene remarks, teasing, touching, startling gesture, songs and unwanted attention are all forms of sexual violence, punishable by up to 2 years [sic] or a fine.' On the right: 'Fill up forms in case of theft, robbery or dacoity.' As the delay moves into its second hour, passengers pick up their bags, jump off the train and walk along the tracks. I leaf through a railway atlas and count the stations on our route. So far, I reckon we've passed through 291 and have 319 more to go. I mention this to Clare, who mouths 'an-o-rak'.

In Varanasi, we stay for three nights at the Nadesar Palace, fabulously converted from a former maharaja's guest-house. After three trips to the Ganges ('The traveller will do well to spend most of his time in a boat': Murray), and one to friends in a nearby village, we drive across the river to the city's other main station, Mughal Sarai, for a 22-hour overnight journey to Guwahati on the evocatively named North East Frontier Railway.

THE NORTH EAST EXPRESS TO GUWAHATI

It's now teatime and a day of torrential rain seems to have flushed out the station rats, which scuttle out of holes and pipes, across platforms and into rubbish bins. Not even the rats, however, can dull one of the great excitements of Indian travel: standing on a platform as your train makes its gradual way into the station. Inside, the North East Express from Delhi is less exciting. We push our way in, past people pushing their way out. Passengers who have already been travelling for 12 hours have mapped out their territories and we feel like intruders. In our compartment, a small cockroach is crawling across the table. It seems to have half a dozen pals biding their time under the armrest where I'm planning to put my pillow. So I sleep the other way round and reflect on the romance of railway travel.

The morning brings the landscapes of West Bengal and then, through the 'chicken neck' of land linking the bulk of India to the North Eastern States, Assam: bamboo huts, paddy fields, elegant stooks of corn, tea bushes, swallows on telegraph wires, people with parasols. There are more things to list as the train is invaded by hawkers, selling DVDs, umbrellas, computer memory sticks, tomato soup, nail cutters, bedspreads, 'night binoculars', hair-straighteners, children's clothes, vegetable pulao (labelled 'Meals on Wheels') and 'multi-knives' with fish-scaling blades and leather-punchers. An ear-cleaner is followed by a head-massager, a rouged and lipsticked hijra (a man of ambiguous sexuality) in a pink sari holding out his/her languid hand for money (good luck if you give it, bad luck if you don't), and finally by Deepak Rajah, a shoe-cleaning boy. He squats on the floor next to his wooden boxes of polishes, dyes, insoles and laces, and cleans my shoes with great concentration. He speaks little English, but through an elderly man on the next seat I ask him about his life. He says he is 17 years old and has been working as a shoe cleaner since he was seven. His father and three brothers are in the same trade. Every day, he gets on a train near his home village, travels 100 miles, picks up what work he can en route, and travels back. He earns 200 to 250 rupees a day, about £3–£4. My shoes have never been shinier.

We're delayed by a demonstration at a station; local people demanding that more trains should stop there. Ours does, for a couple of hours. I pass the time with S R Shakur, the Chief Travelling Ticket Examiner, a railwayman for 30 years who delights in explaining the abbreviations on his now rather dog-eared forms. With his finger, he sketches out a map of Assam's railway network on my kneecap, goes off to do something official and comes back ten minutes later with cups of tea for us.

Just four hours late, we arrive in Guwahati ('The situation of it, on the south bank of the Brahmaputra, is very pretty': Murray). It's a busy city, but its dimly lit museum offers insights into village life ('Industrialisation has relegated the villages to the darker background of contemporary Indian culture.') Attendants doze in the midday heat as a blue haze hovers over the river, so wide and monsoon-swollen that we can't see the far bank. Our hotel is the venue for a conference on 'Minimum Standards'.

THE INTERCITY EXPRESS TO LEDO

After a Somerset-Maugham sunset of towering dark clouds and rumbling thunder, we return to the station for our final train, the 10.30 p.m. Intercity Express to Ledo. I explore Lumding Junction at 3 a.m., go back to sleep, wake four hours later and hear Mr Victor Toppo before I see him. He is talking in the next compartment, animatedly. Mr Toppo talks animatedly very well. 'People in other parts of India think Assam is another country,' he says when he joins us. 'One gentleman in Goa asked me: "Do you need a visa to go there?"' He moves on to poetry. 'Yesterday I bought *Palgrave's Golden Treasury*, which I read as a child. There are many beautiful poems by great poets. Keats, Shelley, Coleridge, Wordsworth and his *Daffodils*.' I glance outside at towering ferns of a sort rarely found in the Lake District.

'We live with nature,' says Mr Toppo, a young deputy bank manager, and points out the Naga Hills, wound with scarves of cloud beyond the forests and tea estates. He tells us that at one point the train will 'bifurcate' and that the Assamese sell their best tea to other people, and 'make do with the dust' themselves. I mention that we shall be passing through an oil town called Digboi. 'You know where the name comes from? British engineers used to say "Dig, boy, dig; there's oil here." ' His station looms. 'The small things I have told you may be of immense use,' he says, shaking our hands as he leaves.

We're now in Upper Assam, a land beyond tourism. The train is almost empty and the carriage attendant says we're the first foreigners he's seen in two years of working on the route. And so, ten days after setting out from the west, we have arrived in the east ('The line ends at Ledo': Murray, with no further comment.).

THE JOURNEY ENDS

We should perhaps have marked the end of our 2,300-mile journey with a bit of fuss, a grand gesture – booked the town band, maybe, to play rousing martial music as we step down onto the long, canopied platform. But we just get off and that's it.

The train's arrival is a daily high point for Ledo's station master, SN Saikia. He has two main-line trains a day to sort out, and four local ones. His office wall is covered with useful maxims ('Avail full rest before coming on duty . . . Awareness and Alertness Alone can Avert Accidents'). Under them is a sort of vast iron slot machine called the 'Block Machine'. It ensures rail safety. Mr Saikia rings his counterpart at the next station down the line, Margherita, bells ring and, if it's all clear, the machine delivers a metal token. 'I give it to the driver and he will proceed to the next station,' he says, delighted by the simplicity of it all. Here, he says, they see only around a dozen foreigners a year, mostly train enthusiasts and birdwatchers (it's a good place for spotting the chestnut-backed laughing thrush).

For this outer edge of India, we have a guide: Shishir Adhikari, a quiet, patient man who leads us towards lunch on the verandah of a wooden roadside cafe where we order delicious banana flower soup. Bamboo towers over the brown river alongside, cicadas hiss and a cat snoozes. We're 15 miles from the Burmese border and this is recognisably the world of Orwell's *Burmese Days*. Shishir takes a call on his mobile. 'You know Southampton?' he asks us. 'My brother is calling me from there.'

He takes us to an unexpectedly interesting oil museum in Digboi,

with photographs of the British community of the 1950s and '60s . . .
flower shows at the club, the cricket team striding masterfully to the
wicket, the golf club cup being presented, frozen moments of high
emotion from amateur drama productions. That night we share our
guest-house bedroom with a frog, two cicadas that jump down my
shirt, and a spider that bites my finger. 'No poisonous spiders here,'
says Shishir calmly.

Next morning, he has asked a friend to meet us over breakfast.
Professor HN Sharma, a retired college principal, offers a thoughtful
take on 'British days': 'You could smell the British aroma – systematic,
disciplined, very neat and clean and cosy. Even in their bungalows,
everything was so decent, so orderly. And your urbanity . . . But
the British Raj indirectly encouraged corruption. It was not
monetary corruption; it was corruption of the head, corrupt thoughts.
They encouraged Indian flatterers. 'We move unavoidably on to
E M Forster.

And so to the sights of Ledo. Or perhaps the sight: the start of the
Stilwell Road, heroically built during the Second World War to give
allied forces fighting the Japanese a route through Burma to China.
It's beyond the tea estates over which coal-tips tower alarmingly
('Excavating happiness from the depths of darkness', says a colliery
sign). Tiny children coal-pick in deep puddles and load the coal into
sacks they have to bend double to carry.

Shishir has a hunch. We drive across rickety metal bridges to Tipong
Colliery and follow a railway track through the forest to a shunting
yard. In an oily engine shed are two steam locomotives. One is bright
blue, a century old and similar to the 'toy trains' that wind their way
up to Indian hill stations. The other, an almost skeletal version of it,
dates from 1851. Made by W G Bagnall of Stafford, it's reputedly the
oldest working steam engine in India. It's called, for reasons no one
knows, David. Railway enthusiasts come here from all over Europe.
The shunting yard staff are used to striking proud poses for
photographers.

On the way back to town, we pass an abandoned stretch of line. A
sign says it once served Lekhapani Station, for decades the most easterly
in India – farther east even than Ledo – but last used in 1997. The
station buildings have gone and only an overgrown wasteland remains,

grazed by goats and edged by huts with lines of washing outside. The track just peters out, unceremoniously. After ten days' crossing India, we've now truly reached the end of the line.

HOW THE JAPANESE RUN THEIR RAILWAY

Sir – Last week I travelled on the new Tokaido Railway from Osaka to Tokyo. Its trains cover the 350 miles in exactly four hours, and are delayed by nothing short of landslide, flood or typhoon. The three uniformed figures in the silver driver's cabin, eyes fixed straight ahead, wear an expression of almost mystic dedication.

On Wednesday I took the last train, due in Tokyo at exactly midnight. About halfway through the journey the train suddenly stopped, and we were told by loudspeaker that that monsoon rain near Nagoya had caused a landslide on the line that was likely to delay the train for about an hour. The message ended with profuse apologies for the inconvenience and extra fatigue caused to passengers, of whose many important commitments the railway authorities were well aware.

When, at about 1 a.m., the train duly reached Tokyo, the loud-speaker informed us that owing to the delay all passengers would get a refund on their ticket of 26s., more than half the total fare. Moreover, since all metropolitan trains had stopped running, special trains would be put on every main metropolitan line to carry the delayed passengers back free of charge to their nearest station. All this duly came to pass.

Millenarian fantasies of a similar situation in London have been teasing my mind since I returned. The train from the north an hour late at Euston; the passengers, a fat refund in their pockets, transported free by special train to Richmond, to Hampstead, to Hackney . . . But in my lifetime perhaps I should count myself happy to see the trains from Whitstable or even Sidcup as little as an hour late, even without apology, on a normal run.

Yours faithfully,

Carmen Blacker,
Cambridge

RIDING AWAY FROM RADIATION

AFTER EARTHQUAKE, TSUNAMI AND NUCLEAR ACCIDENT, THE JAPANESE FLED ON THE BULLET TRAIN. **ANDREW GILLIGAN** REPORTS

They had been evacuated once already, pushed from pillar to post, and told that everything was fine. Now the truth was out, and they were fleeing, in their thousands. The railway station at Nasushiobara, the last one still operating near Japan's nuclear crisis area, was jammed with frightened people. In this ghost town of closed shops and offices, pedestrian-free pavements, and empty petrol pumps, the station was the only place still alive, and the only escape route that most had left.

The Tokyo highway a mile to the west was busy, too – but you needed a lot of petrol to get to Tokyo. At the only garage that still had it, there was a five-hour queue. With radiation now leaking from the stricken plant just down the road, there might not be five hours to spare.

From the town and the whole surrounding region, on foot, by bicycle and using the last fuel in their tanks, the people came to the railway station, a river turning into a flood as word spread of just how serious the danger now was.

'I couldn't sleep and I was watching TV,' said Noriyuki Fukada, an English teacher. 'Then it was announced that there would be a government statement at 6.30. I thought, if the government announces something at 6.30 a.m., it cannot be good.'

It wasn't. Radioactive fuel rods in one of the stricken Fukushima nuclear reactors, the official spokesman admitted, were now 'fully exposed', at risk of meltdown, and radiation had escaped into the atmosphere. Ninety per cent of the plant's own staff were evacuated, leaving only a skeleton team fighting off catastrophe. Most serious of all, an explosion the previous day – the plant's third – might have damaged a reactor containment vessel.

The containment vessels are the last barriers between the reactors' cores and the outside world, the very things the government has spent the past several days promising will protect us. A few hours later, the chief cabinet secretary, Yukio Edano, appeared on television. 'Now we are talking about levels [of leakage] that can impact human health. I would like all of you to embrace this information calmly,' he said. But the beads of sweat were clearly visible on his own brow.

By that point, however, I, and a good part of the population of the district around Koriyama, the major town closest to the stricken plant, were getting out. Mr Edano was telling us to stay indoors and keep our windows closed. But old habits of deference to authority were breaking down after days of conflicting and partial information, evacuations and evasions. Many were taking matters into their own hands.

Koriyama's own station has been closed for days, but the word was that there were still a few trains, for the moment, at Nasushiobara, 25 miles away. In another humbling example of Japanese kindness and hospitality, the family I stayed with on Monday night decided to use some of their precious petrol to drive me there – and would accept no payment. We joined a line of cars heading south.

Arriving at the station, we were vastly relieved to see the long white snout of a bullet train. Their reputation in nuclear matters might have taken a knock, but at least the Japanese can lay on a fast getaway vehicle. Inside the booking hall, there was Japanese-style panic – whose symptoms are not the same as those of Western-style panic. Even without the shouting and fighting, people were clearly under great strain. Many had flared nostrils and terrified eyes.

The electronic departure board showed only two more trains that day, far too few for the swelling crowd. This caused a nasty moment, a low murmur of anger when the mood threatened to turn markedly ugly, but the board turned out to be wrong, as white-gloved railway officials hastily explained through little loudhailers. The TV screens showing the latest 24-hour rolling news were tactfully switched off.

A quarrel broke out in the ticket queue when one man tried to pay by credit card, holding everybody up. But there still was a queue for tickets, and a queue to board, even though it was about half a mile long. Most people were too stressed to talk, or had no English. 'Very happy,' said one man. 'Very happy to get out.'

Two slightly grubby European backpackers – the only other Westerners there – looked every bit as pleased, but were swept off in the crowd before I could talk to them. Other people's backpacks, and suitcases, were of a size suggesting they expected to be away for a while. There were big family groups, too, with children and old people.

Fascinatingly, while thousands were waiting to leave, a small trickle of people actually arrived on the inbound express from Tokyo. Had they not heard the news?

The train left without an inch of spare standing space in any doorway or aisle. As we charged away from the reactor at 110mph, the atmosphere became noticeably lighter, and I felt my own spirits lifting. The difference between fear and relief was only about 75 minutes – though, with the wind blowing towards Tokyo, and higher radiation levels already present in the city, the feeling of deliverance may well be an illusory one.

Mr Fukada, the English teacher, said: 'People are fed up with being told what to do and treated like fools. The problem with radiation is that you cannot know anything – you depend on the government for the information to save your life. Now we are acting for ourselves, but the worry is that we left it too late.'

Perhaps we did. But the train, at least, arrived precisely on time.

ROUND SOUTH KOREA WITH 'THE VOICE'

ON A CIRCUIT OF THE COUNTRY, TAKING IN COLD-WAR ZONE AND MONASTIC REFUGE, **PETER HUGHES** IS ACCOMPANIED EVERYWHERE BY THE SAME SOLICITOUS TONES FROM THE LOUDSPEAKER

It was a bizarre start to a railway journey. The station had no trains. It had no passengers, either. There were tracks, platforms and a ticket office, an arrival and departure board, even a new baggage hall with bays for x-ray machines. But no trains. Dorasan Station is a ghost halt on the main line to nowhere.

Yet the building was both new and contemporary. I was soon to see stations like it all round South Korea. The glass walls, polished flagstones and cantilevered roof came straight from the Korean kit for railway buildings. As with so much I would see, however, it was not quite what it seemed.

My journey would take me by train on a circuit of South Korea, from the capital, Seoul, to Gyeongju and Busan in the south-east corner of the peninsula, east to Gwangju and back north again to Seoul. I was using a Korean Rail Pass, which can be bought in Britain. They are valid for periods of between three and 10 days, allow unlimited travel on all Korail trains, including the high-speed KTX, and represent a discount on standard fares. My journey could be done comfortably with a seven-day pass.

Trains very nearly take you to North Korea. Dorasan station might be closed, but Imjingak, just ahead of it on the line from Seoul, is one of the main access points for visitors to the border.

Dorasan was supposed to be a key stop on the route to reunification for North and South. The station was built in 2002, during one of the fleeting bouts of optimism that periodically suffuse contact between the two sides. The following year they even laid a track across the

Military Demarcation Line to reconnect the Gyeongui Line, the historic railway link between the two capitals, Seoul in the south and Pyongyang in the communist north. But relations reverted to the political permafrost, and any idea of restoring a regular cross-frontier passenger service was put on hold. Dorasan Station, though shiny with hope, remains no more than a 20-minute stop-off for sightseers on bus tours of the border, among them a regular procession of world leaders.

It sits at the edge of one of the world's weirdest slivers of real estate – the Korean Demilitarised Zone, or DMZ, where the Z rhymes with C. It's a scrubby sample of the 20th century, preserved in camouflage, landmines and barbed wire. Here, along a 150-mile-long belt of rough country, is laid a reminder of those archaic days when nations confronted each other with vast armies. It's a last gasp of politics from before the era of unmanned drones and Navy SEALS. As South Korea never signed the 1953 armistice agreement, the two sides are technically still at war. Bill Clinton called it the 'scariest place on earth.'

Around the DMZ has grown a sort of Cold War theme park, a creepy peep show of a world almost at war, where instead of turnstiles there are guard posts and the guys on the gate are front-line soldiers. Their costumes and props – combat fatigues and automatic rifles – are real. There are official tours and you can't enter the zone unless you take one. I started mine at Imjingak.

At the boundary of the DMZ a military policeman, his battledress hung with long white rope aiguillettes, came on to the bus to check passports, saluted and waved us through. The road climbed past a wood on the left. At the verge, as innocent as signs warning of newly seeded grass, little red pennants marked the start of a minefield.

On the top of the hill is a camouflaged blockhouse from where you can look across the strip of wood and heath two and a half miles wide that keeps the two Koreas apart. No photographs are permitted beyond a thick yellow painted line, but the observation terrace is lined with a battery of binoculars. Through them you can see a North Korean observation post from where communist binoculars are undoubtedly trained on you.

Anyone expecting to witness the start of the Third World War has, so far, been disappointed. In fact, apart from a wire fence and a security ditch snaking through a coppice of bristly trees, one wonders what there is not to photograph. The greatest threats have all been underground.

Between 1974 and 1990, four tunnels were discovered, running from north to south. One is more than a mile long and 475ft deep. The North Koreans claimed they were coal mines and painted some rocks black to prove it. The 'Third Tunnel of Aggression', whose existence was disclosed by a defector in 1978, is open to the public. An electric train with open cars took me down a steep tube to a depth of 240ft. I then walked, stooped, for another 400 yards along a rock passage six feet wide, its walls glistening with water. Daubs of yellow paint marked where the tunnellers had placed their explosives; a sodden rubber mat squelched underfoot. I was glad of my compulsory hard hat, which continually banged against the ceiling. I am obviously not built for the People's Army.

Three concrete barriers seal the tunnel's northern end, the first with a steel door and bullet-proof window. In front of it is coiled a tangle of razor wire, curiously illuminated with a strand of little red warning lights. Health and safety.

Amid all the Disneyesque flimflam in the DMZ one never quite forgets that the Third Tunnel came within 35 miles of Seoul; that 30,000 troops an hour could have scurried through it, and that the loopy folk at the far end possess nuclear weapons as well as black paint and binoculars.

Seoul was battered in the war. The city changed hands four times. Parts of it are, well, soulless. Utilitarian buildings, plated with advertising hoardings, crawl with the cryptic characters of Korean script. To my untutored eye, Korean appears almost digital in its designs, with none of the charm and flourish of, say, Chinese. It looks like a code to be broken rather than writing to be read. On the outskirts of the city, planted in clumps, are multi-storey apartment blocks, each bearing a huge painted numeral. As on hotel rooms, the numbering always appears to start at 101. I'd be surprised if the word 'quaint' exists in Korean.

It was time to take another train. Cheongrangri station is new and glossy and dressed in businesslike shades of grey – polished grey stone floor, grey metallic pillars, walls and wavy roof. It was just like Dorasan except that the signs were illuminated, and the big screens shimmered with commercials and a fraught episode from a TV soap. There were both passengers and trains.

It was 7.45 in the morning and at least four information officers in navy-blue uniforms were distributed about the concourse. 'Gyeongju?' I asked one, a smiley girl identified by her yellow sash. 'Platform 7 and 8,' she said, bowed her head and smiled again. The gate would open ten minutes before departure.

At 8 a.m. the public address came to life with a plangent little song sung by The Voice, the girl who looks after your every need by loudspeaker in Korea. She had been on the Korean Air flight to show me how to fasten my seat belt, and in the airport to tell me when the travelator ended. I am pretty sure she came down the Third Tunnel with me to make sure I didn't stand up prematurely in the little electric train. Now she was singing to me in the railway station.

A woman on an electric invalid carriage with a bicycle basket on the front was tracing carefree arabesques on the shining floor. I was so taken with the rapture of her patterns that I failed to spot the mops at either end of her machine. It turned out she was a cleaner. Sometimes we will foreign places to be more foreign than they are.

Train number 1621, the 0825 Mugunghwa to Gyeongju, was waiting at platform seven. It wore Korail's raspberry-and-white livery and seemed to be compressed beneath the large air-conditioning units on its roof. Mugunghwa trains are the stopping expresses that complement the hardly-stopping high-speed KTX, of which more anon. They are the cheapest of Korea's cross-country trains and take their name from a hibiscus, sometimes known as rose althea or the Rose of Sharon, which is the national flower of Korea. Mugung in Korean also means eternity, which is not such a good name for a train.

A fellow passenger, a friendly woman in a blue blazer and taupe slacks, took me in hand and showed me to my seat. 'Ohh!' she exclaimed when she saw my itinerary, as if no one had attempted it before.

Tinkly music gave way to a bracing orchestral piece and then The Voice again. She addressed me in English: 'Our staff will do their best to make your trip comfortable and pleasant. Thank you.'

The Mugunghwa pulled out on the dot of 8.25 and went straight into a canter past apartment blocks 102 to 104 and a golf driving range. It never seemed to dawdle, except in the mountains, but the journey that was about to take me six hours to complete the KTX does in two. So however briskly the Mugunghwa seemed to be going about its business, in Korean terms it was really a stroll. As the speed increased so did the temperature. A sign beside my seat in English read, 'Caution! Heater may cause severe burns.'

After ten minutes the conductor appeared. He wore white gloves and carried a hand-held computer, presumably to check passengers against reservations. Only once in my travels on Korail was I asked to show a ticket and that was because I was in the wrong seat. When he reached the end of the carriage the conductor turned and bowed.

I enjoyed the Mugunghwa. It was a proper train, not one pretending to be an aeroplane. It was sociable, too: the seats can be swivelled to face one another. Some people in my compartment had done just that and were enjoying a jolly breakfast picnic. The Mugunghwa also boasted a small amusement arcade. As well as a cafe it had half a dozen electronic games and, for prospective Korea's Got Talent contestants, two coin-in-the-slot karaoke booths.

We made 20 stops between Seoul and Gyeongju. One was at an unnamed country halt wreathed in cherry blossom. Maegok had grassy platforms; Ganhyeon was preceded by a blaze of wild forsythia. The passengers, none of whom stayed long, were on shopping trips or seeing their children. They were going to meet people, not going to meetings. There is a difference. They were not wearing suits. At Danyang lots of people boarded, mostly women. One old lady with mottled skin sported a shocking pink anorak; another wore an eye shade with a peak like a huge scoop. Fishermen in Dominica wear something similar.

The Mugunghwa also felt at one with its landscape, although it was not until we had been going for some three and a half hours that we entered real countryside. So far there had been snatches of hillside and glimpses of rock and river. There had also been, for me, the surprising sight of church spires spiking the sky from almost every town and village. Around a third of the population professes to be Christian. At times the succession of hills and spires was nearly Alpine, but without the pastures and with the addition of houses tiled in scarlet and blue and whose roofs curled at the eaves like small temples.

South Korea is largely mountainous, so population and production have to be concentrated within a limited area of plains, which comprise about 20 per cent of the land. And concentrated they are. The dynamism of an economy such as Korea's does not take kindly to constraint. There are times when the country seems to have been physically reinforced with steel and concrete; when infrastructure becomes superstructure. It is as if the landscape will fly apart without a strapping of countless flyovers, and the seams let go unless they are stitched with bridges, taped with highways, done up in cable and clipped with pylons.

The train passed small fields, rice paddies and orchards and a woman sowing seed by hand from a tin. But there were also acres of gleaming poly-tunnels. Then, at the southern end of the Sobaeksan National Park, the line climbed through a succession of tunnels, threw off the Jungang Expressway, which had been striding beside us on high bridges, and surfaced among wooded mountains. At last there were slopes too steep and too wild to build on or farm, too rugged sometimes even for trees. Such wilderness was short-lived. The train entered a long tunnel to emerge beneath yet another overpass.

Only one thing worried me about the Mugunghwa: I could see no way to stop it. There was an emergency intercom outside the lavatories but I wasn't sure if the emergencies should be exclusively lavatorial, nor to whom the intercom might connect, plumber, paramedic or driver. The progress of Korean trains, like the progress of Korea itself, seemed inexorable. But we stopped at Gyeongju on time, to the minute, six hours after leaving Seoul.

One of the pleasures of my trains was that they took me to a rich selection of the sights that attract travellers to Korea in the first place. In Seoul there was Changdeok Palace, built in 1405, and one of ten Korean sites on Unesco's World Heritage list.

Changdeok combines the formality of a seat of Oriental Imperial government with the intimacy of a family estate. It has quarters for both empress and concubines. Its tranquillity is epitomised by the so-called Secret Garden, which is a park-like arboretum complete with lotus pool and pavilions. One such summerhouse, beside a lake, served as the royal library and reading room. The emperors were keen on reflection.

Gyeongju is known as 'the museum without walls' because of its concentration of archaeological sites, most dating from between the 7th and 9th centuries. This was at the height of the thousand-year Silla kingdom, which first united the country. Gyeongju was Silla's lavish capital.

The Silla monarchs are buried in Gyeongju. Their tombs, more than 200 of them, are big, round grassy mounds. They are scattered all round town. One cluster of 23 has been contained within a walled park. As cemeteries go it is one of the strangest, and most restful. The biggest tombs are more than 70ft high, nearly four times that in diameter, so though they are large, their contours are soft. It's like walking through a valley of green bosoms.

One, the Heavenly Horse Tomb, has been excavated. Inside you can see facsimiles of its golden treasures, including a crown, a belt and a 1,600-year-old cap of the finest gold filigree. The real ones are in the town's museum.

Another day, another train. According to the electronic indicator board at Gyeongju's Singyeongju station, Train No 113 from Gyeongju to Busan was running three minutes late. All information and announcements are given in English as well as Korean on Korail. When I looked again a few minutes later, the train was on time. Train No 113 was a KTX and the KTX is never late.

Nor do KTX passengers do a lot of waiting, not, at any rate, on the evidence of Singyeongju station. The concourse was vast, yet there were only about a hundred seats and surprisingly few shops, just a small restaurant, cafe, car rental office and convenience store. Singyeongju was a convenience station, little more than a funnel to pipe people on to Korea's high-speed train.

On time, my train slipped unassumingly into the station – no unusual noise, no trumpets, no banging of doors. It had the beak of an aerodynamic duck and the steely colours of a business shirt, blue and grey. I took my seat – 2A – in Car 3. I had opted for first class because if the train had any service tricks to match its speed this is where they would be.

The KTX has been running since 2004. The first trains were based on the French TGV but the technology has become increasingly Koreanised ever since. The whole project, of which bits are still under construction, was budgeted at more than £8 billion. The track is designed for speeds of more than 200mph, though trains of the current generation have a maximum of 190mph.

I am not quite sure what I was expecting, perhaps not the music that preceded every announcement, nor the cinema in Car 1, let alone three breast-feeding rooms, which give a whole new meaning to expressing milk. But the Wi-Fi, complimentary newspapers (one in English), television and phone chargers were all standard stuff for business class. After all, the KTX is essentially a business train. But the conductor still bowed to his passengers.

The carriage was lined from floor to ceiling in grey green carpet, which presumably helped make it as quiet as it was, even in tunnels. They did come as a surprise: on the 28-minute run to Busan, most of the time was spent in tunnels. Nearly half the completed network – 118 miles out of 255 – will eventually be underground. Imagine a super-sonic Central Line. But while you lose the view inside the tunnels, you won't lose your phone signal.

For holidaymakers, with time to potter and who like something to look at through the window, the KTX is not the answer. KTX tracks are laid with a ruler; no crow could fly straighter. But the trains slip under the scenery as much as through it.

Busan is South Korea's second city and largest port. You can get a ferry from here to Japan and buy your railway travel for both countries in a single ticket. Busan's station reflects its big-city status. There were more food shops than I had seen elsewhere, but no more places to sit. Everything was 'to go'. The only people I saw sleeping in Korea were in Busan station. Two young men were slumped over public computer keyboards, whether because they had exhausted themselves with emails or couldn't find anywhere else to get their heads down, I shall never know.

The destination screens flicked between Korean and English and a TV announced with the precision of a language tutor, 'This is the 11 a.m. No128 KTX train bound for Seoul.' For English speakers, railway travel in Korea couldn't be easier.

It was 45 minutes to Daegu, my next stop. A cartoon was shown on the train. It seemed to have been made to reassure anyone anxious about high-speed travel. Why else make the conductor a mouse, the driver a doll and the KTX itself a sort of happy maggot? But then it mutated into a safety video and the passengers – more mice – were seen tugging on the alarm handle and bashing their way out of a window with the emergency hammer. Sesame Street meets Quentin Tarantino.

Until now everywhere I had been could be reached by train, but the Haeinsa Temple was just beyond the reach of rail, about an hour and a half's drive from Daegu. Some 200 monks live in the temple's monastery; for one night I was to join them.

Haeinsa nestles in woodland at 2,300ft on Mount Kaya in the Gayasan National Park. It is one of the few parts of Korea that has never been disturbed by any war. It was because of its seclusion that in 1398 the king himself supervised the transfer of one of the wonders of Korea to the temple's sanctuary. The Tripitaka Koreana is the most complete collection of Buddhist texts in existence. That alone would be significant, but the Tripitaka is carved on more than 81,000 wood-blocks. They were completed in 1248.

Four long, timber-framed buildings with wooden barred windows constructed to store the text are among the largest wooden structures in the world. In these ancient libraries that look like Elizabethan barns, the wooden tablets have been kept for more than 600 years, packed like dark-spined books on three levels of sturdy shelving. Their conservation alone, without any artificial atmospheric control, is remarkable. The buildings, as well as the Tripitaka, have Unesco World Heritage listing.

Each woodblock measures a little over two feet in length by almost ten inches wide. Among them they contain about 52 million Chinese characters delicately chiselled into slabs of birch hardened in brine. When recently they were transcribed and committed to a single CD, just 130 errors were discovered. 'Typos,' a monk endearingly called them.

Haeinsa, which dates from the 9th century, is one of 40 temples where guests can experience monastic life in a programme called 'Templestay'. A doleful woman receptionist showed me to my room.

It was decorated entirely in lemon. Sleeping mats, duvets and surprisingly soft pillows were spread on the lemon floor. The only furniture, a full-length mirror and a clothes rail, stood against the lemon wall. Above the door was a clock. It was the most ominous thing in the room, given the programme to come.

I changed into my temple clothes, a loose-fitting quilted jacket and baggy trousers, all in charcoal grey. I felt dressed more for a martial art than religious devotion.

At 4 p.m. the receptionist instructed us in temple etiquette. Walking in the monastery we should clasp our hands in front of our stomachs and focus on the ground one yard ahead. We should bow on entering the Dharma Hall, 'right foot first', and to any passing monk.

Bed would be early. 'In temple life we have to calm the light at 9 p.m.,' said the receptionist. At 4 a.m. we would make our 108 prostrations. 'Make lines and I teach you how to bow,' she continued, and in a single fluid movement dropped to her knees and lowered her head to the floor, her hands beside her ears, palms up, in an attitude of abject humility.

At 5.40 we had the evening meal. Every last grain of rice had to be consumed. Temple food is not only vegan but excludes vegetables of the onion family. Eaten raw they are supposed to increase anger; cooked, they stimulate lust. Every last grain of rice must be consumed.

At 6 p.m. the monks were summoned to the Dharma Hall, not by a bell or announcement, but by a virtuoso performance of drumming. Four monks took turns at thrashing out a thunderous tattoo on a drum six feet in diameter, suspended from the painted beams of an open-sided shelter. The monks' robes flared theatrically as they played, a stick in each hand, fingers rosined for grip. The rhythms were amazing. They were said to have been handed down over the centuries, but some were pure jazz, syncopated and with little clacking riffs from one stick rattled on the drum frame.

We filed across the temple compound and up steep stone steps to the Dharma Hall. Inside was a cavern of crimson and gold. Candlelight threw flickering shadows across three Buddha statues on a dais and glinted from polished brass. Apart from two lines of massive timber columns in carnelian red, every surface was ornately painted. At 3.30 a.m. we would return for a more elaborate ceremony before making our 108 prostrations. Korean Buddhism is run as punctiliously as Korean railways.

At Gwangju I boarded the KTX to take me back from 9th-century Haeinsa to 21st-century Seoul. On this route there were fewer tunnels and at one point the track had to bend through lumps of hills. But for most of the journey towns and villages were kept at a distance, so the train had the landscape to itself. Now it hit its stride and shot through the country at its exhilarating maximum.

Korea, I reflected, seems either to have been made 1,200 years ago or yesterday. There is little in between. Except for the washroom on the KTX. Incongruously, for a train doing 190mph, the lavatory flush and the water for the basin are pumped by early-20th-century pedals.

CHAPTER 5
AUSTRALASIA

DECEMBER 11 2010

CHRISTMAS CARAVANSERAI

MICHAEL KERR JOINS SANTA AND SOME CAROL-SINGING ROCKERS ON THE INDIAN PACIFIC FROM SYDNEY TO PERTH

The snake, finger-thin and yellow-brown, slithered under Santa Claus's battered old armchair. Santa bent as if to touch it, and for a moment it looked as if he too might get bitten. It disappeared. Where had it gone? This being outback Australia, there was a Snake Dundee at hand who had a pretty good idea. He reached down, grabbed the snake behind the head, and turned what had been a pandemonium-producing reptile into the subject for a photo opportunity.

Meanwhile, Lauren, a teacher in her twenties who had travelled three hours through the bush to a railway siding with her Aboriginal pupils just so that they could meet Santa, was sitting on the earth, her left leg bandaged from ankle to knee. 'Ow! It's really stinging,' she said.

'She's lucky,' another macho type chipped in. 'If the snake bit her, she's a special girl. The snake was attracted to her. It didn't bite you [this to a woman who was not quite as slim as Lauren] because it if had, the *snake* would have died.'

A nurse who had arrived with the children and a doctor who happened to be on the train were less convinced about Lauren's good luck. She was carried on a stretcher to an ambulance that had been waiting as a precautionary measure – the only one within a radius of 190 miles – to be driven to Maralinga, some three hours away, and flown from there to hospital in Port Augusta, north-west of Adelaide. By this time her charges, and the rest of the Aboriginal party, were long gone. Time to get back on our silver bullet.

We had arrived about an hour earlier, intent on bringing festive cheer. For 40 years the Indian Pacific has been crossing Australia, and for the past ten its operating company, Great Southern Rail, has run a Christmas special as a thank-you to the communities that support the train throughout the year. As well as Santa Claus to dole out goodie bags, the company books a nationally known musician. This year, there were not one but two, the veteran Aussie rockers Mark Seymour and James Reyne, supported ('to provide a bit of additional firepower', as he put it) by Cameron McKenzie, who as a session musician has played with acts from Aerosmith to Johnny Cash.

So far, troubadours and Santa had raised the roof at stations in Sydney, Broken Hill and Adelaide. First, the local schoolchildren would take to the stage with Aussie-flavoured carols ('Oh, what fun it is to ride in a rusty Holden ute'), then Seymour and Reyne would play a few of their hits, then stars and school choir would combine in *Rockin' Around The Christmas Tree*. After that, it was time for the man in the white beard.

Santa is a figure unknown in Aboriginal culture, but in the 11 years that Bruce Dent, a retired bank manager, has been playing him, he has become a familiar and eagerly awaited one in this part of the country. The night before we arrived at the railway siding of Watson, Bruce's wife, Colleen, told me: 'At the start the kids were very tentative, but over the years they have got more confident. These days, they're in there like Flynn.'

And so it proved. Watson doesn't even appear on Great Southern Rail's map of the train's route; it's mentioned, if at all, for its proximity to the former nuclear testing site of Maralinga. When we arrived, though, it had become a semi-circular Aboriginal encampment of minibuses and 4x4s. Teenagers waited close to the track; younger children hung back with mothers or fathers, who leaned against pick-ups or sat in the dust with their dogs.

There was no carol singing here. Indeed, when the rockers began playing, they were met with giggling. However, when Santa stepped off the train, to sit down with his sack beneath a tinsel-hung bush, he was mobbed. For a moment, his red tunic was completely lost in the scrum. It was shortly after that that the snake (identified by one bystander as a 'yellow-faced whipsnake' and by another, with equal certainty, as 'a yellow-*tailed* whipsnake') made its appearance, leaving the white people in a tizzy and the black people entirely unfazed.

Maybe we had tempted fate. Shortly after we had left Sydney, on the first evening of our three-night trip across the continent, I came back to my compartment to catch this snatch of commentary over the train's PA system: 'It's very easy to provide statistics that make Australia sound like a dangerous place in relation to snakes . . .'

Easy, too, to get the wrong idea of the sort of landscape you are going to be seeing. Through the window of my compartment – a space with not only a fold-down bed, but a fold-down loo and fold-down sink – it looked much greener than I had expected. Thanks to unseasonal rain in the east, Sydney was having its wettest spring for six years and its coolest for 11. We had to bypass our first scheduled stop, Bathurst, and its waiting carollers because the track was submerged.

'When the River Runs Dry' is one of the songs Mark Seymour delivered at stops along the way. No danger of that at present in the east. Menindee Lakes, on the approach to the silver-mining town of Broken Hill, had the air of an inland sea, a spooky one with drowned tree stumps. It was near there that I saw my first and only kangaroos of the trip: six of them on a roof, cutouts in wood hauling Santa's sleigh north to the Pole.

Our own Santa, Bruce, 6ft 3in with silver hair and moustache, wasn't interested in going that far afield. 'I've been to the furthest points north, south, east and west in Australia,' he told me. 'I'm not that bothered about going abroad. I like to see my own country.'

Most of the passengers on our 22-carriage train had boarded with similar intent, many of them pensioners taking a trip they had promised themselves for years; a chance to see 'the wide brown land' celebrated in Dorothea Mackellar's poem *My Country*.

Dr Andy Killcross, 37, a GP from Manchester, was enjoying the ride, too. But he was there to explain and promote the work of one of the few Australian institutions of which no Australian has a bad word to say: the Royal Flying Doctor Service. Having taken a job at a hospital in Sydney, intending to stay only 12 months, he saw a post advertised in the RFDS, based in Port Augusta. That was eight years ago. He's now married to an Australian, and they are expecting their first child.

The service, he was keen to stress, is not just for aero-medical evacuations. Preventive medicine, from immunisation to a mental health project for teenagers, is a large part of its unsung work. It's the emergencies, though, about which people most want to hear. He talked of a flight to an injured miner in the desert in South Australia, and a landing in the dark on an airstrip lit by flares of burning kerosene. 'Not the kind of thing I'd be doing if I'd carried on as a GP in Manchester.'

He had been called out, too, when a passenger had a stroke on the Indian Pacific near Cook, a place that's normally home to only four people who maintain a boarding house for long-distance train drivers: 'Suddenly the train arrived with all these passengers. And then we came taxiing down the main street in our plane . . .'

On the ground, he was told that a second woman was ill; it turned out that she had a potentially fatal heart condition. Given the narrowness of the train, it was impossible to get a stretcher in to the stroke victim. One of the staff went in on hands and knees, she was put on his back, and then he carried her to the train door. Both patients made it to hospital.

Cook is on a 300-mile stretch of track that doesn't have a kink, let alone a curve: it's the longest straight in the railway world. It runs through the Nullarbor ('treeless') Plain, where, for mile after mile, the only vegetation is bluebush and saltbush. Here, a bird on a wire was the cause of great excitement at the windows of the Queen Adelaide restaurant car, and even a birdless wire added a little variety.

'Look!' said a Kiwi: 'Big hole! What is it — an asteroid crater?'

'I think you can safely say so,' an Aussie responded. 'Who's going to be able to find it again to check?'

We were safe, too, from the trill of the mobile. On the Nullarbor, even the smartest of smart phones had to admit that it had 'No Signal'.

Our arrival at Cook was a little more routine than Andy's, but there were enough of us to keep half the population, one man, one woman, behind the counter in the souvenir shop for all of 20 minutes. Santa, in full gear, was dragged into several groups for a photograph. Tourist dollars were taken for 'stubbie holders', teaspoons, cuddly koalas and laminated pieces of A4 paper testifying that the holder had crossed the longest stretch of straight railway in the world. An ancient-looking notice on a blocked-off door read: 'Any arsehole that steals from this camp will be gut shot and left for the eagles to feed on.'

That's the kind of promise I can imagine having been made by one of the tough-looking men who brought their families out to greet our Christmas caravanserai at Rawlinna. This sheep station has 70,000 sheep, but as they are spread over 2.5 million acres finding them at shearing time requires an aircraft. Mustering one paddock with the aid of motorbikes can take eight hours – and that's assuming that they are all 'in the right place'. The station hands, leaning against their 4×4s and knocking back the stubbies, looked like an audience that might be hard to please.

Urging them to come a bit closer, Mark Seymour said: 'We didn't bring a PA. Just got our guitars, so it's not so loud.'

One of the hands responded with a laugh: 'You did bring a train, though.'

There were no carols here – not enough children for a choir – and maybe a bit less singing along, but there was as much toe-tapping recognition of the Seymour-Reyne repertoire as there had been everywhere else.

Last time he had played places this remote, Reyne had said earlier, he had been younger and thirstier. He and his band had been warned by local police not to overdo the drinking. 'This time', he joked, 'I've eaten my way across. They do feed you well.'

They did. Dinner menus ran to four choices of main course and two of dessert – which on the last night, of course, included plum pudding. After that, Seymour, Reyne and McKenzie sang for the penultimate time in the car park behind Kalgoorlie station, while the wind whipped at the pompoms of the primary-school choir's hats.

After a last 'Great Australian Breakfast', we entered the outskirts of Perth, and the last stretch of a journey of 2,720 miles, from the Indian Ocean to the edge of the Pacific. Trackside maintenance work brought us to a halt on an incline. On the other side of the window were gardens mulched with bark chippings, over-tidied trees, a pre-office jogger glancing at her watch. Suburbia was swallowing a train that had crossed a continent.

9 JUNE 2009

TOURIST FEARED HE WOULD DIE CLINGING TO OUTBACK TRAIN

BY **BONNIE MALKIN** IN SYDNEY

An American tourist has told how he feared he would die as he spent two and a half hours clinging to the outside of a train travelling through the Australian outback at speeds of up to 70mph.

Chad Vance, a 19-year-old student from Alaska, jumped on to the Ghan, which travels from Adelaide to Darwin, as it pulled out of Port Augusta. He had hopped off to stretch his legs during a stop, and panicked when he saw it moving off. He managed to squeeze into a small stairwell, but as the train gathered speed and night fell he realised his decision could be fatal.

'I was worried I wasn't going to survive,' he said. 'If I'd fallen off at that speed and hit the nasty-looking rocks below, I don't think I would have made it.' He clung on for two hours and 20 minutes before Marty Wells, a crew member, heard his cries for help and brought the train to an emergency stop. 'Chad is a very lucky guy. When we rescued him his skin was white and his lips were blue,' Mr Wells told a newspaper. 'We were still about three hours away from our next scheduled stop and in that time he could have easily died of hypothermia or lost his grip.'

Mr Vance boarded the Ghan in Adelaide on May 28 for the journey to Alice Springs. He lost track of time in Port Augusta and arrived back at the platform as the train was moving off. He said he knew it would pull up outside town to change drivers, so he decided to chase it. When he caught it up, he banged on the windows of the first-class dining carriage. The passengers ignored him because they 'probably thought I was some crazy kid', he said.

After five minutes, the train started to pull away again and he made the 'instinctive' decision, which he admitted was a 'pretty crazy idea', to climb back on board. Wearing only jeans, boots and a T-shirt, he endured freezing temperatures before he was rescued.

'He was shaking uncontrollably for several hours and complained of numbness to the left side of his body and arms and said his face was also stinging,' Mr Wells said. 'I've never seen anything like this before, and I sure hope I don't ever see it happen again.'

6 NOVEMBER 2010

RATTLING BACK TO A BYGONE AGE IN 'THE LAST PLACE GOD MADE'

NEW ZEALAND'S TRAINS, LIKE THE COUNTRY ITSELF, OFFER A GLIMPSE OF AN OLDER WORLD. **JAMES OWEN** RELISHES THE CHANCE TO SLOW DOWN AND TAKE STOCK

Waiting in Picton's picture-postcard station, all trim white wood and red brick, brought to mind the cliché that travelling in New Zealand is like being in England in the 1950s. On the bench beside me was a young boy who kept glancing up approvingly from his tightly held copy of *Thomas the Tank Engine* at the stout, blue-painted train that we were waiting to board.

The carriages beside the only platform had old-fashioned handles on their doors, and farther down I could see porters loading baggage, and even an observation car. There was an almost palpable sense of occasion among the locals queuing up to buy their tickets. Yet that stemmed, I had learned to my surprise, not from any feelings of nostalgia but from novelty value.

We were not, it seemed, about to rattle back into the past on a piece of the nation's heritage that looked as if it must have long been ousted by a more modern service. The attraction of this train was still more basic than that. New Zealand has no passenger network to speak of, and while air travel would have been a regular experience for most of the youngsters taking their seats, few of them had ever ridden by rail before.

'Here, you travel by train for the journey, not to get somewhere,' explained Raewyn, who was guiding a tour group of Australians. A combination of mountainous topography and a small population (and hence revenue) had meant that the Empire had never constructed an extensive railway here. In recent times, what services there were have been greatly reduced following several changes of ownership and much asset-stripping. Now, all that remains are a few commuter lines, mainly around Wellington, and a track – chiefly aimed at tourists – that slides slowly down the country from Auckland to Christchurch and then over the Southern Alps to Greymouth.

Once a day, the train sets out from Picton along a 200-mile stretch of this that the marketing men have named 'the tranzcoastal'. Picton is a harbour town on the northern rim of South Island, named for one of the heroes of Waterloo and flanked by a guard of other military men whose deeds were still fresh in the minds of early settlers: Nelson; Marlborough; the Iron Duke himself. Soon we had left behind the hills above the port, and were running down to Blenheim, through a flatter landscape of orchards and then past long green rows of vines smudged by an early tinge of autumn.

Across a formica table from me was Chris, an architect. He had flown up from farther south for a meeting with a client in the Sounds, the fjord-like fingers that reach out from Picton into Cook Strait, and was taking the chance to go back by train. Beyond the window were the images that I had expected of New Zealand – a farmer repairing wire, newly shorn sheep white against the yellowing grass – but talking to Chris and others of his generation had made me appreciate that a new identity was emerging here. It was one that looks much less to colonial Britain and more instead to the once-shunned native culture. It was noticeable, for instance, how those under 50 used Maori rather than English names for local trees. Even sheep are no longer big business: farmers now favour dairy herding.

Another influence in the past 20 years has been immigration from Asia and the Mediterranean. New kinds of cooking have thrived, the coffee has suddenly become drinkable and chardonnay flourishes on the fertile plain across which we were trundling. If the lowering hills beyond were reminiscent of Scotland, then it was a Scotland basking in near-tropical sunshine.

I leaned over the rail of the open-sided observation car to feel the cool of the rushing air against my face. Above open farmland a bird of prey hovered on the same wind. I began to let my thoughts drift, lulled by the sluggish rhythm of our progress. Then a long blast of the hooter woke me from my reverie. The red-and-yellow diesel engine was beginning to curve through Dashwood Pass, and workmen on the track had to be alerted. The carriage swayed suddenly, and those of us inside lunged for handholds, including a German woman who had lived for years in the South and was more pessimistic about the country's future.

'They have high expectations here,' she said, 'but not enough people to pay for them. Technology has made it easier for hotheads to get together and cause trouble, and there aren't enough police to stop them. And,' she went on, no doubt reflecting on her own future, 'care for the elderly is becoming a real problem, too.'

Kwan was younger and thinking only of the fun she was having. She was finding it chillier than her native Singapore, and had donned a large blue woolly hat to brave the open car. Her parents had brought her to New Zealand on holiday, and they had taken the train all the way down from Auckland so that her father would be spared driving. She seemed determined to record every foot of the journey with her camera.

The breeze smelled of salt, not from the ocean but from Lake Grassmere, a shallow lagoon among the dunes where seawater is allowed to evaporate and the residue harvested for domestic use and for bleaching paper. Now we could see the grey sand of a beach, and the spare white limbs of trees on the foreshore, gaunt survivors of the desiccating effects of the wind and sun. Some two hours and 80 miles out from Blenheim, the train began to run alongside the blue of the Pacific. Propelled by a light swell, frothy spume flecked the boulders beside the line.

Joe came from Hawkes Bay, on the North Island, and was giving his children their first taste of the South. They had known that it had a harder climate than where they lived, but they had been surprised by its more varied and wilder landscape, especially its rocky spine. 'This has been the best part of the trip for us,' he said, as we pulled into Kaikoura, in the shadow of those same mountains. 'Doesn't everyone like trains?'

We waited a while as Joe and several others got down to the platform and began to look for their luggage. The sun picked out a piping of snow that ran along the range, and I savoured the sound of the syllables of its highest peak, Tapuae-o-Uenuku, or 'footprint of the rainbow'. Offshore, its mirror image, the 10,000-ft deep Hikurangi Trench, is the larder of the whales, dolphins and marine birds – albatross, petrels and even blue penguins – that are Kaikoura's great attraction.

The engine hefted its load once more, and we followed the coast, rolling through a bucolic landscape of lightly wooded hills coursed by swiftly running brooks. The green-and-blue pattern of the table on which I rested my elbows was intensified a hundred-fold in the verdant shades of the farmland and the great depths of the sea. For much of the way, the road ran beside the line, disappearing into its own tunnels as we slid through ours from light into darkness and back again. A bus, not travelling at any great pace, overtook us easily.

A succession of smooth, grey sandy coves was soon just a memory as the track started to weave inland, darting back occasionally to the water to rinse off the day's heat. The late afternoon sun blew fire into the glassy surface of the waves. Here the presence of man became less evident. Wooden fences grew rickety and the tines of Surrey rail were left bent and broken.

Through stubby spinneys of akeake I could see the bend of a river, as silvery as the underside of a fern. 'They say it's the last place God made,' an Australian voice said beside me. 'He put in all his favourite bits from elsewhere.' Not far away was the farm where Charles Upham, the only soldier to win the Victoria Cross twice, had lived quietly for 40 years.

The voice belonged to Dennis, who was relishing the sheer abundance of nature visible from the observation car. 'In Oz there's just bush, and it just keeps on going.' Daniel nodded in agreement. His wife's people used to own 50,000 acres 'up on the place where *Waltzing Matilda* was written'. There, drought was a fact of life. One year they had lost almost half their sheep to it. By comparison, as a New Zealander would say, this well-watered land was 'all good'.

The sound of the train had startled a black-faced herd, which scurried away through the shaggy grass towards the hills to our right. Shorn of their cloak of trees – more than 95 per cent of the country's timber has already been felled – the bare ridges stood out sharply as we dropped down to the Canterbury plain, another major wine-producing region about 40 minutes' drive from Christchurch.

'The Garden City' has the reputation of being the most English in New Zealand, and as we neared it order once more began to reassert itself in the countryside. Regimented lines of pines, planted for regeneration, gave way to a *Midsomer Murders* notion of England: a neatly tended cemetery; gabled cottages; somewhere called Amberley. Only the long, long bank of white cloud in the distance held a hint of the exotic. Right on time, after four hours and 21 minutes, we drew into Christchurch Station.

Even after just a few hours away from the crowded world, it felt odd to be back in a city. On a train, you feel temporarily removed from responsibility, free to enjoy travel for itself. Now I had to rely once more on myself, and on others. A taxi that had been ordered failed to show. Decisions had to be made about where to sleep and what to eat, and in which order. Later on, the tranquillity of the vast park at the heart of Christchurch was ruptured by the squeal and roar of what I hoped was South Island's only Lamborghini.

It felt good to be up early the next morning and back once more into a wilder realm. The city was still slumbering under a blanket of fog when, 800 feet above it, the minibus that had picked me up from the hotel shot out into sunshine. I was to spend the morning on a jet boat, skimming like a dragonfly across the sapphire-blue Waimakariri at nearly a mile a minute. As we sped up the gorge, stopping briefly beneath the tallest bridge on the railway line, I marvelled at how serene was our progress, despite its rapid rate. How still, too, the world beyond remained, as if we were no more than another bubble of air rushing through the rapids and across the bright stones.

At four, I found the train waiting at Arthur's Pass, at some 3,000 feet the highest point on the road over the mountains. For more than an hour, what had become the 'tranzalpine' had wound its way up from the west coast on its return journey to Christchurch. Passing at first through a lusher, more tropical landscape, it had then hauled through the five-mile-long Orita Tunnel, the longest in the Empire when finished in 1923 and, at a gradient of one in 33, one of the steepest in the world. Despite a delay of an hour caused by a load of coal being shed ahead of it on the line, it was now ready for the last leg of what some train buffs rate as being among the top ten short railway journeys in the world.

The sky was sullen, two parts copper to one of lead, but the scenery sufficiently majestic to distract from that. Either side of the carriage rose near-sheer hot, grey, rugged rock. The absence of other life was almost total. No animals made this their habitat, and only the presence of a beehive suggested that nearby of plants. In winter, the station can be snowed in for several days, but even though the sun now bore down on the high slopes around us, the train itself was deep in shadow.

Bucking occasionally on the rail, we began to cross a series of viaducts built a century before over the bends in the river. Their sections had been made in Britain and then sent over by sea. Light flittered through the wooden slats at the sides of the bridges, put there to protect the trains from the 200mph winds that can barrel down the canyon in stormy weather. The water over which I had raced in the morning had only been a few inches deep in places, but during the winter rains it can rise to more than 30 feet.

Most of those on the train were tourists. The service, which was only instituted in 1987 in place of a failing passenger line, is the most profitable in New Zealand – indeed, one of the few that makes any money at all. More than 200,000 people a year travel by it, and around me were visitors from Malaysia and Canada, as well as a group of Saudi engineers who had flown in for a conference on public utilities.

'This is very different from what we are used to,' Abdullah told me. 'At home, it is all desert. And there are no cinemas.' The first part I might have guessed, but the second was news to me. If you want to watch a film in its original format in Saudi Arabia – that is to say unedited, in public, in the dark and perhaps sitting next to someone of the opposite sex – then you need to leave the country to do so. As the views became ever more spectacular, we talked earnestly about faith, women's rights, taxation and the advantages of multiple wives.

Something about the conversation brought John Cleese to mind and then, as if the line had read my thoughts, we passed a corrugated iron shed on which track workers had chalked the words 'Fawlty Towers'. Below, the cliffs fell straight to the valley floor, and as we jolted over the bridge next to which the boat had stopped earlier, I remembered a little nervously that it was high enough to fit Christchurch Cathedral beneath it.

Nowhere else in the country do the mountains descend to the sea as swiftly as here, and after about two hours we began to wind through a series of tunnels and viaducts known as the Staircase. The train bent in a series of C and S shapes, hastening now as if trying to keep pace with the faltering sun. The light on the Waimakariri fell more subtly, a change matched by that in the steadily more domesticated world beyond the window. Moraine gave way to flat grasslands, pine to palm. Windbreaks appeared, then wheat, and finally clapboard houses behind manicured hedges. White fence posts flickered past, like images in a zoetrope. The line of hills grew more distant.

A sign on a vast metal shed, used for seed storage, told us that we were at Darfield. Often it lies under a distinctive arch of cloud caused by water in the atmosphere condensing as it begins to be drawn upwards over the island's backbone. The day had gone now, leaving only vestigial traces of pale orange in the sky. As the dusk thickened, the tilled earth beside the train turned from mauve to black. A twinkling of fairy lights could be seen on the heights behind us, while ahead Christchurch already shimmered with neon.

I thought back to the calm of that journey the following evening, when somewhere over the water between Auckland and Sydney the captain informed us that an engine had failed and we would have to turn around. There was something of a bygone age about the train, but it was all of a part with what I had found in a New Zealand entirely comfortable with itself. There had been a moment, when I had been waiting for the green-lipped mussels that we had fished out of the bay to cook in the billycan set up on the shingle where the canoes were beached, when I had stopped hearing the thoughts in my head. I was listening instead to the sound of the water lapping against the shore.

What I had found was a place where the striving that drives life in Britain was virtually absent. There seemed to be no urge on the part of those I met to just accumulate more stuff, to get somewhere ahead of everyone else. For the first time in many years I had had the time, and had felt the need, to reflect. Take life, like the train, at its own pace, and enjoy it for what it shows you.

There had been a moment, too, on that afternoon ride from Picton, when I had felt more in harmony with the world than for many years. I had been watching what I thought must be deer, standing half-hidden in the shade of trees a hundred yards from the track. Some instinct had startled them, and they turned their backs on the train and began to bounce away through the grass, their motion as graceful as any ballerina's.

I followed their movement with my head, and my eye caught that of Joe, the man from North Island. He had been watching the same thing. For an instant, we had been admitted to an older world, one that still existed if you knew where to look and if you gave it room to breathe. We had come into it only for a short time, but for just long enough to still the ticking of the clock. I had forgotten how good it was just to be, to float on the water rather than to seek to part it. 'All good, mate?' said Joe. 'Yes,' I replied, 'all good, it's all good.'

CHAPTER 6
CROSSING CONTINENTS

───────────

10 FEBRUARY 2007

HIGHGATE TO HANOI

IN AN EFFORT TO RECAPTURE THE ROMANCE OF TRAIN TRAVEL, **CHRIS HEATH** DECIDED TO GO NON-STOP FROM HIS HOME IN NORTH LONDON TO THE CAPITAL OF VIETNAM. ON THE WAY HE DISCOVERED, ALONG WITH THE DRUNKEN FOOTBALL FANS, FURIOUS PROVODNIKS AND PECULIAR CONTRABAND BISCUITS, THE BEAUTY OF THE JOURNEY IN ITS PUREST FORM

For all that flying has opened up our world, the rise of commercial aviation has also stolen something from us. It has removed the journey from our lives, in its truest and grandest and messiest sense: as a continuous line upon the surface of the earth that connects two distant places. Despite the real-time sky map on your seatback TV, and the occasional glance through an aeroplane window at the terrain far below, flying is about being somewhere and then, magically, reappearing somewhere else. It is Star Trek teleportation, albeit in a slightly more sluggish form.

The journey described here, 13 days by train from north London to Vietnam, was originally planned as a trip just from Moscow to Beijing via the Trans-Siberian Express, until I realised how much farther the line could be extended at either end. The lure was irresistible. I wanted to see what it was like to be on a train for so long; but, more than that,

I wanted to know what it would feel like to move a third of the way round the globe without cheating, pulling the landscape past you and around you and beneath you, mile after mile.

It begins with the London Underground. At 10.40 in the morning, the southbound Northern Line train from Highgate is nearly empty. I am the only person in the carriage with an overstuffed rucksack; and the only person to have brought a roll of lavatory paper with me, just in case. My second train, the near-empty Eurostar from Waterloo to Brussels, connects with the third, the Brussels-Cologne commuter run, which departs at dusk. I am impatient to leave London far behind me, but it's not proving easy. The seats in front are taken by some middle-aged British men on a gently laddish outing. As soon as we set off, they get out their box of Shiraz and some plastic cups.

'Three-litre box,' one of them says, beaming.

'That's four bottles, isn't it?' He makes it sound as though they've got away with something.

'Superb stuff,' another comments, his tone of voice serious in a way that seems impossible in a post-Alan Partridge world.

The German woman next to me breaks from her sudoku puzzle to take a piece of fruit out of her bag, but she fumbles it. It drops to the floor and rolls forward, under one of the Englishmen's seats. She taps him on the shoulder and explains. He picks it up.

'Is it a blood orange?' he asks.

'It's a pear,' she points out.

'A very nice pear, if I might say,' he comments, as though he feels obliged to say this but his heart isn't really in it. She goes back to her puzzle.

After Liège, I escape to the catering car. A mistake. I have exchanged the Shiraz-box revellers for drunken Tottenham fans. How European commuters must dread, in midweek during the football season, the travelling football supporter. Tomorrow, Tottenham play Bayer Leverkusen. This evening, a handful of inebriated Tottenham fans have hooked up here with three Hamburg fans, whose team last night lost to Tottenham's greatest rivals, Arsenal, but only after unexpectedly taking an early lead. These facts are enough for a certain empathy and friendship.

Between endlessly congratulating Hamburg for giving Arsenal a humiliating scare, there are songs to sing:

'F*** off, Arsenal! F*** off, Arsenal! F***! Off! Ars-! En-! Al! F*** off Arsenal!'

'Tottenham 'til I die, Tottenham 'til I die, Tottenham 'til I die.'

'F*** off, Arsenal! F*** off, Arsenal.'

People in this and the next carriage glance over disapprovingly, but nobody says anything. It is both baffling and impressive how little bored the Tottenham fans get by the same, endlessly repeated chants. One will start up the next bawdy, idiotic hymn, and the rest will all rush in with such glee, as though it has just struck them, with an accompanying rush of joy, 'This one? I love this one, and I haven't heard it for years!' When, in truth, it has only been — 'F*** off, Arsenal!' — six or seven minutes since it was last heard.

By the time we draw into Cologne, even the most rudimentary wit and rhyme seems beyond them. It is as though they have been desperately trying to communicate something, and now, with the drink taking its toll and time running short, they must pare their message down to its essence. Here, for the benefit of future generations, is that essence:

'Tottenham, Tottenham, Tottenham, Tottenham,
Tottenham, Tottenham, Tottenham, Tottenham,
Tottenham, Tottenham, Tottenham, Tottenham,
Tottenham, Tottenham, Tottenham, Tottenham,
Tottenham, Tottenham, Tottenham, Tottenham.'

I have been travelling away from London all day, and I am beginning to despair whether I will ever leave Britain at all. With the arrival of the 21.29 from Cologne to Moscow, it happens in seconds.

The moment my ticket is snatched from me, and not returned, by the fearsome middle-aged woman with illicitly blond hair who stands outside the carriage, barking at me in a language I can't understand and shoving me aboard, I have — I will come to realise — not only left Britain far behind me, but Western Europe as well.

Though it is not yet half past nine, when I open the door of my assigned second-class compartment the lights are off; I turn them on to see a woman on the bottom bunk scowling at me, making it clear that she has just been woken and doesn't appreciate it, and a man on the top bunk either sleeping through this commotion or pretending to. I am to be in the slender horizontal gap between them. I don't much look forward to lying awake for hours squeezed into the middle bunk, so I decide to have some dinner and then linger over drinks in the dining car until I am ready for bed. I ask the male carriage attendant in which direction I should go. He shakes his head. No food until . . . he traces his finger down the timetable in Russian script on the wall, and indicates four o'clock in the morning. He shrugs. I eventually manage to establish that cans of beer are available from a fridge a couple of carriages down. When I return, in the absence of anywhere else to sit I wedge myself in the narrow corridor on the threadbare carpet, and open a beer. A few minutes ago, on the platform, I was pumped with the romance of riding the rails east through the night. That feeling has somewhat faded.

After I have been squatting here a few minutes, the male carriage attendant comes up to me. He starts asking me, in broken English, why I am doing this, and says something about first class. It eventually dawns on me that he is trying to open a negotiation. I nod. In the end I'm led not to first class but into an empty compartment in this carriage that I'll have all to myself. Fifty euros exchange hands. 'No receipt,' he says, a trace of worry in his face that I might misunderstand the nature of this upgrade. It is barely 10 o'clock when I pull the door shut, absurdly relieved. I sit there in the dark, watching occasional flashes of Germany, drinking beer and nibbling on biscuits – thankfully, in a wise moment of just-in-case, I had bought some dry biscuits and a bar of chocolate at Cologne station – until I drop off.

At 3.30 a.m. I'm woken by Polish passport control rapping on the door, but after that I sleep through the night. In the morning, I doze, enjoying the solitude, free of grumpy bunk buddies and Tottenham fans and the Western world, letting my hunger grow until I can bear it no more. I wait until we pull out of Warsaw at just past 11 a.m. before I unlock my door and ask the carriage attendant in which direction the restaurant is.

He shakes his head, as though slightly sad that neither his regret nor my money can help us this time. 'After Brest,' he says. Five o'clock this afternoon.

I decide to save the chocolate for lunch. Soon afterwards I change my mind. Outside the window, Poland looks as you would imagine it in a depressing movie: factories belting out smoke, people on bicycles carrying tatty plastic bags, men sawing wood, chickens, sheds, paint peeling wherever paint has been painted – all of this in muted colours under a low, dark sky.

We reach Brest as what little light there has been today begins to fade. 'Where are you going?' the Belarus passport inspector demands.

'Hanoi.'

'Hanoi?'

'Vietnam.'

'Good luck,' he says, in a voice that suggests such folly is almost beyond sympathy.

We reach Moscow early the next morning. The Trans-Siberian Express doesn't leave until late evening; after a troublesome day in Moscow I am helped aboard by Sergei, my escort from a local travel agency, badly needed to interpret the impenetrable sea of Cyrillic script on the departure-announcement screen. Aboard, Sergei speaks to the provodnik, the person who runs the carriage – in this case a man called Stepan – and then briefs me. He tells me that I will have the two-berth cabin to myself until Beijing, six and a half days away. He also tells me that I should be very careful when the train passes through Gorky (these days known as Nizhny Novgorod) because Gorky is full of criminals.

Finally, just before midnight on Friday night, two and a half days after leaving London, I set off on the Trans-Siberian Express. I press play on my iPod, programmed to shuffle, and of the 1,532 songs currently available it chooses Robert Wyatt's heavenly yet mournful version of Chic's 'At Last I Am Free', which seems about right. And when it is drawn to follow that with the Osmonds' 'One Bad Apple', I can only blame myself.

I love sleeping on trains – that glorious sense of stillness cosseted within motion and of the world flickering by behind glass in the dark – but this first night towards Siberia I toss and turn and struggle to settle on the surprisingly hard sleeper bed. Whenever I wake, I see the same grey-white shapes of fir trees covered in snow. (Gorky, however, I sleep through, untouched by larceny.) In the morning, the view is the same. The afternoon, too. I haven't seen a patch of clear sky since I left London. It strikes me that we might well have just been travelling down some kind of forest-and-snow themed train line, trees planted for 20 or 30 yards either side of the track, with some kind of different terrain altogether hidden beyond.

During the day, I set off to explore the train a little, and to find the restaurant car. One of the minor challenges of life on the Trans-Siberian Express involves passing between carriages. These are coupled to each other in the old-fashioned way, where two curved metal plates rise up, one over the other, like a rough metal saddle. The seals round these areas don't quite meet, and there are plenty of gaps above and below, so as you move from one carriage to another you are effectively exposed to the outside elements. As you head deeper and deeper into the Siberian winter, this becomes more and more of an issue. My travelling library offers cautionary tales. In *The Great Railway Bazaar*, Paul Theroux reports losing the skin of his hands on one of the frozen external car door handles, and in Eric Newby's *The Big Red Train Ride*, he is told that should one be trapped between two carriages in mid-winter death may result within 20 minutes.

It's not just the cold. Simply passing through is a little tricky: between the two carriage doors you have to step on to the ever-shifting hump where the two metal plates meet, and then off again. These are frequently covered in ice, and so the trick is to keep in motion parallel to the tracks, so that if you slip a little – as sometimes you will do – you are falling towards one of the doors. (If you were to slip sideways, there are inviting holes plenty big enough for a leg to fit into, and just small enough that, with the movement of the train and the relative motion of the two carriages, a leg might not fit back out again.) Added to this, you have to decide, based on your level of paranoia about being frozen to death inter-carriage, whether you prefer to try to have at least one of the doors open at any time, a process that involves a kind of rocking technique in which you reach forward to open the new carriage door at the same time as bouncing back off it so that you may reach back and close the previous door, on which you then rebound one more time to send yourself into the new carriage. It certainly makes you think twice about how much you want breakfast.

In the dining car the menu is in Russian only. (The Trans-Siberian Express is not a tourist train, and no particular concessions are made to tourists who wish to travel on it.) The waitress speaks maybe 10 words of English, all of them reluctantly. Only two other tables in the dining car are occupied; at one, a man with white hair in a corduroy jacket is washing his meal down with vodka. It is five past 11 in the morning.

When I make my way back down the two carriages that lie between the restaurant car and my compartment and try the compartment door I think is mine, it is locked. I check the provodnik on duty at the end of the compartment; it is not Stepan. Slightly perplexed by my absent-mindedness, I open the equivalent compartment in the next carriage and am shouted at by the alarmed occupants. I try the next carriage on, but these have four berths to a compartment. My compartment seems to have disappeared. Finally, out of options and slightly flustered, I go to the provodnik in the first carriage I tried. (Rather disconcertingly, on this trip my mind seems to have randomly cast half the people I meet as Russian versions of semi-familiar faces; I will never look at this man without thinking of the actor Pete Postlethwaite, someone I have given fairly little thought to in my life before now.) 'Stepan?' I say to him. He gestures that Stepan is asleep. It is the right carriage after all. I act out my predicament; it seems that he, finding the compartment empty, has taken it upon himself to lock it.

He lets me in, then returns a few minutes later and starts shouting at me. My sin is that, having been told that I will be alone in this carriage until Beijing, I have spread my possessions over both berths. He is furious. He returns with my ticket and points to where it says that I have one berth and shouts, 'One! One!'

The compartment itself has a kind of faded luxury, with its wooden veneer, its scuffed table next to the window, and its frustratingly filthy windows. Most striking are the matching large mirrors on either side: when you stand up, you can see repeating versions of yourself and the mirrors tapering away towards infinity.

That afternoon, the piped music starts up for the first time. I have read about this. There is a speaker above the window in each compartment, and traditionally the provodnik supplies music or inspiring speech of his choice for his travellers. In the Communist era, the speakers couldn't be turned off, and my guidebooks warn me that even now some speakers will only allow their volume to be reduced to a minimum. Today's opening number is accordion-led harmony-singing in waltz time. As annoying as I find it, it strikes me that perhaps I should leave it on to allow myself the most authentic trans-Siberian experience. But the second song is the kind of tinny, feeble and yet annoyingly shouty pop techno beloved in the post-communist East. Before its end I have located the off-switch under the window.

At around four in the afternoon – it already feels like the middle of the night – we roll into Balyezino. Moscow is already 1,000 kilometres (625 miles) behind us. These trains stop several times each day, stops that are scheduled for between two and 23 minutes. The guidebooks advise that you may get off the train at the longer stops, to stretch your legs or to buy provisions from the hawkers waiting on the platform, but that you should always check precise timings with the provodnik. I'm a little nervous to leave the train at all, but decide it is time to give it a go. I try to ask Pete Postlethwaite for guidance and he offers me two gloved hands of fingers, twice; unfortunately, I have no idea whether this means 20 minutes or a particularly emphatic 10. In the freezing outside, refusing to leave the train more than a couple of paces away, I buy some rissoles and potatoes. I eat them cold with my fingers as I watch the millionth snowy fir tree pass in the dark.

Before bedtime, we pull into Perm, formerly home to one of the USSR's most famous labour camps and also, apparently, the town Chekhov's three sisters were so keen to leave. Late at night, lying with my head below the window as we pass from Europe to Asia, I am giddy with relief to glimpse some stars; at last some sign that the sky still exists.

The next morning, the sky is there still. I have rarely been more happy to see a sunrise. I was beginning to feel that the sun was some kind of Western opiate-for-the-masses conspiracy that the East had abandoned, and I realise how much the endless days of gloom have been affecting me.

Now, from the restaurant car at the crack of dawn there's a beautiful display of the whole pastel paintbox. Even the old-style smoke-belching industrial plants we pass look gorgeous, and between towns the landscape has opened up a little: still trees, and still snow, but sometimes you can see for a couple of hundred yards either side of the track.

In celebration, I spend 20 minutes painstakingly comparing Russian words on the menu with the lists of foods in my Lonely Planet guide. Eventually I hit on a match, and order the mushrooms. The waitress shakes her head. Not possible. I ask for a fried egg. Not possible. I give up and ask for some fried pork for breakfast. It arrives with a fried egg on top.

Today, I decide, it is time to travel the length of the train. There turn out to be about 10 further carriages on the other side of the restaurant car, and they all seem fairly full. Most of the passengers are of Chinese appearance, and are in four-berth compartments; the reason why none of them is ever seen in the restaurant car is apparent from the huge piles of food stacked high on each compartment table, and the further bags and pails at the ends of the carriages. Eventually, I reach the very back of the train. The small window in the final door is completely frozen over. I hack away at it with a rolled-up copy of *Private Eye*, the edge of my guidebook and a coin until I have made a small hole through which I can look and take photos. If I stop scrubbing for more than a few seconds, it freezes over again. Between scrubs, I watch the railway line racing away behind, the dry snow whipped up by the motion of the train swirling and dancing over the rails.

We officially entered Siberia 2,102 kilometres (1,314 miles) down the line from Moscow, just after daybreak on day three. (You can find out where you are at any point in the journey by jamming your head hard against a window on the right-hand side of the train – no windows open in the winter – and trying to catch the number on the next of the kilometre posts that stand right by the track. Then you can compare it with the running guide offered in Bryn Thomas's *Trans-Siberian Guidebook*, the best trip companion for that very reason.) Distance is always measured from Moscow. More perplexing, and one more thing that adds to the surreality of life aboard, is that along the length of the line time is also always Moscow time. You pass through six time zones before reaching the Chinese border, but the station clocks still tell Moscow time so that, near the journey's end, you will pull into Borzya at what your stomach and the sun will tell you is lunchtime but every clock will tell you is not yet six o'clock in the morning.

Omsk, the next town down the line, is where Dostoevsky was incarcerated for four years: his mixed feelings about this experience are recorded in his book *Buried Alive in Siberia*. I get off here for just a moment, and clamber over the two sets of railway lines that separate our train from the station shops. As I do so, I hear a whistle blow, and sum up the situation only just quickly enough – another train is arriving at the station and is about to cross over into these nearside tracks; if it stops, I will have little hope of making my way around it and back to my train in time. I scamper back in front of it. I realise that there have not been many days on this trip when I haven't been worried that a train was about to leave me behind.

In truth, there is no such train as the Trans-Siberian Express. The railway line crossing Siberia to join European Russia with the Pacific coast was completed at the beginning of the last century, but to Russians the different trains that travel upon it are simply known by their names and route numbers. Though many other trains travel along portions of these tracks, there are three main routes collectively being referred to as those of the Trans-Siberian Express. The longest-established, and the only one that remains within Russia throughout, is from Moscow to the eastern port of Vladivostok, down which trains run once every two days: the Trans-Siberian route. The Trans-Mongolian route (weekly) branches south after 5,655 kilometres (3,534 miles) and heads through Mongolia before terminating in Beijing. The Trans-Manchurian – the train I am on, once a week as well – also terminates in Beijing but doesn't branch south until around 6,300 kilometres (3,938 miles) from Moscow, avoiding Mongolia and heading directly into Manchurian China. This train is known as the Vostok.

The various accounts I had read of those who had ridden these routes over the years had led me to believe that the train would be packed with tourists – most of them reading, or failing to read, *War and Peace* – and also of curious Russians who would miss no opportunity to coerce you into vodka-drinking games and chess matches. I imagined that it would be a blessing to escape to my compartment in between the dizzy social whirl that would propel me up and down the corridors.

One of the surprises of my first days on the train is that it isn't working out like that at all. The shortage of tourists, at least, seems to be down to the season – frozen November is not a popular choice – and also to my chosen train. Tourists tend to favour the Mongolian route, for its more deluxe first-class cabins and its showers – on the Vostok you wash as best you can in the toilet – and, of course, because you get to go through Mongolia.

After a couple of days, I discover, however, that there are three other tourists on the train – three Swedes, travelling together. Improbably, they run dinosaur theme parks in the United States.

Still, on the fourth day, I do get some unexpected new company. Returning to my compartment, I find a pile of bags and a man returning home to China; he is travelling with friends who will rotate in occupying the other berth – I think being stuck with me may be the short straw – from now on.

One slight frustration in riding the Trans-Siberian Express as a tourist is that the schedule is not arranged so that places of interest are necessarily passed in daylight. It has been frustrating to miss the Europe-Asia marker, and the crossing of the Volga, so I'm relieved that at least the eastbound Trans-Manchurian passes Lake Baikal during daylight on our fifth day. The lake is the world's deepest and contains about 20 per cent of this planet's fresh water. From the train you get no sense of its immensity – we pass beneath its thin southernmost finger – but it's still a liberating change of scene. I had imagined it would be frozen, but in early December this part of the lake is wet and blue and steaming.

We stop in Slyudyanka at the lip of the lake; when the train used to pause here for 15 minutes it was considered possible to race down to the water and back, but these days they don't even lower the steps. Instead, food sellers gather round the open doors. Most of them proffer a foot-long fish, which I presume is the lake's famous omul. Assuming, quite correctly, that nothing so interesting will be added to the restaurant car menu, I buy one – handed up to me loosely folded inside the competition-and-puzzle page from the local newspaper – and also point to what looks like a bread roll to eat with it. This turns out to be a potato doughnut, and the fish itself, slightly smoked, is like a rich, tasty, dark-fleshed kind of trout. I wash it down with some apple juice

I've bought at a previous platform which, on being opened, and despite the green fruit on its packaging, turns out to be peach.

Just before we pass the 5,508km (3,442 miles) post, I spot two deer grazing. Aside from the very occasional bird, these are the first wild animals I've seen since we left Moscow.

It is around sundown on this, my fifth day aboard the Trans-Siberian Express, when I realize that in some way I no longer really expect this train ever to reach a destination. To find a comfort level on such a trip as this – to accept it as it is, to embrace it and also to be institutionalised by it – is to let go of the fantasy that journeys once had beginnings, and some day will end. It now feels as though this track beneath me will roll on forever, through slightly bleaker and odder and less frequent destinations that I will see for two or 10 or 23 minutes. Outside, the view will change very slowly. Somewhere in the back of my head I distantly remember some other life, beyond these wooden veneered and mirrored walls, where my sleep wasn't punctuated by the dull hammering noises of axes chopping ice from the underside of the train before its endless motion resumes; but I'm not sure how much I really believe in it any more.

Perhaps you could argue that nearly all modern tourism, to a greater or lesser extent, involves a kind of gliding through places without really engaging with them; and that a long train journey like this is simply an extreme version. Beyond the satisfying of basic bodily needs, there's really little to occupy yourself with. You can read, you can listen to music, you can stare aimlessly out of the window, and you can pretend to think about the world – that's about it. Fortunately, these are four of my favourite things to do.

We arrive at the Russian border town of Zabaikalsk in the late afternoon of day five. The next few hours are somewhat anxious and disorientating. First, you are turfed off the train in Zabaikalsk and then the train disappears from the station without you. It could be a very disturbing moment; luckily, I have read that it is only going a few hundred yards to a shed where, to prepare for the different-gauge Chinese tracks, each carriage must be lifted up and placed on a new undercarriage. I have also managed to ascertain from Stepan that the train will not be leaving before midday Russian time – more than two hours from now.

There is nothing to do in the waiting room but wait. The couple of hundred people from the train simply spread themselves around; those who can take seats and the rest crouch or sit on the cold floor. Instead, I decide to head off over the footbridge into town to waste some time and find some food. I find a row of commercial establishments, though it's impossible to tell what they sell without going into each. The first sells carpets, vinyl flooring, stationery and David Beckham posters. The second, shoes. The third, building supplies. The fourth is a laundry that also sells hi-fis and computers. The fifth, thankfully, is a café. Afterwards, I find a grocery store around the corner and stock up on supplies – in homage to my Cologne-Moscow experience I buy some thick, square, rather grim local biscuits loosely packed in a clear plastic bag; on them they have a weird design of a rather plain bespectacled Russian girl's face.

Back at the station, I sit on the freezing marble floor, getting up every few minutes to check for the train's return, terrified of missing it. Eventually, several hours after its disappearance, it grinds its way in front of the platform. Chilled, I huddle in my compartment and taste one of the bespectacled girl biscuits. As I eat, I notice the strange, loping Russian script down the side: ??pp? ?o???? I stare again at what is left of the girl's head.

The penny drops. She is not a girl, and she is not Russian. What I am eating is bootleg biscuit – Siberian Harry Potter merchandise.

A few miles down the line, we reach Manzhouli, the Chinese border town. Once more, Stepan pushes me off the train, and this time I am unable to get any further explanation or time-frame or guidance from him. I have absolutely no idea what is happening. It is now late at night; outside it is wincingly cold; the platform is frozen solid, and slippery; I don't know where I'm going. Much farther along the platform some, but not all, of the disembarking passengers head for a room in the station, and I follow them. Eventually, the dinosaur Swedes arrive too, so I stand with them. They have no idea what is going on, either. I guess I am expecting us eventually to be shepherded through the customs channels in the other half of the room, and then back on to the train, but for about an hour nothing happens. I think I would have waited until told otherwise, but eventually the Swedes decide to try getting back on to the train and so, not wanting to be left completely alone, I follow.

We're allowed on and a few minutes later the train leaves. I have no reason to believe that if I had remained in the customs hall for some never-to-happen customs/passport ritual the train would not have left without me.

Nine days after I last slept on a still bed, I finally reach Beijing. I must stay here for two nights to wait for the train to Hanoi. I head down to Tiananmen Square to see Chairman Mao's body (but the schedule has been changed so that he is no longer receiving visitors on Friday afternoons), then eat at a restaurant where there are 17 different types of mushrooms soaking in plastic bowls on a table near the entrance. I order the mushroom soup. Later, I am dozing at dusk on my hotel bed, and when the headlights of the cars at the traffic lights outside slowly begin to accelerate, I find my body bracing itself, my train-washed senses instinctively assuming that the hotel room is pulling out of its station.

On the impressively modern train south to Vietnam I am booked into a lower-berth bunk in a four-berth cabin. (These are the smartest seats on offer. Most of the Chinese are in three-level bunks in open-plan carriages.) My first discovery is that there are plenty of storage spaces on a Chinese train – under the bunks and in a compartment above the corridor – but that all of these are far too narrow to accommodate a rucksack. If you want to travel in comfort on a Chinese train, bring pretty much anything you want with you, but pack thinly.

A journey up and down the train will later confirm that there is only one other passenger of non-Chinese appearance, a young Frenchman whom the carriage attendants – in China called *fuwuyuen* – move from next door into my compartment, presumably to put all the foreigners together. He introduces himself as 'Merry – like Merry Christmas.' I assume that this is an easy guide to his name's pronunciation, rather than its spelling, and that his name is some French male version of Mary, but when I ask him for clarification at the end of our journey he will explain that his name really is Merry. 'My parents were fond of the book *Lord of the Rings*,' he explains. He is named after a hobbit.

The *fuwuyuen* hands out the light slippers to be worn while walking around the train, and then a moment later returns and, with great solemnity, hands first Merry, then me, a grey-clothed book. He stands there expectantly, as though he has just shared the sacred totem of a secret religion as part of an initiation ceremony, and is anticipating some grand reaction. Merry politely flicks through the book, and so do I, and then hand it back. The *fuwuyuen* seems slightly disappointed. But what else were we to do with what he had given us – a hardback copy in English, without its dust-jacket, of a Joanna Trollope novel called *Marrying the Mistress*?

At breakfast, the Chinese in the packed dining car mostly watch the TV mounted near the car's ceiling. At the table opposite, a man in a smart jacket finishes his meal and shaves with his electric razor at the table. About a dozen female *fuwuyuen* line up in the dining car corridor where they are given a lecture. On the TV, after what seems to be a satirical political Chinese cartoon, there is, bizarrely, footage from a fashion show: models parading up and down, up and down. A caption eventually explains that this is a Vivienne Westwood collection filmed in Paris. If that alone wasn't surreal enough, the music playing in the background is Suzi Quatro's 'Can the Can'.

It strikes me that all of this – Joanna Trollope, Vivienne Westwood, Suzi Quatro – serves to remind that when a culture opens itself up to another, as China has to the West, the remarkable thing is that, more often than not, it neither gets the best of that culture (as we might hope) nor its worst (as we might fear) but instead receives a sometimes baffling mishmash. Whatever they learn from us, or think of us, it is from our good, our bad, our mediocre, our indifferent and our irrelevant.

The border formalities between China and Vietnam are far less troubling than those between Russia and China. At the Chinese station nearest the border, Nanning, we are pulled off the train and put into a waiting room. Only two carriages remain of the dozen or so that left Beijing, and of the 20 or so passengers aboard now, most are non-Chinese. After a while, we are put back on the train and it races through the dark – faster, it seems, than before – towards Vietnam. There are no lights anywhere. Passing between China and Vietnam you feel as though you are doing something that is being allowed only reluctantly; the sense you get is of two countries who prefer to sit with their backs to each other and their arms crossed, as if each would rather pretend that its neighbour is not there.

At around 1 a.m., we reach the Vietnamese side of the border. We get out in a darkened station and are ushered into an indoor area where we have to fill out departure cards, undergo customs inspection (my copy of Ryszard Kapuscinski's *Imperium* is studied for some time, then returned without comment) and pay the equivalent of about 30p to a man in a booth, after which one must lean through the glass window of his booth so that he can place a plastic cone in one's ear to measure its temperature.

On the final leg of my journey I have new travelling companions: a holidaying Japanese electrical engineer who mostly listens without speaking, although his English is good, and a grey-haired, balding retired trucker from San Diego who can talk for all of us. I had seen him in the Nanning waiting room chatting amiably to a Chinese woman but she, it turns out, was only for while he was in China. He comes here often and quotes, approvingly, an old Vietnam hand who explained the country's appeal as 'good f***ing women and cheap f***ing beer'. He puts it his own way. 'Wine, women and song,' he says. 'And who really gives a damn about song?'

He is already talking again, it seems, when I wake in the morning: about Vietnamese funeral traditions, and rice-field grave sites, and the narrowness of Vietnamese houses, and their unique rice-fired bricks, and how he needs to get rid of his Chinese cans of ready-made coffee given to him by the Chinese woman before he flies to Ho Chi Minh city today because last time they killed him on the excess baggage . . .

'You know what today is?' he asks.

I shake my head.

'December 7?' he prompts, and grunts despairingly when this fails to draw a response. 'Pearl Harbor Day,' he says. And he's off – talking about how fewer and fewer veterans of that attack are still around, seemingly oblivious to the third person in the compartment, the Japanese engineer. When I, embarrassed by this whole conversation, silently refuse to respond to his questions, he offers unnecessary elaborations such as 'That's where the Japanese bombed'. I have no idea whether he is not thinking, or whether it is deliberate, but he never acknowledges what he is doing. The Japanese man says nothing.

The American tells me proudly that he has been to 47 of the USA's states. I murmur, untactfully, annoyed with him, that I have been to 49. He just looks at me. It's as though either he doesn't believe me, or that he can't believe I would cut across his storytelling like that. In the end he decides to simply ignore what I have said, and resumes his blocked flow. 'Forty-seven's a lot of states,' he says.

My final railway mile takes me over the Long Bien bridge, whose construction was directed by the architect who designed the Eiffel Tower and which was regularly bombed by the Americans during the Vietnam war. The line curves south into the centre of Hanoi; when I later wander up this piece of track on foot I discover it bustling with activity, the rails used by the locals for cooking, washing and anything else they so choose as they reclaim this land as their own in the spaces between trains. (I'd quite like to see the proud people of Highgate try that.)

I have arranged to spend five days in Hanoi – to decompress, to explore a city I have never visited, and also because I thought that it was important to feel that my journey had a destination, rather than just turning right round again. I do some conventional sightseeing but mostly I just walk around Hanoi's streets and shops and lakes and restaurants. For one day I rent a bicycle (one dollar, no deposit) but otherwise I walk. It's a wonderful city, though it takes a little getting used to. The insane traffic, in particular. On any street, there is a constant melange of bicycles, cyclos (the pedalled rickshaw-type contraptions available for hire), motorbikes, and a few cars, heading in your direction, often 15 or 20 abreast. You soon learn to do as the locals do: you simply step into the stream and carefully wade through, not minding that vehicles of different speed are dodging inches either side of you. It seems to work, and I feel quite safe.

Still, over dinner on the last night – I've ignored the many snake, pigeon and tortoise dishes on the menu, and also Beef Testicles Stuffed With Hotch-Potch, and opted for something semi-sensible involving eels – when I open a copy of the supremely stolid English-language paper, the *Viet Nam News*, I find this headline: 'Top Foreign Scientist Still In Coma After Traffic Accident'. I read on. Dr Seymour Papert, a 78-year-old MIT professor and one of the world's leading experts on artificial intelligence, in town for a conference, has been severely injured after being hit by a motorbike while crossing the road near his

Hanoi hotel. The report says:

'Papert was discussing ways to build a mathematical model to describe Ha Noi's notoriously chaotic streets when the accident occurred, according to Uri Wilensky, a professor of computer science at Northwestern University, who was crossing the street with Papert when he was hit.'

After dinner, I visit a bar I have read about, far from the tourist areas, away by the river, not far from the railway bridge. I am the only customer, and I sit on the artfully abandoned sofa on its terrace and watch the water go by in the dark. A train comes in over the bridge, just as mine had done a few days earlier. When I head back towards the hotel, slightly nervous at how rough and out of the way this neighbourhood seems, some girls walking ahead of me start screaming, and running in all directions. Darting to get out of their way, I step on something soft. The rodent that has been the cause of this commotion – a chunky mouse, or a small rat – seems less traumatised by this than I do. Walking on vermin, scientists toppling over around me in darkly ironic traffic accidents . . . how many omens do I need that it might be time to head back?

For all those lucky enough to have one, going home is the final step – part triumph, part admission of defeat – of all travels. I felt every mile roll under me from north London to South-East Asia but now, by the miracle of air travel, all my progress comes undone. It is like watching a film on video, falling asleep at its end, and then awakening to find it rewound to the beginning. The journey back is so much easier – two flights, less than a day in transit, changing in Hong Kong – and so uneventful that, after all that has come before, it is no journey at all.

4,887 MILES – AND *ANNA KARENINA* UNFINISHED

THE TRANS-MONGOLIAN FROM MOSCOW TO BEIJING TOOK **ADRIAN BRIDGE** AND FAMILY ACROSS CONTINENTS, TIME ZONES AND GEOPOLITICAL DIVIDES

After months of preparation and years of wondering what it must be like to board the Trans-Siberian, the moment when it finally came was so much better than I had expected. There was the train itself – the Rossiya (Number 2) – brightly painted in the Russian national colours of blue, white and red, and looking magnificent in the late evening light on Platform 4 of Yaroslavsky station in Moscow. There were the smartly uniformed *provodnitsas* (train attendants) standing territorially by their carriage doors while they scrutinised tickets. There were last-minute dashes to buy extra provisions (cold bottles of beer in my case); there were tearful hugs and protracted goodbyes. And then, when all of us were safely on board, there was a blast of martial-style music as the guards on the platform gave a final cheer and a wave and the train slowly pulled away. In the carriage corridor there was a spontaneous round of applause. We had just begun the greatest train journey in the world.

As a rule, the Trans-Siberian means the 5,772-mile journey that begins in European Moscow and ends up a stone's throw from Japan in the Pacific Ocean port of Vladivostok. Travelling with two teenage children, my wife and I decided to vary the itinerary to take the classic route as far as Irkutsk, deep in Siberia, before dipping south towards the plains of Mongolia, the Gobi Desert and down to Beijing. Our journey – known as the Trans-Mongolian – was almost as long (4,887 miles), offered more geographical and cultural variety – and, of course, linked the two great bastions of Communist power over the past century, Moscow and Beijing.

We didn't get off to the greatest of starts, though. Caught up in the drama of the departure, I opened one of the bottles of beer and, with Moscow's Stalinesque towers still in view, proceeded to spill half of it on the freshly cleaned corridor carpet. Maria, our archetypally fierce-looking *provodnitsa*, was not amused. We were not going all the way to Vladivostok, but we were to spend the next four nights on board. She gave me a withering look.

MOSCOW – NOVOSIBIRSK (0-2,072 MILES)

Having been slightly apprehensive about what our four-bed, second-class compartment would be like, we were pleasantly surprised. It was clean (and thanks to Maria's daily vacuuming it remained that way). It was certainly cosy, but the bunks were wide and long enough (my 6ft 2in son did not complain). There were fresh sheets and blankets and a small table on which we could tuck into our supplies – bread and peanut butter, pot noodles and the daily meals that were provided in polystyrene containers (typically buckwheat and meat; pork and peas; teeth-ruiningly sweet wafers).

I could happily have curled up with *Anna Karenina* and not emerged until we arrived in Irkutsk four nights and five time zones later. But there was so much to see. More precisely, there were so many birch trees to see. For someone attuned to the visual harshness of urban life, it was a balm to stand in the corridor watching the endlessly green sweep of the Russian countryside passing by. The corridor – and in particular the all-important samovar dispensing boiling water at the end of it – was also the place to socialise. Our fellow travellers comprised a mixture of foreigners (some Britons, Germans, French, Japanese), generally intrepid-traveller types in their twenties and thirties but some well into their fifties – and plenty of Russians. One of the great things about this journey is that it is not exclusively aimed at tourists; the Trans-Siberian is a regular working train used by ordinary Russians.

We shared many of the early scenic pleasures with Alexander, a kindly train engineer from Kolomna, just south of Moscow, who was travelling to Barabinsk for a few days' work. On the second evening of the trip, as we pulled away from Perm, we hit a glorious stretch incorporating streams, dramatic rock faces and beautiful forests, all bathed in the last of the day's sun.

'This is the real Russia,' exclaimed Alexander, beating his breast. 'I love this country; it is wonderful – also for me.'

The following morning, shortly after the train crossed the Ural Mountains and the line marking the end of Europe and the beginning of Asia (1,104 miles), I encountered Nikolai, a young Russian from Omsk with a broad smile and flashing golden teeth who reminded me of the Jaws character in the James Bond films.

Nikolai ushered me into his compartment and introduced me to his friends Victor and Walli. 'Omsk very good! London very good! America very good!' he declared. I nodded in agreement at the first two statements but hesitated at the third (this was pre-Obama). We all smiled. The Cold War seemed a long time ago.

I enjoyed such encounters enormously but could always retreat back into the sanctuary of our own compartment. The slender Japanese couple we befriended farther down the corridor had less room for manoeuvre in the compartment they shared with two larger-than-life Russians, one of whom spent the entire journey wandering around in his boxer shorts. 'A very interesting cultural exchange,' was how they termed the invitation to join their roommates for a vodka-fuelled breakfast every morning at nine. A French couple in a similar arrangement quietly upgraded to a two-bed, first-class cabin.

It sometimes felt frustrating not being able to see and experience more of the vast country we were passing through. But while we might not have been getting out and into Russia, Russia came to us in the form of the constantly changing cast of passengers – and the hawkers and babushkas who greeted us at every station. They sold woollen shawls, cuddly toys, pieces of smoked fish and genuine Siberian fur hats. My 15-year-old son thought the hats were cool, so I haggled (not very successfully) to get one for about £35. There was no time to try to get the price down further: Maria was signalling that the 20 minutes allocated for the stop was up.

NOVOSIBIRSK – IRKUTSK (2,072 MILES-3,222 MILES)

In an animated exchange in the restaurant car towards the end of our third evening, a Russian army officer heading home to Vladivostok was insisting that his country's ice hockey team was the best in the world, a claim hotly contested by Shayna, an equally passionate ice hockey fan from Canada. Like us, Shayna and her boyfriend, Hans, were taking the Trans-Siberian to Irkutsk and then the Trans-Mongolian to Ulan Bator and Beijing. But Beijing still felt a long way off as our train – at that point somewhere between Novosibirsk and Krasnoyarsk – trundled through a spectacular red Siberian sunset on its long passage east.

Not long afterwards the lights in the restaurant car were dimmed and the music – let's just call it Russian pop – was turned up. It was disco night on the Trans-Siberian.

There was some good-hearted jigging, an attempt at forming a snake and some rather indiscreet importuning of the Western ladies by inebriated Russian officers whose intentions, it can confidently be said, were not entirely honourable. A young Russian by the name of Vladimir began showing just a little too much interest in my 16-year-old daughter and I decided it was time for us to retreat to our compartment.

When we had been considering this trip in London – and especially the four-night, 3,222-mile stretch from Moscow to Irkutsk – we imagined it would go on forever and that we would easily get bored. At times our children were bored – silver birches weren't really their thing and there were few fellow teenagers – so they resorted to their books and iPods. But for my wife and me the time flew by. There was the scenery – beautiful pine forests, meadows filled with wild purple flowers, the lovely hills surrounding Krasnoyarsk. There were the constant references to the map (a fellow traveller had pinned a huge one above his bunk) and the timetable in the corridor. There was the simple excitement of arriving at places such as Nizhny Novgorod and wondering what they were like. There were the quirky things you saw along the way: a woman dressed in Sunday best in a yard full of geese; cargo trains bearing tanks and military vehicles; tantalising glimpses of gold-plated onion domes. And there was space: the sheer, vast space of Russia. Mental space.

As our third day drew to a close, many of us due to get out at Irkutsk the next morning were almost sad not to be going all the way to Vladivostok (by now only another three nights away). We had got rather used to the rhythms and rituals of the day, the gatherings by the samovar, the chats at the corridor windows, the trips to the restaurant car (the beef stroganoff and rice wasn't bad). We had got used to the bizarre way in which, no matter how many time zones you cross, Russian trains run to Moscow time (we were due to arrive in Irkutsk at 6.03 a.m. the following day but the station clock would read 1.03 a.m.). We had got used to the regular tickings-off we received from Maria – she once shouted at one of the German travellers for having spent more than five minutes in the communal bathroom (containing a large sink but no shower). Four nights on board suddenly didn't seem like long enough. I was only on page 30 of *Anna Karenina*.

IRKUTSK – ULAN BATOR (3,222 MILES-3,917 MILES)

The journey from Irkutsk to Ulan Bator got off to an alarming start. Within minutes of scrambling up into our compartment for the 5.13 a.m. departure we became aware of a commotion at the end of the carriage. A young Mongolian was throwing up into a black bin liner and being shouted at by an extremely angry blue-uniformed woman. The woman, our new *provodnitsa*, was adding to his pain by kicking him. She made Maria look like an old softie.

Many different kinds of train ply the Trans-Siberian and Trans-Mongolian routes; having enjoyed the relative comfort of the No. 2 (Rossiya) so far, we were now on the rather different Mongolian-run No. 6 (Moscow-Ulan Bator Express). The carriages were less homely, the cabins more cramped and the attendant – Botrama – was clearly not someone to fall out with. That said, the train was perfectly comfortable and it was great to be moving again. Lake Baikal (the oldest and deepest lake in the world, as well as one of the largest), was a beautiful spot to break the journey, but it was good simply to be tuning back into the sounds and rhythms of life on board a train.

Switching trains brought us into contact with a whole new set of travellers, most of whom were also heading for Beijing. I spoke to one Englishman who was bravely making the journey with children aged eight, 10 and 12. I also ran into Jörg, a German who combined a fanatical passion for travel with an equally fanatical passion for sport (he had even seen FC Vladivostok play at home). Of such characters are long train journeys made.

In subtle ways, Beijing was beginning to feel nearer. After a lovely stretch running right along the edge of Lake Baikal, we moved away from the territory of birch and pine into lusher pastures. For a long period after passing Ulan Ude we followed the course of the Selenga river, the leisurely twists and turns of which afforded great views of the train itself (this one coloured a deep green) coming around the bends. The hawkers at stations (selling smoked Omul fish, jeans and berries) were also beginning to look different. Many of the people were Buryats, an ethnic group of Mongolian descent, and their features were distinctly Asiatic.

We got rather longer than we would have liked to study them at the Russian town of Naushki, the last stopping point before the train crossed into Mongolia proper. We spent more than four hours at the station, a nondescript affair that had a definite end-of-the-line feel about it. Immigration and customs officers scrutinised documents and searched cabins for stowaways or illicit goods. There were multiple forms to fill in. Orders to open suitcases were barked. The bad old days seemed closer again.

It took a further three hours to cross into Mongolia and go through similar procedures there. Train travel is great – until your train is stationary. It was with immense relief that just before 1 a.m. we finally chugged back into life. Although sleep is always fitful on trains, I dozed off more quickly than usual. I knew that by daybreak we would be deep inside Genghis Khan country.

ULAN BATOR – BEIJING (3,917 MILES-4,887 MILES)

After all those birch trees, it was a novel and welcome experience to wake to the rolling hills and steppes of Mongolia. In the distance we caught sight of the occasional wild horse. As we pulled closer to the capital, Ulan Bator, we saw row after row of the traditional gers – tents – in which more than half of the Mongolian population still live. On the outskirts of Ulan Bator, engraved on a hillside, we spotted the features of Genghis Khan himself, the national hero who has once again been returned to his pedestal following the loosening of ties with Russia after the collapse of communism. We broke the journey here again, sampling the delights of local life: riding, archery (a huge hit with my son), Mongolian throat-singing and . . . fermented mare's milk (as bad as it sounds).

For the final leg of the journey from Ulan Bator to Beijing we were again travelling with Mongolian Railways, but this time a much more modern version. This one (No. 23/24) had plush carpets, television screens for each bed and a power point in each compartment (essential for iPod recharging). It was by far the most comfortable train we had taken so far. Which was probably just as well. The grassy hills we climbed on our way out of Ulan Bator soon gave way to the much harsher, more arid landscape of the Gobi Desert. Our attendant came round to lock all the windows against dust. Soon all we could see was sand with the odd little clump of grass. Relief came in the occasional sighting of a double-humped camel.

At the desolate town of Choyr, little boys ran furiously alongside the slowing train in the hope that we would be tempted to buy lumps of jade and amethyst, or paintings of Mongolian warriors on horse-back. I wandered out to the front of the station and spotted a bizarre silver statue of VVT Ertvuntz, the first (and only) Mongolian cos-monaut. It was a dusty, inhospitable landscape. The train represented a welcome refuge.

As at the border between Russia and Mongolia, the crossing into China was a rather sweaty affair involving more officious border guards and customs officers, and lengthy checking procedures. But there was the added diversion of the changing of the bogies: a process that involved the lifting of each carriage of the train to adjust the width between the wheels to fit them for the narrower gauge used in China.

And there was no mistaking China when we did finally reach it. Uniformed guards lined the platform at the red-neon-lit Erlyan station and loudspeakers broadcast Viennese waltzes at high volume. It was brash and over-the-top, and extremely regimented. Welcome to the People's Republic.

We were almost at our journey's end. The following morning it was a relatively short hop to Beijing via Datong and Zhangjiakou, the point where the old caravan route between China and Russia crossed the Great Wall. We didn't see the wall itself, but along the way we passed some spectacular rocky scenery and fields full of maize and sunflowers (though a thick haze marred the views.) Through the haze I picked out the occasional red flag among rather ramshackle housing and nondescript developments. Was this really the new superpower?

Beijing, too, was shrouded in smog (it often is). The Chinese capital is not an attractive city at the best of times and, for all the emphasis on the glitzy and the new, it remains a hard place to love. Arriving was almost anticlimactic. But it was the journey that counted. We had got there by train. The trip, all 4,887 miles of it, really had been an extraordinary experience (even the teenagers grunted as much). We had started in the heart of the old communist order (Moscow) and ended in the heart of the new communist order (Beijing). We had met scores of intriguing, inspiring people. We had learnt how to cope without showers on demand and instant gratification. We had drunk to the end of the Cold War with Russians and dined with Japanese. We had enjoyed sunsets over Siberia and the wildernesses of Mongolia. We had crossed time zones and great geopolitical divides. We had seen silver birch trees, silver birch trees and more silver birch trees. We had enriched our lives.

We could of course have flown and saved ourselves the trouble. But then we would have missed everything.

CHAPTER 7
CLOSE TO HOME

---

9 APRIL 1965

THE LINE OF LINES

FOR **JOHN BETJEMAN**, IT HAS TO BE THE
GREAT WESTERN. HERE HE EXPLAINS WHY

Railways were like ships. Their crews felt a loyalty to the company
and a pride in its name. Sometimes there were fights – even pitched
battles between the South Eastern and Chatham and the London,
Brighton and South Coast, involving planks and crowbars. The
London and South Western and the Great Western were deadly
rivals, and, when the latter opened a new route to Exeter via
Westbury, the London and South Western went so fast that it jumped
the rails at Salisbury and there was a fatal accident. The rivalries had
more advantages than disadvantages. Crews were proud of the
uniform of the company, the livery of its locomotives, the colour of
the rolling-stock, and they took a pride in the stations and in keeping
up traditions peculiar to the line. When the companies were
regrouped under the Railways Act of 1921, the Great Western
Railway alone was allowed to retain its name among the big
companies. As a result, there are, even today, Great Western
traditions that survive. You will still find officials who, out of their
own pockets, buy the round pill-box hats of the Great Western and
wear the company's badge of twin shields bearing the arms of the
Cities of London and Bristol. And, on some of the dining cars to the

west, watercress and radishes are served with the cheese, a luxury unknown to other companies.

Now I have to be personal, because nearly all of us have an affection for one particular line, and I hope Midland men, North Western men, South Western men and devotees of other railways will forgive my partiality for the Great Western. I have used it all my life. It took me to and from school and university. It has taken me to my happiest holidays. Swindon was for long my nearest large town and I came to know its railway people well. Here the WEA (Workers' Education Association) was founded in the days of Reuben George. There was great solidarity among the railway workers and, during the years of unemployment in the Twenties, whole streets of two-storeyed houses down in the railway part of the town near the works would subscribe for the help of fellow workers out of employment. The railway men built one of their churches, St Saviour's, in their spare time, with their own hands. To be in the works at Swindon was an honour and a family tradition, and known as being 'inside'. All that has gone with the reorganisation of the works and the decantation into Swindon of a huge overspill, as planners call it, of people from London.

But still the Great Western remains the line of lines for me, and perhaps this is partly because, safe in its carriages from telephones and interruptions, I have been able to write and read and, by looking out of the window, to know just how much longer of peace is left to me. But chiefly, I think, it is because the railway was built on a grander scale than any other. Over it all is stamped the personality of its first engineer, Isambard Kingdom Brunel. His grandfather was a French Huguenot, his father, Sir Mark Brunel, was the engineer of the Thames tunnel, the first underwater tunnel in the world. His son, Isambard, designed the Clifton Suspension Bridge, Bristol, in 1831, at the age of 25, and, two years later, was appointed engineer of the projected railway from Bristol to London. Tom Rolt, in his splendid life of I K Brunel, describes him as 'the last great figure of the European Renaissance'. And such, indeed, he was. He was no narrow specialist, and belonged to the times when engineers were also architects and artists. He inspired all who worked with him, this lively little man who died aged 46 in 1852, it is said of the excessive smoking of cigars. He is associated with great successes and great failures. The failures were the atmospheric railway along the Devon coast from Exeter to Newton Abbot, and his vast iron-clad ship, the Great Eastern, and, though he did not live to see its demise, the broad gauge for English railways. Yet the Great Western, Saltash Bridge, Clifton Suspension Bridge and the Box tunnel are some of his triumphs.

Like many great movements in this country, the Great Western was born in Bristol. Its heartline was that from Bristol to London, though later the company spread to Devon and Cornwall, South Wales, Birmingham and Chester. It is this heartline that is described here and its story is fascinating. Even as late as 1825 there was a fear that the French, who were then what the Germans have since become to us, a potential menace, might dominate the English Channel. The Kennet and Avon Canal, begun in 1794 and completed, with its chain of 29 locks, at Devizes in 1807, provided an alternative water route between London and Bristol. But it was slow, and sometimes even the 80 miles by Thames from Reading to London took three days. There was also the increasing threat to the prosperity of Bristol from the growing port of Liverpool, so that a fast link to London was essential.

In 1833 some Bristol merchants formed a strong committee to build a railway and another was formed in London. The London secretary was Mr C A Saunders, a vigorous Wykehamist, who had eschewed the university for commerce. The banker George Henry Gibbs and Mr Charles Russell, the MP for Reading, were behind the scheme. Young Brunel at Bristol had shown himself successful with his design for the Clifton Suspension Bridge and he was employed by the two committees to survey the line. He worked for 20 hours a day, travelling all night by coach, taking notes and staying in acute discomfort until, by May 31, 1838, the London section of the line, as far as the east bank of the Thames at Maidenhead, was ready, and the directors travelled on the first train from Paddington in 49 minutes. Three hundred people had a cold luncheon in a tent at Maidenhead, as Gibbs's diary records, toasts were drunk and the journey back took only 34 minutes to travel the 22 miles. By June 1841, the whole line from Bristol to Paddington was completed. The Bristol terminus at Temple Meads, with its wooden Tudor roof of vast span, still remains in part of the station. The trains at the London end stopped under the arches of Bishop's Road Bridge, until 1851, when Brunel designed 'a station after my own fancy . . . with engineering roof – and admitting of no exterior, all interior and all roofed in'. He asked Matthew Digby Wyatt to supply decorative ironwork. The station has well served its purpose since 1854 when it was completed.

In the year of his engagement to the Great Western, young Brunel took in Daniel Gooch, who was 20 and working with his elder brother on the Manchester and Leeds railway. He employed Daniel as super-intendent of locomotive engines, and it was Gooch who built the Firefly-class engines for the Great Western in the 1840s, which were derivations from Stephenson's North Star, which had hauled the first Great Western train. Gooch outlived Brunel and was made a baronet for his work as a locomotive designer. When Brunel died, he wrote, 'By his death the greatest of England's engineers was lost, the man of the greatest originality of thought and power of execution, bold in his plans but right. The commercial world thought him extravagant, but although he was so, great things are not done by those who sit down and count the cost of every thought and act. He was a true and sincere friend, a man of the highest honour, and his loss was deplored by all who had the pleasure to know him.'

It was Gooch too who decided that some flat country by the Wilts and Berks Canal, below the old market town of Swindon, in the Vale of the White Horse, should be the site of the new works for the railway. It was a good half-way house between the longer and leveller line from London and the more steep inclines westward to Bristol. Gooch looked after the locomotives, Gibbs helped with the money, Saunders organised timetables and schedules, Russell got the bills through Parliament and Brunel saw to the track, the tunnels, the cuttings, the viaducts, bridges, sheds and stations. I suppose all four of them, backed by the Bristol committee, must have had to do with the lay-out of New Swindon, the first railway town in the world, and probably the first industrial estate, with a church by Sir George Gilbert Scott, an institute, recreation ground, allotments and houses. These two-storey houses built of limestone in Tudor style with little gardens in front, known as 'the company's houses', survive in Swindon today, as do St Mark's church and the Mechanics' Institute.

Steam railways are an English invention. What makes the Great Western the grandest of the early ones is that, by Brunel's direction and with Gooch's concurrence, it was built broad gauge. When George Stephenson built the first steam locomotive at Killingworth in 1814 the distance between the wheels of ordinary carts in that district was 4ft 8½ins, the same gauge as British railways today. Brunel thought, and rightly, that trains would be swifter, smoother and more capacious if built to a 7ft gauge, and his directors agreed with him. Because of this, bridges and tunnel entrances on the Great Western are wider than on narrow-gauge lines. The most beautiful of his constructions on the London-to-Bristol line are the Wharncliffe Viaduct over the River Brent at Hanwell, Middlesex – built in the Egyptian style he had favoured for Clifton Suspension Bridge – and the brick railway bridge over the Thames at Maidenhead. This last consists of two arches of 128ft span rising by only 24½ft. They were the flattest brick arches ever constructed and critics at the time thought that when the wooden centrings were taken away the arches would collapse. Brunel knew better and they have carried trains ever since. The most daring engineering feat was the tunnel through the limestone hill at Box, between Chippenham and Bath. A hundred men were killed in its construction. It is two miles long and descends at a gradient of one in a hundred towards Bath. Mr O S Nock, the railway writer, has discovered that the rising sun can be seen at its appropriate altitude and azimuth from the Bath end on April 9, which is Brunel's birthday. It may well be that Brunel thought of this when he constructed what was then the longest and straightest tunnel in the world. At the Bristol end of the line, where limestone for building was available, Brunel took pleasure in decorating the tunnel entrances. Towards Bath they were in the Classic style, recalling ancient Rome. Between Bath and Bristol, they were Gothic and Tudor, so as to be a prelude to the medieval port. At the Number 2 tunnel, in the castle style, the machicolated parapet partially collapsed, and Brunel thought it looked so romantic he left it as a ruin. A journey in the front or the back of a diesel in and out of tunnels between Bath and Bristol is an architectural delight.

The early railways, and the Great Western in particular, were thought of as fit only for landowners and the rich. Carriages were stage coaches joined together, generally in threes, and mounted on iron-wheeled trucks. On the Great Western railway, till quite lately, there were looped straps hanging by the doors of first-class carriages, in which passengers in corner seats might rest their arms, as in a stagecoach. Second-class carriages had hard upright seats and, until 1844, when Gladstone compelled railways to provide sheltered carriages, there were no closed third-class carriages at all. Even then, Mr Saunders, the secretary, only built boxes containing ten transverse plank seats, each holding six people, in a carriage without windows and without light and with only slats for ventilation. Passengers of this class were only allowed on slow trains late at night and, of course, they were not allowed into the sumptuous refreshment rooms at Swindon when the train stopped on its four-hour journey between Bristol and London, before the days of dining cars. The food in this refreshment room was so disgusting that it is the subject of a letter from Brunel to the caterers:

> Dear Sir,
>
> I assure you Mr Player was wrong in supposing that I thought you purchased inferior coffee. I thought I said to him I was surprised you should buy such bad roasted corn. I did not believe you had such a thing as coffee in the place; I am certain I never tasted any. I have long ceased to make complaints at Swindon. I avoid taking anything there when I can help it.
>
> Yours faithfully,
> I. K. BRUNEL

Since those days, the Great Western has been subjected to many humiliations. The last 177 miles of broad gauge were converted to the cheeseparing narrow gauge of the rest of England, in a single weekend in 1892. Regrouping in 1921 left the line its name. Nationalisation, when it was renamed Western Region by bureaucrats, took away most of the individuality that remained. Perhaps, because it was once so great a line, its fall today is the saddest of all.

MAY 21, 2011

WESTWARDS WITH THE LIGHT

BRIAN JACKMAN RETRACES A CHILDHOOD
JOURNEY FROM LONDON TO THE HOLIDAY
BEACHES OF ST IVES

Back in the age of steam before the railways were nationalised, the biggest moment of my year was the day we set off by train for our family holidays in Cornwall. Sometimes we travelled on the Atlantic Coast Express from Waterloo, speeding through the fields of Hampshire past trackside billboards bearing the slogan 'You are entering the Strong Country'. How true, I thought in my innocence. That's where we are going: to King Arthur's land with its granite moors and rugged cliffs. Only when I was older did I realise the posters were advertising beer brewed by Strongs of Romsey.

But the greatest thrill of all was to board the Penzance-bound Cornish Riviera Express at Paddington, the London terminus of the Great Western Railway. The GWR – translated by rail aficionados as God's Wonderful Railway – was established in the 1830s and its mainline route to Penzance pioneered by Isambard Kingdom Brunel, the top-hatted engineering genius of Victorian England. It was above all a holiday line transporting summer visitors to the West Country, and its flagship service was the Cornish Riviera Express. Introduced in 1904, it rose to fame in the 1930s, and it still departs every morning from Paddington.

In the golden age of steam its carriages with their distinctive chocolate-and-cream livery were hauled by King Class and Castle Class locomotives, 79-ton fire-breathing monsters built in Swindon and painted a deep, rich Brunswick green. That is how it was the last time I travelled on the Cornish Riviera, in the years before the GWR was nationalised in 1948, when it took six and a quarter hours to reach Penzance. But as I now discover, today's high-speed trains (HSTs) have cut the journey time to five hours.

Paddington has changed out of all recognition. Infinitely cleaner and altogether more efficient with its automated indicator boards announcing arrival and departure times. But along with the grime the romance of the age of steam has also been swept away and replaced with a terminus more akin to a shopping centre filled with coffee stalls and sandwich bars. Nor is the first half hour of the journey much to write home about. As we hurry through Slough it is hard to ignore John Betjeman's unkind phrase about friendly bombs. Only when we have left Reading behind and are following the Kennet into rural Wessex does the countryside become compulsive viewing.

As I look out of the window the years fall away and I remember the excitement of spotting familiar landmarks such as the Westbury White Horse. Carved on the chalk flanks of Salisbury Plain and measuring 107ft from head to hoofs, it trots boldly across the downland scarp in full view of the train. Its shape has been radically altered over the centuries, but some historians have conjectured that it was first cut as long ago as 878, to commemorate King Alfred's victory over the Danes at the battle of Ethandun.

The Westbury Horse marks the last of the chalk, the great geological divide where the South Country ends and the West Country begins, and I hear my father saying 'Must be doing 70 now,' with something like awe in his voice as we head towards Taunton, flying across the Somerset Levels with the Quantock Hills on one side and the Blackdowns on the other. Nowadays maiden aunts in Civic Hondas think nothing of zooming around the M25 at such speeds; but to my father and me at that time it seemed unbelievably fast.

Next stop is Exeter St David's, the starting point for one of the most scenic mainline rail journeys in Britain. The best of it lies on the left-hand side, where the Turf Hotel signals the beginnings of the Exe estuary; but spare a glance to the right as you pass Powderham Castle's parkland oaks and fallow deer. The estuary opens out, revealing a mile-wide expanse of glittering channels and shining mudflats alive with oystercatchers, and suddenly I am a child again with my nose pressed to the corridor windows as we race along at the edge of the tideway. At Starcross even my parents would set aside the books that occupied them for most of the day-long journey, my father pointing out the tower that marks where Brunel's atmospheric railway once ran along the shore. Then, when we had flashed past Cockwood's pocket-sized harbour, the protective arm of Dawlish Warren would come into view, and that first longed-for sight of the sea, flanked by red sandstone cliffs laid down 280 million years ago when dinosaurs roamed the Devon hills. It was only after the train had turned inland again at Teignmouth, following the route of the migrating salmon as they headed up the Teign estuary past Newton Abbot, that I thought of returning to my seat for a picnic lunch of cold chicken sandwiches – a rare treat in those austere post-war years.

Back in the present again, all the hedgerows in Devon's apple-blossom valleys are decked out in white for the blackthorn winter; but the spring sunshine tells a different story and primroses lie thick as clotted cream by every woodland edge. The old-time express trains used to talk to the rails, beating out a steady clickety-clack rhythm as they laboured up Dainton Bank – the third-steepest main-line incline in Britain. But today's streamlined HST diesels simply take it in their stride. Capable of speeds up to 125mph, we purr along as smooth as silk, crossing the River Dart at Totnes on our way down to Plymouth.

Now comes another five-star moment as Brunel's iconic Royal Albert Bridge carries us over the Tamar to Saltash. Painted the same shade of grey as the warships at rest in Devonport docks, this ironclad masterpiece opened in 1859, and when Brunel died in that same year his name was placed on the portals at both ends of the bridge as a lasting memorial to the man who put the Great in Great Western. To cross the Tamar is to travel out of England into another country, and on the other side, as if to underline the point, Saltash station greets passengers with a sign in Cornish. Kernow a'gas dynnergh, it says. Welcome to Cornwall.

On the 80 miles of track between Saltash and Penzance the old-time steam trains went huffing and puffing across more than 40 viaducts – most of them dreamed up by Brunel to carry his precious line across Cornwall's deep wooded valleys. Beyond Truro the woods give way. Gorse takes over and Carn Brea monument appears on its moorland hilltop, presiding over a post-industrial landscape of abandoned tin mines. The monument – a 90ft tall obelisk – was erected to the memory of Francis Bassett, an 18th-century mine owner. Now it presides over a post-industrial landscape of overgrown spoil heaps and abandoned tin mines. The hard rock miners are long gone. Their engine houses stand open to the sky; but their pride remains, and the black-and-white Cornish flag flutters defiantly from a Redruth church tower.

At St Erth it is time to leave the Cornish Riviera to complete the last leg of its 305-mile journey to Penzance and await the arrival of the two-coach shuttle service to St Ives. London now seems a world away. There are palm trees on the platform, and good coffee to be had at a station buffet that has made it into the list of Britain's top ten railway cafes. The single-track branch line to St Ives opened in 1877 and was the last to be built to Brunel's 'broad gauge' specification. It was converted to standard gauge 15 years later and used mostly for transporting fish. Now holiday visitors are its main cargo, and although it takes only 12 minutes to complete the four-and-a-bit miles to St Ives, there is no lovelier rail journey in Britain; a slow train to yesterday, dawdling along the dizzy cliff tops of St Ives Bay.

From the right-hand side of the train I can see it all as we set off around Lelant saltings with the waters of the Hayle estuary almost lapping at our wheels. But soon we are climbing above the gleaming expanse of Porth Kidney sands and then cutting through the solid rock of Carrick Gladden Head to emerge above Carbis Bay. Among the passengers alighting here are several heading for the Carbis Bay Hotel. Readers of Rosamund Pilcher's best-seller *The Shell Seekers* will recognise it as the Sands Hotel. Built in the late 19th century, it was given a complete makeover in 1991 and enjoys an unrivalled position overlooking the bay.

The sea is calm and so emerald-clear I can see the bottom through two fathoms of water, and as we come round the last bend there lies St Ives on its knobbly promontory, a salt-encrusted barnacle of a town with a picturebook harbour, bathed in the luminous Atlantic sea light that has bewitched generations of painters, and with the wet satin sands of Porthminster framed by palm trees below. No wonder St Ives has been voted top British beach resort by the website TripAdvisor, and sixth best beach destination in the whole of Europe. You can swim at Porthminster, surf at Porthmeor in the shadow of the Tate St Ives – even sunbathe on the harbour sands, where Smeaton's pier makes a perfect windbreak. John Smeaton was an 18th-century Cornish engineer best known for building the Eddystone

Lighthouse; like everything else in St Ives, his pier is built of solid granite that glints and sparkles come rain or shine. The light is dazzling and everything is as it always was: the crying gulls, the rooftops smothered in ochre lichens, the smell of pasties in the cobbled lanes; and the branch line from St Erth deposits me in the very heart of it.

Down by the harbour the Sloop Inn is still in business as it has been for 600 years. But now – joy of joys – St Ives has also come of age as a foodie heaven. And so, to celebrate my return, where better than the Porthminster Café, to feast on a sublime monkfish curry with a view to match, looking out across the beach to where Godrevy Light sits on a horizon as blue as the Aegean.

A PLACE I KNOW

JOHN WELLS RECOMMENDS LEWES
STATION BUFFET

There are several reasons why I particularly like Lewes Station buffet. I am fond of that part of Sussex, having grown up in Eastbourne; there is a faint smell of the sea, the South Downs against the sky, the Castle high on the hill above the jumble of flint walls and hung tiles and red rooftops, and opposite, on a level with the tracks, the iron hurdles of the Cattle Market.

Lewes Station is full of history. When they were digging the railway in the last century they uncovered the tombs of a Norman duke and his wife under the high altar of St Pancras Priory, and the line still skirts the ruins.

I'm also very fond of travelling by train – possibly because I don't drive, or because my grandfather, who died 10 years before I was born, ran the engine sheds at Watford Junction, and I spent my early childhood travelling with my grandmother on her widow's pass.

At The Runaway – Lewes Station buffet, unlike most, has a name, presumably a thigh-slapping reference to the local prison – the spirit of *Brief Encounter* still hangs in the air. *Brief Encounter*, admittedly, cleaned up. No more steam, no more joke Railway Sandwiches curling under grubby glass covers, and no funny working-class accents behind the counter. It is militantly middle-class. A lot of people who go there are humble enough, the kind of travellers you might meet in any brilliantly lit and Muzak-ed Megaburger-Pizza-Fayre at a large mainline station. And local people, who aren't travelling by train at all, meet there. At The Runaway they come face to face not only with the England of Trevor Howard and Celia Johnson, but with a ringing Conran-Habitat challenge to pull their cultural socks up.

For all that, the mood is extraordinarily welcoming. The details on the menu board change every day. There are very good homemade soups and curries, baked potatoes with various homemade fillings, and homemade bread pudding and cakes, as well as salads, pizzas, baguettes, cheese and reasonable wine.

Classical music warbles quietly in the background, the tea is made in gleaming little stainless steel teapots, there are real flowers on the tables, the china is clean, there are fresh wholemeal scones . . . They also do hot buttered toast and very good drinking chocolate. Talk at the tables is quiet and slightly self-conscious, in homage to the film. Other station buffets have a one-armed bandit: at The Runaway there is an improving Quiz Machine.

It's quite a wrench when the London train rumbles along the edge of the platform and it's time to leave.

FLEETING DELIGHT

SIR – Charles Spencer (Features, January 11) invites readers to suggest delights of winter. Mine are sights of Britain from a railway compartment, which suits the weather – as long as the heating works and the snow has not stopped the train. I have in mind sights such as Lincoln, Rochester and Durham cathedrals, approached by rail. Since they are framed for only a limited time, the impact is intense. The panorama from a train window beats anything visible from a car, which usually delivers little more than the sight of a motorway embankment.

Rupert Nicholson
Shipley, West Yorkshire

HOW THE ROYAL TRAIN SECURED THE ENTENTE CORDIALE

SIR – The Queen kindly takes scheduled trains to save money (report, December 18). It would save the country money if instead a royal train were used in pursuit of diplomatic aims. To do without one is a false economy.

In the 19th century, royal trains shuttled backwards and forwards to Windsor with foreign potentates. During such a visit by King Louis-Philippe in 1844, for example, the term *entente cordiale* was coined.

Queen Victoria and Prince Albert got on well enough with Louis-Philippe, but he failed to make a good impression on the French people. A mob stormed his palace in 1848, and the King, having abdicated, fled to England under the name Mr Smith. This time he had to catch the scheduled rail service from Newhaven.

John Harrison, Feltham, Middlesex

SIR – It was customary between the two world wars for the King and Queen not only to use their own train but also to be escorted by the regional general manager of their ultimate destination.

For trips to Balmoral (originally Caledonian Railway territory, subsequently that of the London, Midland and Scottish), this required my great-grandfather, Donald Matheson, to travel from Glasgow to London with his own carriages and two engines, the latter to help push the train extended by Royal carriages over Shap. Somewhere around Watford an equerry would appear with a message requesting Mr and Mrs Matheson to join their Majesties – King George V and Queen Mary – for dinner. This meant dining with two rather introverted people at a table the size of a small card table. Such 'casual dining', however, was the basis of an enduring friendship. A personal telegram of condolence came from their Majesties on Matheson's death in 1935.

Nigel Kenyon Tilston, Cheshire

SIR – Twelve years of class warfare by stealth has moved our monarchy closer to Peter Simple's King Norman and Queen Doreen model (Letters, December 21).

First the Royal Yacht went, then the Flight. Now it is public train services for the Queen, with national coach services no doubt next.

Commander Alan York RN retd
Sheffield, South Yorkshire

RAILING AGAINST BUSES

SIR – Professor Mark Hill (Letters, September 6) cites 'replacement bus service' as the three most ghastly words in the English language. I can think of worse, but what does the phrase mean? Surely a train running when the road is closed is the replacement bus service? Correctly, Southern Railway's replacement buses display 'railway replacement service' on their route blinds, but this in itself says something about the frequency with which they need to be called in.

Paul King
Hassocks, West Sussex

TRAVELS WITH 'GEORGE'

BENJI WILSON MEETS MICHAEL PORTILLO
AT WORK ON HIS NEW RAILWAY SERIES

No one is quite sure when Michael Portillo became popular, but popular he undoubtedly is. At Paignton station the Devon Belle, a magnificent 2-6-2T steam engine, is all stoked up and ready to depart, but Portillo is holding everyone up, doing a piece to camera for his new TV series. Yet when he does finally get on the train and it chugs away, the response he gets from passengers could hardly be further from the derision he received on losing his seat in the 1997 General Election. Hands are shaken, pictures are taken: it's smiles all round. 'People are very pleased to see me,' he says, sounding slightly surprised. 'Or maybe it's the TV camera.'

It is Portillo's television work, from *This Week* to *Dinner with Portillo*, that has taught us to love him, and *Great British Railway Journeys* on BBC Two is his latest excursion. Over four weeks Portillo covers the length and breadth of the country with but one accomplice, whom he calls 'George'. George is *Bradshaw's Railway Companion*. Written in 1840 by George Bradshaw, a mapmaker by trade, it was the first national railway timetable. Bradshaw assembled the information from all of the various railway companies and then added details and recommendations from his own travels. In the programme, Portillo takes 'George' with him on four railway journeys, from Liverpool to Scarborough, Buxton to London, Preston to Kirkcaldy (his mother's home town) and from Swindon to St Ives.

Portillo's battered Bradshaw becomes a prism through which he compares and contrasts Victorian Britain with our own. 'The world today would be unrecognisable to George Bradshaw,' he says, 'yet some of the seeds of today's world are there in the book — he sees how technology changes everything. He understands globalisation, he talks about migration, mass movements of people — and he sees how all these things are connected to railways. In fact he sees the entire world changing because of railways.'

As we chuff-chuff away down the Devon coast in bright sunshine it is hard not to be swept away by the romance of it all, although it is a romance that few commuters on a sweaty 08.04 to Manchester will recognise. One wonders what Bradshaw would think of our railways today, but Portillo, 56, says that rather than mourning the passing of a golden age, we should be hailing a railway renaissance.

'My feeling is that the thing is somewhat cyclical,' he says. 'We dealt with Dr Beeching's cuts of 1963. But when I was travelling through Scotland the other day I found out that 62 stations have opened since 1993. I've observed that trains are very well used, and very full. It's true that they're not used in the same way. I mean you don't get people pouring down to Torquay to take their holidays the way they would have done even in the Fifties or Sixties; but what you do get is mass commuting across long distances that George Bradshaw would probably never have foreseen. And just to complete the thing, we've built a new railway line from the Channel Tunnel to St Pancras: people are talking about high-speed rail as being the future of surface transport.' (He's not to know that at the time of writing people are talking about the Channel Tunnel in the same way they talk about Fred Goodwin.)

Portillo, of course, is more than just an impartial observer when it comes to Britain's railway network. He was Minister of State for Transport from 1988 to 1990, and it was his party that privatised the railways, for good or ill. Naturally, he thinks it was for the good. 'I remember when I was in government: that was a period when we electrified the East Coast Main Line, when we built the Channel Tunnel, when we put the tram system into Sheffield, when we built the Heathrow Express . . . you begin to get the point,' he says. 'What I would say now is, whatever your views about privatisation, there are more trains and more passengers. And that's just a fact. So something right must be happening.'

Hearing him in hustings mode reminds you of the politician who could have led the Conservative Party in 2001. He says that he 'really doesn't want to talk politics', but come on, Michael – there's an election coming down the tracks as surely as the Devon Belle. With his party ahead in the polls, surely the inveterate politico must feel a hankering for office?

'I can be very, very straightforward about this: there is no part of me that so hankers.'

But does he feel intellectually stretched, making television programmes, flirting with Diane Abbott, messing about on trains?

'I'm not sure that I want to be as stretched as at one time,' he says. 'People get older and they want to achieve more of a . . . not a work-life balance because I probably work as hard as ever, but a stress-life balance. I love the creativity of making television. You have to make the words work with the pictures, and you have to tell a story to people. You find out so many things that you didn't know, you go to so many places that you wouldn't have gone . . .'

Which does sound a little like . . .

'Yes, a lot of that is true in politics, but in politics it did occasionally happen that the people you met weren't completely friendly! Now, if you'll excuse me, I'd better go and make some films.' And with that, he strides back to his steam train, smiling at the passengers lining the way. They all smile back.

SIR – Michael Portillo's *Great British Railway Journeys* is a splendid programme. Carriages are clean and relatively empty; they glisten in the appropriate livery. Trains seem to be running on time, it is always summer and there is no mention of replacement buses.

Michael Spragg
Great Yarmouth
Norfolk

RAIL FAMILIES

SIR – Ross Clark's article on railway lines (May 23) reminds me that my mother's grandfather and his younger brother lived near Langley in Bucks. John Nash, who lived at the Old Rectory, had 10 children. His cousin Henry Nash, at Upton Lea, had 11. The families referred to them as the Broad Gauge and Narrow Gauge Nashes, since John had the GWR main line built through his land while Henry had the Southern Railway.

W F N Tolfree
Shaftesbury,
Dorset

NORTH BY TRAIN – AND BY THE BOOK

SIMON HEFFER FINDS A JOURNEY TO EDINBURGH
ENRICHED BY AN LNER GUIDE

The journey from London to Edinburgh up the East Coast main line has, for me, never had any rivals as the best railway journey in Britain. It has everything: landscapes from fenland to moors and mountains, tiny villages and great cities, and even, as the line curves round from Berwick to Dunbar, the sea.

We do not, though, make as much of the touristic possibilities of railway travel as, say, the Americans. If Amtrak ran the East Coast main line, each train would have a special observation car with running commentary on the fleeting features of the world outside and the passengers would be issued with leaflets explaining what they could see from their seats. But this is Britain. The inquisitive traveller can, with the aid of Ordnance Survey maps and a set of Pevsner's *Buildings of England*, plot for himself the sights along his route, but such research is not always practicable.

Our grandparents were more fortunate. Recently, at a second-hand book market, I found a pamphlet called *On Either Side: depicting and describing features of interest to be seen from the train between London (King's Cross) & Edinburgh (Waverley), Fort William, Inverness and Aberdeen*. Published in 1939 by the London and North Eastern Railway, it points out architectural and physical features the traveller can look out for, and gives a potted history of the towns through which the line passes. It is not exhaustive, but certainly thorough enough to prove illuminating to all but the most expert antiquary. Armed with this splendid guide, I felt the time had come to travel again from London to Edinburgh.

We were fortunate that our first-class carriage had clean windows, but one consequence of modern efficiency became immediately apparent.

As the train roared through the London suburbs at nearly two miles a minute, it was hard to keep up with the LNER's steam-age plan.

The first hour out of London, to just beyond Peterborough, is the part of the journey that has changed most. 'Hornsey boasts itself one of the healthiest districts about London,' says the guide, 'and it would be difficult to find a more salubrious area within easy reach of the great city.' What was then an already vast stretch of suburbia is now lost in a sea of post-war ribbon development, and it is here that the factories, industrial units and discount warehouses that line the railway out into the Fens begin to make their mark.

In 1939, these were golf links; indeed, the booklet gives the impression that one long course stretched from Alexandra Palace to Biggleswade. Stevenage – now a sprawling new town – is described as 'a populous village, famous in old coaching days'.

The first of five great cathedrals visible from the train, at Peterborough, is one of the few features of that city untouched since before the war. All around, though, the countryside is as it was. The stretch from the south includes, right next to the railway, three fine medieval churches at Buckden, Offord Cluny and Yaxley. To the north we change from the flatness of the black-earthed fens to the undulations of the green wolds.

In Nottinghamshire the land becomes more industrial, and little can now be seen of the magnificence of the Dukeries. To the east, though, on a clear day – and this was – one can see on a hill the silhouette of Lincoln cathedral, 15 miles away.

For a while the railway skirts the industrial area around Doncaster, with its cooling towers, collieries and ironworks. As York nears, though, the land becomes empty and green again. South of York the railway has been diverted from its original course, through Selby, because it passed over the 'Super Pit' opened in the 1980s. At York, dominated by the Minster, the original course resumes.

I did not spot, north of Thirsk, 'the first of the LNER wonder signal boxes' which, the booklet says, 'controls four-and-a-half miles of track'. Of more significance, though, the book begins to tell of the turbulent history of this part of England north of the Humber, principally in wars against the Scots.

Northallerton was twice burned by them, in 1319 and 1322. After

Darlington, where railways were born, there are more reminders of bloody times. At Neville's Cross many Scots noblemen were killed and their King, David, was captured in 1346, after he had responded to the French king's call to make war on the English after Crécy.

Durham provides the most spectacular view on the journey: the magnificent cathedral and castle both seen clearly from the train, towering over the little town. Minutes later, at Chester-le-Street, is Lambton Castle, seat of the Earl of Durham, and on a hill above it the Grecian-style monument to the first earl, copied from the temple at Theseus. There are still, though, the decaying pit villages of County Durham along this stretch, harbingers of the great industrial spectacle at Newcastle, with its bridges over the Tyne.

As the railway comes closer to the sea, the historical references become older still, as these were the landing grounds of the Saxon and Viking invaders. They recognised the strategic importance of Alnmouth and its fine natural harbour, above which the railway passes. Holy Island, home of English Christianity, is clearly visible soon afterwards.

The descent into Berwick provides a further ravishing prospect: the 28-span railway bridge curving in front of the train over the Tweed. Berwick was a bustling port in the 13th century, but has never grown to more than a small border town since Edward I had 7,000 of its inhabitants massacred in 1294.

Five minutes after leaving the station, the modern traveller is in Scotland and the countryside seems at once craggier and less hospitable.

The run round the coast to Dunbar and Edinburgh gives one frequent and arresting glimpses of the sea crashing at the foot of cliffs, with small fishing villages perched above them. More pacific are the views of the Forth, and of the Fifeshire coast opposite seen on a clear day. Arthur's Seat, Edinburgh's extinct volcano, is the first sign of the Scottish capital. On a good day the journey from London will have taken not much more than four-and-a-half hours, on a bad one it can take up to seven – which at least gives you more time to read the guidebook. Perhaps British Rail will show some initiative and update and reprint it.

UPS AND DOWNS

SIR — It is curious that you use the expression 'down at Henley-on-Thames' (Peterborough, May 19), although writing from London. If it were 'down', the Thames would never get to London. The capital has a habit of regarding everywhere as 'down' when in fact most places are up. You might write about going down to Buxton, or Penrith — even Ben Nevis. All these places are 'up' on the map, and in a geographical sense too. In Birmingham, we talk about going down to London, and we are right.

A J Sutton
Birmingham

SIR — Mr Sutton (letter, May 22) is incorrect. It is not 'down' to London. This has nothing to do with height above sea-level, but was introduced by the railways 150 years ago in order to avoid confusion. Thus it was always the 'Up' line to London and the 'Down' line from London. Volume 1 of *The History of the Great Western Railway* reproduces a timetable of 1841 showing this clearly, and it has been standard practice ever since.

D E Jones
Solihull
West Midlands

SIR – Railway timetables are not a sufficient explanation of life's 'ups' and 'downs' (letter, May 22). One always goes up to Oxford and Cambridge from anywhere and can, sadly, be sent down from these places – even to London.

Tony McCarthy
London W4

'RAILWAYS ARE TO THE ENGLISH A MORAL ISSUE'

CHRISTOPHER HOWSE REFLECTS ON THE REOPENING BY ENTHUSIASTS OF A BRANCH LINE THAT WAS CLOSED BY BEECHING

Corfe Castle stands perfectly picturesque on its green Dorset hill above the Isle of Purbeck, one of those ancient monuments more beautiful as a ruin. At its foot runs the branch line from Wareham to Swanage, and the sight of the 4-6-2 West Country-class locomotive Eddystone chuffing past would bring a tear to the eye of anyone brought up on the Reverend W Awdry.

This, however, is no Thomas the Tank Engine story but a triumph by the Swanage Railway Society, which has rebuilt the 11 miles and 70 chains of track wickedly uprooted by British Railways in 1972. The first through-service from London on the restored line chugged into Swanage on Wednesday afternoon, and aboard were Frederick Sills and his son Peter, who was 15 when they travelled on the last Swanage train. 'It's absolutely amazing that the clock has been turned back and history reversed by the Swanage Railway volunteers,' the elder Mr Sills said. 'They have performed miracles.'

By contrast, grand public rail projects are sinking into a slough as the economic tsunami washes away their ballast. This is despite an optimistic announcement by Network Rail, the day before the Swanage triumph, of the 'biggest expansion of Britain's railways since the age of Brunel', at a cost of £35 billion. Of this, £2 billion will go towards the £16 billion needed for London's Crossrail project to link the Great Western at Paddington to the Great Eastern at Stratford, via a 13-mile tunnel.

Crossrail is a touchstone. Only now has the project even reached the planning-blight stage, 19 years after it was announced. It has missed the psychologically useful deadline of the London Olympics. 'The tragedy is that 10 years of dithering means that Crossrail will be nowhere near ready in time,' Boris Johnson, the Mayor of London, laments. Completion will now be in 2017 – if ever. More than one transport anorak likens it to the aircraft carriers promised to the Royal Navy – always being given the go-ahead but never being built.

Funding is the problem, since Crossrail depends on private finance to top up public commitments. Funds are expected from BAA and Canary Wharf, or at least they were. Now everyone has stopped flying, and the bankers have deserted Canary Wharf, and owls shall dwell there, and satyrs shall dance.

'If we cannot deliver Crossrail,' says Lord Adonis, the transport minister, 'how will we be credible in delivering any other major scheme through joint financing?' Quite.

It's such a shame. Britain is good at big engineering projects like this. The tunnels that now link St Pancras to the fast line under the Channel mean that it is quicker to get to Paris than to Liverpool – and considerably more pleasant to most people when they arrive.

Railways have been a roaring, groaning, crowded success over the past two decades. There were 12.5 billion passenger journeys last year, more than in any year since the big spike just after the Second World War. Like cinemas, predicted in the 1950s to become empty dinosaurs, railways have won a new following. Because of the peculiar way they are run, though, we have become accustomed to seeing prices rise and trains getting more packed simultaneously. Yet this week there was talk of two train operators possibly being forced to relinquish their franchises by the numbing economic wind.

It does not help that the lovely summery English myth is of a railway so deserted that it could never possibly make money. The ideal is the Gloucestershire station of Adlestrop, where, in Edward Thomas's poem, 'No one left and no one came/ On the bare platform.' Adlestrop closed in 1966, but tourists still take photographs of the station nameplate in a bus shelter on the edge of the village.

How strange it is that the metal monster of the industrial age, the searing power of steam, should now be seen as part of a rural pattern of English and Welsh life. (Tourists photograph the station sign at Llanfair PG on Anglesey, too, and, as a bonus, trains still call there.) In Scotland, things are a little different: the railways are a skeleton, even if one of the world's great train journeys is to Mallaig, where ferries leave for the Hebridean isles.

In England, the iron road's trespass is forgiven, enfolded as it is in groves of the wrong kind of leaves. Even railway viaducts, which one might expect to be reckoned as ugly as gasworks or wind farms, are ornaments of the landscape. On the line that cheers every railway tourist, the 72 miles from Settle to Carlisle, a celebrated view is of the Ribblehead Viaduct. Its 24 arches carry the line 104 feet above the moors of North Yorkshire. It is designated a Scheduled Ancient Monument, although its last stone was laid only in 1874. The traveller cannot see it so well from the train, although the line does curve, but there's a station half a mile away to get out at for a walk closer. The pattern of the sun and hurrying clouds in the drizzly atmosphere equals anything by the Romantic painter Caspar David Friedrich.

That is one reason why railways are to the English a moral issue. It would have been wrong to close the Settle-to-Carlisle line, just as it was wrong to close the Swanage line. The satanic figure of railway damnation was Dr Beeching, Richard to his wife, but cloven-hoofed and more redolent of sulphur than the smokiest furnace coal. His report in 1963 (published after the end of the Chatterley ban, but five days later than the Beatles' first LP) proposed the closure of a third of the railway system. The Beeching Axe fell.

In 1950 there were 21,000 miles of railway. Three thousand closed before Beeching. Now there are 12,000. Worse was proposed, such as the ending of the East Coast line at Newcastle; today the easiest way to Edinburgh (quicker than air) is by that line.

In response to Beeching, Flanders and Swann's song *Slow Train* is firmly in the tradition of *Adlestrop*. 'No churns, no porter, no cat on a seat,' they sang, mourning the coming loss of Mow Cop and Scholar Green (closed 1964), Tumby Woodside (closed 1970), Midsomer Norton (closed 1966), Cockermouth, for Buttermere (closed 1966), Long Stanton (closed 1970) and Kirby Muxloe (closed 1964).

They manage these things better – and worse – in France, or Spain. Both had their Beeching years, and both networks receive huge public subsidies. Over the past two decades they have laid hundreds of miles of high-speed lines, newly surveyed routes across virgin territory. Their advantages are open country and fierce planning laws. They cleverly used EU funding. So now the two-hour journey from Madrid to Segovia, across the Guadarrama mountains, takes half an hour, through a tunnel. That I regret. Travelling by train is a pleasure, and pleasures should last.

The ideal train journey is in a corner seat in an empty compartment, with well-upholstered seats. A corridor provides access to an efficient bar and a place for the children to play. There is a loo and no traffic jams. It is the best way to see the country (at a steady pace); the easiest place in the world to doze or to read. You reach your destination rested and lively, whether it's Córdoba or Corfe Castle.

NOW THEY'VE GROWN UP THEY WANT TO BE MODEL TRAIN DRIVERS

AN EXHIBITION OF MODEL TRAINS THIS WEEKEND IS EXPECTED TO ATTRACT THOUSANDS OF FANS. WHAT KIND OF PEOPLE ARE THEY? **HUGO DAVENPORT** MET SOME OF THEM AT A SHRINE FOR THE MOST DEDICATED

'I object strongly when people say we're playing with trains,' says Roger Bickle, emphasising the point with a frown of disapproval as deep as a railway cutting. 'I do *not* play with trains; I operate a model railway. What I've done is to try to recreate a certain part of the Great Western Railway, in a certain part of Devon, at a certain time in history, as correctly as possible in every detail.'

Bickle, a bearded and bespectacled solicitor in his mid-fifties, is willing to concede that there might be an element of nostalgia in his passion for the vanished glories of the Great Western. 'It was,' he says, 'the railway of my childhood.' But playtime? Never.

He is one of 50 or so people who recently paid £72.50 to gather at Missenden Abbey, in Buckinghamshire, for a weekend of lectures and practical work on the finer points of soldering and blackening, landscape design, wagon loads and other arcane tricks of the modeller's art. It would be difficult, in his purist company, to find anyone unable to work up a head of steam at the sacrilegious notion that their love affair with the railways had anything in it of arrested development.

For serious railway modellers, it has always been galling to be dismissed as overgrown schoolboys (or, increasingly, girls) struggling vainly to recapture their childhood, and happier to retreat into a precise and orderly world of their own devising than to engage with the mess and uncertainty of the real one. The Missenden modellers have no desire, as their co-organiser Harry Drummond puts it, to be associated with 'those funny people who stand up at exhibitions and make train noises.'

Indeed, they insist that no other hobby can offer such a variety of incontrovertibly adult pleasures, from delving into social and industrial history to studying geology; from the artistic enjoyment of painting backdrops and buildings to the more craftsmanlike satisfaction of working with wood and metal. 'Do you realise,' asks another enthusiast with a steely glint in his eye, 'that in Germany they always ask you at job interviews whether you have a hobby – and if you don't they reckon there's something seriously wrong?'

The Great Missenden weekend is an annual pilgrimage where the deeper mysteries of the scale-model locomotive are celebrated with an unswerving devotion that pays scant heed to fashion. It started two decades ago at Hassocks, in Sussex; one or two participants have been coming for 20 years, and others turn up from as far afield as Ireland and the west coast of America.

At the same time model railways have, once more, become big business. After the lean years of the Seventies, when the flashier charms of computers and video games upstaged the innocent simplicities of the train set, this revival has transformed the fortunes of companies such as Hornby, spawned a whole series of cottage industries started by redundant engineers or draughtsmen, and given the hobby a cash turnover to rival that of angling.

At the more commercial end of the market, the 64th International Model Railway Exhibition (Imrex) today begins a six-day extravaganza at the Royal Horticultural Halls in Westminster. It will be opened by the Rev W Awdry, creator of the ubiquitous Thomas the Tank Engine, and boasts 25 layouts featuring railways from Britain and the Continent. Last year it drew 36,000 visitors; this year the organisers confidently predict more.

Both events are a mere fraction of the ever-growing list of exhibitions and societies promoting the joys of model railways. There are 750 clubs and up to 400 exhibitions each year, and according to John Geach, secretary of the Model Railway Club (it was the first, formed in 1910, and manages Imrex), modellers themselves have become increasingly specialised. 'It's a much more serious adult pursuit these days,' he says. 'Increasingly it has become the hobby of people who are either craftsmen — the watchmaker syndrome — or historical researchers, who wish to reproduce exactly rolling stock or a complete environment. It's much more the activity of the man who wishes to be polymathic.'

Back in Bucks — where according to John Brewer, editor of the magazine *Railway Modeller*, 'most of the chaps are historians; they seem to take great delight in knowing more and more about less and less — the talk is all of God's Wonderful Railway (the Great Western's nickname) and Mud, Sludge and Lightning (the Manchester, Sheffield and Lincoln) and of rivalries between supporters of various defunct lines.'

Clary Edwards, a retired railwayman, gives an account of the perils of live steam — models driven, like the real thing, by a boiler — and reveals that he once managed to burn down most of an ivy hedge when trying to top up the water tank of one of his trains in the garden. His neighbour was not amused; the modellers are.

Over lunch, Hubert Carr, a civil engineer, gives a learned discourse on 'seatings', used to bed the rail on its sleepers. The Rev Ian Pusey, rector of Bletchley, explains that he loves modelling because it is totally different from the emphasis of his working life, which is 'all about people'. He admits that the modelling world does turn up 'extremists' verging on the obsessional, but says there are not many. Nobody cares about your background and you can simply be yourself.

They file back for an afternoon session led by Barry Norman, an expert landscape modeller. Norman hands out little rectangles of blockboard and soon has them pulling the fibres painstakingly from lumps of carpet underfelt to make meadow-grass. For a bunch of serious-minded historians who would not be seen dead playing with the trains, the pleasure on their faces as they set about the task is remarkably boyish.

BOPPING ON THE BERWYN BELLE

CATH URQUHART JOINS THE PASSENGERS
WHO WORK UP A HEAD OF STEAM ON THE
LLANGOLLEN-TO-GLYNDYFRDWY RAILWAY

Disco trains are all the rage in Europe, I had heard. Gorgeous Lycra-clad ravers clutching bottles of Evian water squeeze aboard carriages converted to mobile dance-floors, which transport their hip-hopping young passengers across half a continent before disgorging them, sweaty and disorientated, at some fashionably early hour of the morning.

So when I was invited to ride Britain's first disco train, I went prepared for an adrenaline-pumping boogie. That this trainload of assorted pleasure-seekers was to trundle through the Welsh mountainside worried me not; after all, ravers seeking the old-fashioned stationary acid-house party have even been drawn to such unlikely locations as Romford or Dorking. But as I arrived at Llangollen Station in North Wales, it became clear our disco train was to be an altogether more genteel affair. The Berwyn Belle is a lovingly restored steam train, the pride of the Llangollen Railway Society, its half-dozen carriages named after tongue-twisting Welsh mythological characters.

The end carriage was devoid of seating, but had a wooden dance-floor in the middle, and a bar at one end. These, the brochure explained, were the 'sumptuous surroundings of the function car Gwenabwy'. Three middle-aged men in waistcoats were happily building a stack of amplifiers and speakers at one end of the dance-floor. It transpired they were 'Day to Day', a slick combo from Shrewsbury. No, they didn't mind playing while on the move. A band was better than a DJ on a train, as the records jumped. Of course.

At first sight, the assembling passengers did not display quite the youthful exuberance I had anticipated: gin and tonics replaced bottled water; and any hint of Lycra had been cunningly disguised by layers of polyester and viscose. But a few drinks were to prove that, when it came to energy and enthusiasm, there was little to choose between the dance-floors of the Berwyn Belle and the sweat-soaked disco trains of the Continent.

It is 30 years since Dr Beeching announced the cuts that halved Britain's railway network. Llangollen Station, served by the railway since 1862, was closed, but since 1975 steam enthusiasts have reopened it and gradually rebuilt five-and-a-half miles of track westwards to the village of Glyndyfrdwy. Today, tourists and a few regular commuters use the line, which winds through spectacular countryside above the River Dee. To raise money, the society also holds special events on board – wine-and-dine evenings, the nightclub train, a Christmas Day party. Extra visitors are expected this weekend for the railway's summer Steam Gala, and next month for the International Eisteddfod at Llangollen. Last year, the society even launched a share issue, which has so far raised £200,000 towards its £500,000 target, the amount needed to help volunteers build another five miles of track to the town of Corwen.

'They're a little eccentric in Llangollen,' said David Morgan, a lawyer and steam train enthusiast. 'On St David's Day – March 1st – last year, they held a launch ceremony for their share prospectus. It was at Glyndyfrdwy station in the middle of a blizzard, with the snow and mist swirling, a Greek Orthodox priest swinging incense and chanting, and a Welsh choir singing in the background.'

Our disco train was at least luckier with the weather. Llangollen Station was bathed in early evening sunlight as we prepared to board. The engine was building up a head of steam as it shunted to the front of the train. A guard with mutton-chop whiskers stood by, flag in hand; I half-expected khaki-clad soldiers bound for the front to lean from the carriage windows and bid a fond farewell to their sweethearts. Instead, I stood too close to the engine and got a faceful of soot.

Brushing myself down, I met Wendy Proffitt from Wallasey, who was very excited about the trip; she had been born in Glyndyfrdwy in 1941. 'My mother was evacuated there during the war,' she said. 'We lived there until I was six months old, then we moved to Wallasey, but came back every year to visit. We could get on the old steam train near Wallasey and go straight through to Glyndyfrdwy, before Dr Beeching made his cuts. This is the first time I've been back there by train.' She and her friend Wendy Maddox, 51, stood silently on the platform, temporarily overcome by nostalgia for the days of steam. But not for long; they were with a party of friends from the Wirral, and were soon egging each other on to climb up to the footplate and pose with the driver for pictures.

The Berwyn Belle has been used for wine-and-dine evenings on the Llangollen Railway since 1987, but dancing is a new departure. The train runs the short distance to Glyndyfrdwy and back twice during the evening, with one course of dinner served on each leg. Although the maximum permitted speed is a soup-sloshing 25mph, we kept to a sedate 15mph for much of the journey, as we tackled platefuls of tasty home-cooking – a pleasant surprise for a traveller who equates eating on trains with overpriced sandwiches and Max Pax coffee.

Nick Patching, the company secretary for Llangollen Railway, joined me for a drink on the fourth leg of the trip, as the band struck up and a few brave souls took to the swaying dance-floor. 'The railway is operated under a light-railway order from the Health and Safety Executive, so there are no restrictions on things like dancing,' he said. 'And you don't need a licence to serve alcohol if the train is moving or capable of moving.'

Back in Gwenabwy's sumptuous surroundings, many of the 50 guests had by now taken the view that they did not need a licence to drink alcohol if they were moving or capable of moving. The band were well into their stride, belting out Sixties favourites such as *Honky Tonk Woman*, but steadfastly refusing to gesture to their surroundings with a few choruses of *Chattanooga Choo Choo*. I found the motion of the train encouraged a spot of gentle, reggae-style skanking, best executed with one hand placed firmly on the bar for support, but the Wendys and another dozen enthusiasts by now filling the dance-floor were ambitiously twisting and jiving the night away.

Frank and Sylvia Spence, a middle-aged couple from Southend-on-Sea in Essex, regularly drive up to Llangollen for the weekend, though more for the train than the disco: Mr Spence is a great expert on the age of steam. He even keeps a small train in his back garden. 'We've got 250 shares in the railway between us, so we qualify for four first-class tickets for this line each year,' he said. 'We've been coming up here 10 years. Then the track was only half a mile long.' Sylvia smiled and looked politely off into the distance.

Nick Patching told me that Pete Waterman, erstwhile producer of Kylie Minogue and Sonia, is also a train enthusiast and is busy buying up diesels. Did Nick fear a possible competitor in the disco train field? He thought perhaps not.

The dancers were going strong. 'Oooh, have we stopped?' said one, swaying to balance herself against the motion of the train. We had been standing at Llangollen Station for the past 10 minutes. I walked down the platform. The guard with the mutton-chop whiskers looked heavenwards as the disco carriage swayed and rocked in the night.

SWEPT FROM DATONG TO SHEFFIELD

ON A JOURNEY TO BEIJING, **NIGEL RICHARDSON**
RETURNS TO A TIME AND A PLACE HE THOUGHT
HE WOULD NEVER VISIT AGAIN

Journeys lull the mind into journeys of its own, the hypnotic rhythm of trains being particularly effective at transporting the memory. It was June, 2010 and my partner and I were sitting on the 0833 from Datong to Beijing in northern China. At the same time I was sitting in the lounge of a suburban house in South Yorkshire in the late 1960s. My mother was sweeping the carpet and I was lifting my feet so she could reach beneath my armchair. I never dreamed I would end up back there, after all these years and miles.

That morning the journey had started with a car ride from the hotel in Datong to the railway station in the north of the city. It was no hardship to be leaving Datong, which is one of the main cities of China's coal-mining industry. The town in which I grew up once held an equivalent status in England. Perhaps the smell and texture of coal on the air of Datong had already woken my memory buds when I boarded the train.

In snatches of greenery and outside shops, people were doing their morning exercises as we drove to the station – ballroom dancers twirling to a tinny tape recorder, routines with swords, or tennis racquets, or scarves, slo-mo t'ai chi. Outside the station itself, three women in their thirties were flicking and volleying a shuttlecock between them with a level of skill I would have died for in my footballing youth.

Carriage J, Seats 24 and 25. We settled in to seats of pale blue fabric with white antimacassars on the headrests. The carriage was filling up. Opposite us, occupying three seats, sat a one-child family: mother, father and daughter. The carriage attendant appeared, uniformed and tiny with a badge-like, expressionless face. Perhaps it was the black gloves she wore but she looked as if she might be capable of cruelty (more than most of us, that is).

The attendant passed along each bay of five seats bunching back the curtains into wall-mounted clasps – the equivalent, I supposed, of cabin crew lifting window blinds for take-off and landing – then returned to her domain at the end of the carriage. I pulled my paperback, *North and South* by Elizabeth Gaskell, from my backpack and pushed the pack up into the overhead rack. A strap was left dangling and every so often, for the rest of the journey, I would catch someone in the carriage eyeing it as it bobbed about.

The attendant reappeared with a mop and bucket and swabbed down the aisle of the carriage. For this activity, I noticed, she had removed her black gloves. At 0831 a policeman passed through the carriage with an electronic security wand, and scanned randomly selected luggage in the overhead racks. A large cardboard box caused the wand to bleep. The policeman stared hard at the box, stared down at the wand in his hand, then moved on with a shrug.

The train left on time. As it started to move, the couple and their daughter opposite us, who had not spoken to each other so far, began to eat. They began with plums, which the mother produced from a tuck box by her feet. Virtually everyone in the carriage – bar us foreigners – was suddenly on the chomp and slurp: fruit, chocolate bars, pot noodles made from hot water obtainable from a water heater at the end of the carriage, and constantly replenished flasks of tea.

I opened my book and read about 'choking white wreaths of unwholesome mist', then stared from the window into choking white wreaths of unwholesome mist. In and round Datong, coal-fired power stations and factory chimneys painted in jaunty red-and-white hoops have grown a smog that lies in a band reaching three quarters of the way up the sky. Above it, if you are lucky, you might see a cupola-like hat of blue, but even that is often obliterated, as if the pollution were a retractable roof that slides open and closed at will.

The smog thinned and we were passing through countryside. A field of earthen cones marked a peasant cemetery. A cart pulled by an ambling bullock passed down an avenue of poplars. The man sitting opposite us motored his way through a grenade-sized melon, eating the skin and seeds as well as the pale green flesh. When nothing was left his wife handed him a paper towel.

At a town called Tianzhen we spotted something familiar through the left-hand window: the Great Wall of China. The Great Wall of China! I wanted to shout out but no one was batting an eyelid. The young women sitting on that side of the carriage were reading fashion magazines and thumbing their cellphones, and besides, big deal, they had seen it a million times, this Great Wall of China. They were Chinese!

The train followed the Great Wall along the base of an arid, pleated mountain range beyond which lay Inner Mongolia. The same red-sand colour as the deforested foothills, this section was surprisingly intact, with blockhouses every half mile or so. For several miles the wall rode the contours of the hills, and just as I was beginning to hope it would escort us all the way to the outskirts of Beijing it abruptly snaked north up a mountainside, not to be seen again.

The family sitting opposite had started on the pumpkin seeds. Their hands delved into a plastic bag they had left on the little table beneath the window and they nibbled the seeds from the husks, spitting the husks into their cupped hands and throwing them on the floor of the carriage. The length of the carriage, the husks of pumpkin seeds were being tossed carelessly down until they speckled the linoleum floor in their thousands.

A gong sounded on the carriage tannoy and the quavering wail of Chinese opera started up as the train crossed a valley of glistening emerald rice paddies. At this moment the attendant reappeared, this time with a broom – and still without her gloves – and proceeded to sweep the carriage floor clean of seed husks. She performed this task impassively, without saying a word – but with absolute authority. In each bay the five passengers – two on one side, three on the other – would lift their feet in unison as the attendant approached, and plant them back down when she had swept the husks clear.

When she arrived at our bay I lifted my feet as I had seen others do – and the strangest feeling crept over me. A sound drowned out the Chinese opera on the tannoy. It was a wheezing sound, like an emphysemic climbing a steep hill. It was the sound of an ancient wooden carpet sweeper that my mother had used when I was a child.

And that was when I returned to a time and place I thought I would never visit again.

I would have been eight or nine years old. Every morning after breakfast – this was at weekends and in the school holidays – I would retire to an armchair with a third cup of tea and my mother would choose that moment to sweep the lounge carpet with her old sweeper. This rickety contraption bearing the name of the manufacturer – Ewbank – on the front in faded gold letters must have dated from before the Great War and apparently had belonged to my father's grandmother. Without either of us saying a word I would raise my tartan-slippered feet and the sweeper would clean the carpet beneath in two or three swift strokes.

The carriage attendant moved on but my mind was snagged on the old Ewbank. What on earth had happened to it? I thought back to the day my brother and I had hired a skip to clear out my mother's house after she moved into a nursing home. I remembered the various things we consigned, with varying degrees of guilt, to the skip. But I had no recollection of the sweeper.

Surely I hadn't chucked that too? It was a family heirloom, a link with the great-grandmother I had never known – just like the book on my shelf, *Chambers's Cookery for Young Housewives*, which, as the title page says, was awarded by the Gateshead School Board to Elizabeth Marriner of Shipcote School in March 1898 for winning the school cookery prize (there's a recipe in it for boiled cow-heel).

Then I thought back to the reckless mood my brother and I had been in the day we filled the skip. We had enjoyed smashing things and the sweeper had no doubt gone the way of the moss-coloured sofa, the rubber plant and so on. What a lot of fun we had had, especially with the horrible oil painting! I had hated this still life from the moment my parents bought it in about 1978, and now I got my revenge. I took a Stanley Knife to it, and when I had finished shredding the canvas I bashed the wooden frame to smithereens on the side of the skip. Most gratifying.

This train journey was turning into the story referred to in *North and South* 'of the eastern king, who dipped his head into a basin of water, at the magician's command, and ere he instantly took it out went through the experience of a lifetime'. What caused me to lift my head from the basin – or lift it halfway out, at least – was the recollection that the subject of the wretched painting had been chrysanthemums.

This in turn made me think of a dinner we had had two weeks before in Shanghai, when my partner, Miren, had ordered chrysanthemum tea. It had arrived as a whole flower head in the bottom of a long glass of hot water, and together we had watched it grow and sway, like those lava lamps from the Sixties.

From Shanghai a fortnight before to this train speeding across China's northern plains was but a short journey, and it was completed by a nudge on my arm. The woman sitting opposite me was indicating the bag of pumpkin seeds. 'Have some before we finish them,' she seemed to be saying, and mimed how to throw the husks on the floor.

CHAPTER 8
GOING FORWARD (AND BACKWARDS)

LOST IN FRANCE

NICHOLAS SHAKESPEARE FOLLOWS IN THE TRACKS
OF HIS AUNT, WHO TOOK A TRAIN TO PARIS IN
1937 AND WAS STRANDED THERE WHEN THE
GERMAN TANKS ROLLED IN

One March day in 1937, 'feeling very ill and alone in the world', my aunt Priscilla caught the Paris train from Victoria Station in London with £5 in her pocket. She was 20, unmarried and pregnant, and had decided to go to France, where she had grown up, to have an abortion.

In 1937, a first-class train-and-boat ticket to the Continent cost £5.15. The luxuriously appointed Train Bleu mocked her with its advertisement: 'Sleep your way from the City's fogs to the Riviera sunshine.' She tried to sleep, but could not.

When the train pulled into Newhaven she noticed a tall man looking at her. His face was lined and he must have been about forty. Speaking in French, he introduced himself. Her heart sank: she disliked intensely talking to people on trains, a trait she inherited from her father, a broadcaster and prolific author called S P B Mais.

S P B Mais was my grandfather. He also happened to be the first writer I ever knew. 'In the train and across the Channel,' he observed in *I return to Switzerland*, 'the Englishman regards his fellow traveller as

Cain regarded Abel, and only looks for a chance to eliminate him.'
Priscilla wondered how anyone could find her attractive in her present
state, but was beyond caring.

Once on a blacked-out train during wartime, while on his way
to record a talk to British troops stationed in France, S P B Mais
reflected on the anomalies of his race. 'It is only when notices are
put up in every railway carriage warning us not to talk to strangers
that we feel the strongest temptation to talk.' Priscilla and the
Frenchman were soon swept up in a conversation that lasted to
Paris and beyond. 'For train travel,' as Ludovic Kennedy put it in
his fine anthology of railway journeys, 'being constricted both in
time and space, magnifies character, intensifies relationships,
unites the disparate. Ordinary people become extra-ordinary, larger
than life; and in the knowledge that they will not meet again,
expansive, confiding, intimate. Let us talk now, you and I: later will
be too late.'

By the time they reached the Gare du Nord, the tall French stranger
– Vicomte Robert Doynel de la Sausserie – had fallen in love. He
married Priscilla the following December. Shortly afterwards, the
Germans invaded France, and for the next four and a half years, my
aunt, the young and beautiful Vicomtesse, disappeared from sight.

*   *   *

Seventy years on, I board a Eurostar carriage at St Pancras with the aim
of finding out what on earth happened to her. I have little to go on –
Priscilla was adamantine in her refusal to talk about this period of her
life; but by visiting places mentioned in her letters I hope to shade in
my aunt's story during the Occupation. I travel mindful of Paul
Theroux's mantra: 'Almost anything is possible in a train.'

I last took the train to Paris a decade ago and cannot reconcile the
two experiences. The service has improved beyond recognition.
Gleaming waiting rooms; a minimum of bureaucracy and queues; and
efficient. The young woman beside me booked her ticket a mere couple
of hours earlier. She is a reminder that walking down a train corridor
is still an adventure. A student at the Royal College of Music, Evelyne
Berezovksy received an urgent summons from her father, the Russian
concert pianist Boris, who wanted her to page-turn for him. She will

appear on stage this evening at the Salle Pleyel, where Chopin performed, in the clothes she is wearing.

'Is Evelyne a Russian name?' I ask as she vets her face in a small mirror.

'I was named after Evelyn Waugh.'

When I reveal that I made a documentary on Waugh that was broadcast shortly before she was born – and which her father might well have watched – she invites me to the concert. But I am leaving next morning for Caen.

According to the French writer Jean D'Ormesson, the best way to describe the two years that separate the moment from Priscilla's arrival in Paris to the September day when France declared war on Germany is to say that it was like a period of time outside time. 'Other years led somewhere, formed part of a continuous pattern, and you could make plans in them. But 1938 and 1939 were just an interval, a blind alley.' They were years, D'Ormesson wrote, out of the real sequence of history. 'They didn't count. They were a nightmare, a reprieve, an imaginary stretch of time, an error, an exception, a night in which we were like condemned men dreading the dawn.'

Priscilla and Robert were married in Paris on 16 December 1938. I have a photograph of them standing outside the church of St Honoré d'Eylau in place Victor Hugo. Her father has refused to come over to join the cortege. (When he sees the photograph, he remarks that she looks fifteen years old). The other faces belong to her husband's aristocratic family, who own a château in Normandy where my aunt and Robert spend their weekends and holidays; leaving from the Gare St Lazare, and following the same route as the train that would carry her English friends to safety in June 1940. It's one of a number of mysteries, why Priscilla should choose to remain in France after Germany invaded. Her refusal to flee is no less mysterious, in its way, than the circumstances of her marriage. Perhaps she accepted as a fait accompli that German troops would soon be overrunning the English countryside. Another foreigner who stayed in France was Arthur Koestler, for whom defeat this time seemed as final as the closure, on 16 June 1940, of the British Railways office at 12 boulevard de la Madeleine. 'We did not know that England would carry on the fight alone; nothing in her conduct during the last pre-war decade, nor in the first nine months of the actual war, led one to suppose it.'

At the Gare St Lazare, I settle into my velvet seat and stare out of the window as the long-limbed train eases past the platform's black metal pillars. S P B Mais championed the idea of awarding a prize for the most colourful flowerbed at railway stations. Here I see only weeds growing between a line of tracks.

Aside from your fellow passengers, one of the blissful things about train travel is the counterpoint between life within the train and life without, touched on in William Stafford's poem 'Vacation':

There is dust on everything in Nevada.
I pour the cream.

Made redundant by the *Daily Telegraph*, where he had worked as a leader-writer, Priscilla's father would finance his summer holidays by providing advertising copy for railway companies. In the 1930s, he helped to promote the romance of travelling by train with a series of brochures commissioned by the Southern Railway ('Let's get out of here'), the London, Midland & Scottish Railway ('Royal Scot and her 49 sister engines') and the Great Western Railway. In 1926, he had met a servant girl in the Sussex town of Plaistow who at 16 had never seen or heard a train. Now, for a fee of 15 guineas per thousand words, he would exuberantly describe the pleasure to be derived from steaming through a 'western land of Celtic mysticism' while at the same time tucking into an excellent luncheon ordered from the printed menu. Transported by engines bearing resonant names such as *Tintagel* and *Trelawney* (a rival railway company christened its trains *Merlin*, *Lyonesse* and *Iseult*), S P B Mais took fierce pride in his reputation as 'the Ambassador for the English Countryside', and to the end of his days remained a passionate and unrepentant Englishman. 'I am like a fox-terrier attached, and deeply attached, to an old master from whose side I have never before strayed. Just round the garden of England – and what a lovely garden it is – has been good enough for me.' He titled one of his 200 or so books *See England First*; in another book, 'train' was misprinted as 'tram', causing confusion to a number of travellers plotting a holiday in Scotland. He dispensed this advice to the train-traveller: 'To double the joys of travel write them down at once and let not the sun go down upon your virgin tablets. Your notes need not be longer than those included in that admirable folder produced by the London and North Eastern Railway called "On Either Side," which is just as fascinating as any novel. It shows you just the points of interest that lie on either side of the carriage window as you travel from King's Cross to Edinburgh and Inverness . . . It isn't only small boys who wander where all the interesting branch lines go, what spire this is and who lives in yonder mansion.'

S P B Mais lived for his happiest years on the south coast directly opposite France, in the ship-building village that supplied 26 vessels for the siege of Calais and from which Charles II escaped to Fécamp. Even so, he was strangely proud of his inability to master a word of French. His feelings towards France, and in particular that part of northwest France associated with his French son-in-law, may help to explain why he did not attend his eldest daughter's wedding. In 1930, he had joined a conducted tour from Cherbourg through Normandy and Brittany. The contrast between the sweet-smelling clean English villages and the dirty, unkempt, ill-smelling French ones was so great that he nearly cancelled his trip after the first day. He had never slept before in such a dirty hotel. The charabanc in which he drove to Bayeux and Caen and thence to St Malo was uncomfortable and falling to pieces. The roads were straight and monotonous, the countryside dull, and the villages all exactly like one another, with long streets of dead grey houses innocent of paint. 'The country people, all dressed in black, looked as unhappy as the houses they lived in.'

This was the self-same region in which his eldest daughter had settled, and where she was stranded when German tanks rolled into Paris, 'steel pachyderms let loose from the zoos of hell,' in the words of one who witnessed the sudden, devastating invasion.

It is true that the two-hour journey to Caen takes me through a flat and unremarkable landscape. I look out at the furrowed fields of late September and hedgerows known as bocages: uneven mounds of greenery in which trees, bushes, brambles all patchily intertwine – like Priscilla's life.

My first stop: the archives at Caen, where ardent genealogists have untangled the lineage of Robert's family back to 1066. I search for Priscilla's name in vain, eventually finding this: 'Robert/married an

Englishwoman (no children)/divorced.' It's as though a bocage has grown over her name.

Bombed to flatness, the gaiety of Caen is swiftly exhausted. Even so, I am detained there – a rail strike prevents my moving on, called in protest at President Sarkozy's plan to raise the retirement age. Intriguingly, on the unique occasion that S P B Mais travelled through France to write a book, *The Riviera – New Look and Old* (1949), he, too, found himself stuck. 'As all the restaurant car and *wagons lits* staff in France are on strike . . . there were no *couchettes*, and no meals for twenty hours.'

At the sight of those empty and redundant carriages, I find myself thinking of the humiliating Armistice inflicted on the French.

No train journey through France can be undertaken without the memory of Marshal Foch's static railway carriage in the Forest of Compiègne. In June 1940, the carriage was towed from a museum in the Invalides to the siding where originally it stood, in order for Hitler to revenge himself on the Peace of Versailles – likewise signed in this, Foch's mobile office. Outside, draped over a commemorative granite block, a great swastika flag obscured the inscription: *Here on 11th November 1918 succumbed the criminal pride of the German people.* Feldmarshal Keitel explained: 'The historic forest of Compiègne has been chosen in order to efface once and for all by an act of reparative justice a memory resented by the German people as the greatest shame of all time.' Across the table, Hitler and Goering uttered not a word; no concession was to be made to the defeated French before they had supplied their signatures. Afterwards, Hitler had the carriage transported to Germany and destroyed.

The destruction of Compagnie Internationale des Wagon-Lits dining car No 2419 was rarely the fate of railway carriages in England, where for as little as £15 you could buy an obsolete Victorian carriage from the Great Western Railway and have it delivered to your own site. On his journeys through southern England, S P B Mais frequently complained how, atop every hill with a view, his eyes would settle on the inevitable railway carriage converted to a tea-room, its verandah enclosed with coloured glass, and a notice proclaiming it to be the Lucky Dip café. Sybille Bedford, a writer who grew up in France and who came to England in 1935, once lived on the South Coast 'in one of those converted old railway carriages by a beach,' where, in an upper bunk by a one-candle light, she used to read herself to sleep.

Grounded in Caen by industrial action, I make a detour to the coastal resort of Houlgate, one of Priscilla's favourite destinations. It lies 45 minutes away and is reached by a bus that leaves from beside the train station. On the beach, a solitary pillar commemorates a conquest more ancient than the upstart German one: the departure of Duke William of Normandy for England. The archives revealed that among William's closest companions on board was Robert Doynel's ancestor. An old retainer will later recall for me how Robert, during the Occupation, clung to this belief, repeatedly uttered: 'William of Normandy left with his fleet from Normandy. A fleet will return from England to liberate Normandy.'

Nothing is stiller than a French beach town in late September. Houlgate's ornately tiled villas are shuttered and the only figures are cockle-pickers stooped over the tide-pools. But along this coastline the Allies landed, as Max Hastings next day reminds me.

I chance upon my former editor seated alone at the Auberge Normande in Carentan, tucking into a plate of lobster tails and ordering another glass of chilled white wine. I have interrupted him rereading Trollope's autobiography on an iPad. He caught the ferry over this morning and has come to Carentan to embrace his French chef, to ensure that he returns next year to cater for a weekend in Hungerford ('He said the least awful place to have lunch was here'); and at 4 p.m. is leading a group of US generals on a tour of Omaha Beach. Alas, even had he elected to invite me, I cannot join him for dessert because I have organised to visit the château where Priscilla spent much of her short married life. As well as for Max's chef, Carentan was my aunt's local railway station.

The person driving me to the château, ten kilometres away, is, like Max, an expert on the Normandy landings. A former shipping agent, Michael Yannaghas retired to the nearby provincial capital of Saint-Lo, christened by Samuel Beckett, after the RAF destroyed it, as 'the capital of ruins'. A base for German submarines, Saint-Lo was bombed eight times between June 6 and 22, 1944. In rural Normandy they still talk of that summer as 'the time of bombardments'. Nine out of ten houses were flattened, says Michael, who lives, he tells me, 'in the middle of a battlefield'. He has dug up in his garden: a grenade, a fighting dagger, an entrenching tool – 'and thousands of bits of shrapnel, oh yes.' But he comes from a family accustomed to digging up things in fields. The Venus de Milo was unearthed in his great-great uncle's field on the isle of Milos. 'He sold it to the French consul who gave it to Louis XVIII' – the armless effigy being ferried back to France by a sailor from Normandy.

Priscilla's château at Boisgrimot, outside the hamlet of Sainteny, was the scene of the fiercest fighting in Normandy and a symbol of the difficulty encountered in bocage country. ('The casualty figures were extraordinary,' reads a history of D-Day, calculating the attrition at Sainteny: 7,000 GIs in five kilometres). Michael points out mounds of earth used since time immemorial to partition off land. 'Everyone thought "nice little hedges in Bodmin" – where they had all trained. In the month of June the foliage is thickest. Effectively you can't see anything. A US colonel said the bocage was far worse than anything he had found in the Guadalcanal.' The Germans fought back hard. The 80,000 dead they left behind are buried in six military cemeteries in Normandy, with fresh bodies still being unearthed as recently as 2003.

Priscilla's château stands milk-white and vacant at the end of a long gravel drive. Destroyed by bombs in July 1944, and sold with panic-stricken haste by the Doynels, it has recently endured a sterile renovation. Visible through a window among builder's ladders and paint tins is the sole remaining family relic: a floor-to-ceiling stone fireplace engraved with three ducks – the Doynel crest.

We call on the son of the former butler. At mention of her name, 80-year-old Joseph Carer claps his head: 'Priscilla Mais!' His face reddening, he takes off his spectacles. His father used to collect her by horse and carriage from Carentan railway station . . . He remembers how beautiful she was, her blonde hair, her green eyes, her fur coat. His eyes are watering.

So what went wrong? Why, immediately after the Liberation, did she divorce Robert and return to England? I go back to Paris and take a train to a town near the Swiss border to find out.

The second author I ever met was the Argentine writer Jorge Luis Borges who spent part of his youth in Switzerland, where he is buried – and where, as a teenager, he tasted the first of several catastrophic love affairs. Tolstoy is not the only writer for whom the end of an affair is connected with a train. In May 1952, heartbroken after his rejection by yet another woman, Borges walked on his own through Buenos Aires. He stood on a bridge over the railway tracks outside Constitution station, amid the roar of trains as they departed for the south, the pampas, and experienced a sort of ecstasy. At the sight of those trains – 'weaving labyrinths of iron' – Borges had a revelation that revealed to him the great diversity of the world, and at the same time he heard an infinite voice rising from 'the invisible horizon'. It was as if, he wrote, he was attending the Day of Judgment.

On the platform at the Gare de Lyon, I am conscious of the TGV's electrical hum and the grating of my suitcase rollers. Priscilla, clutching her rapidly packed valise, would have heard different noises: dog barks and the shouts of German soldiers.

Early on 5 December, 1940, during the coldest winter in memory, French policemen rounded up all women with British papers. The procedure did not vary. A bang on the door in the freezing darkness, often in the presence of a Gestapo officer; half an hour to pack – and no whisper of where they were going. The arrest was conducted in the blackout, without warning. Since October, the Germans had required British women still at large in France to sign daily at the local Commissariat; on 16 October, a new decree gave warning that anyone sheltering a British subject must declare her presence, or be shot.

'Urban railway stations', wrote Sybille Bedford, who had watched wounded German soldiers helped into trains in 1915, 'for those not inured by daily use, are places of angst and trauma.' Among those civilians crammed shivering into an unheated train that day was my aunt. Her companions formed a diverse group, from stable boys' wives to Indian royalty. Some didn't speak English, but had married Englishmen. Others had been trapped in France, on holiday when the Germans invaded. They numbered governesses, nurses, couturiers, dancers such as Margaret Kelly (founder of the Blue Belle Girls), plus 500 nuns from 90 orders. Most were rounded up in Paris and spent the day waiting at the Gare de l'Est. The door handles were removed and rumours spread that their destination was a concentration camp in Frankfurt.

By chance, I am in Paris on the winter day when the chief executive of the French national railway delivers this public apology: 'In the name of the SNCF, I bow down before the victims, the survivors, the children of those deported, and before the suffering that still lives.' He makes his landmark contrition in the suburb of Bobigny, from where 20,000 Jews were shipped to Nazi camps. France was the first European country to give full rights to the Jews. And yet between 1941 and 1944, the SNCF was to carry a total of 76,000 European Jews in 76 cattle cars to the French-German border, and thence to Auschwitz.

Consequently, the British women were relieved when their train came to a halt two days later in Besançon, in the Daubs. German soldiers marched them through the snow to a barracks where they lived for five months. What happened to them there is a little known story, even in Besançon.

At the Hotel de Paris in the old town centre, a businesswoman is seething to change her room. She has a double bed and a shower, but no bath — as specifically she had booked.

The receptionist shakes her head. There are no rooms left.

'My colleague — does she have a double?'

The receptionist nods.

'And bath?'

'Yes.'

The woman storms off, and I tell the receptionist that my aunt was three months in Besançon without a bath.

The Caserne Vauban has been closed since 2006, but the Brigadier in command of the 19th Regiment — which is stationed in Besançon and formerly occupied these barracks — unlocks the gates for me. I spend an afternoon wandering through the long empty corridors and courtyards, trying to envisage the place as it would have been in 1940.

The secrecy surrounding the initial round-up was well-kept, even from the Germans who ran the barracks. They were unprepared utterly for the arrival of an estimated 3,900 Englishwomen (no exact record exists of the number), some with screaming babies, some old and ill, all hungry and anxious and cold. The chaos and the filth were indescribable. The barracks until very recently had housed 20,000 French POWS captured in the Maginot Line, who had been sent to Germany, leaving their mess behind. Priscilla was marshalled into a third-floor room in Batiment C with 48 fellow British passport holders. Inside were old straw mattresses in all stages of decay on the damp floor, old shoes, helmets, and urine and excrement everywhere.

Pretty much all agreed with Elizabeth Hales, a 63-year-old New Zealand artist: 'The worst thing in the camp is the sanitary arrangement' – 20 privies on the ground floor for 3,900 women. These swiftly blocked and were closed off, forcing queues to form in the snow outside for the 'tinettes'. My aunt wrote of these hazardous long sheds, each with a deep trench and planks across the holes on which to perch: 'Most of the older people couldn't cope with the straddling so they performed on the side and everything got frozen up and one sometimes slipped and fell in.' A row of white crosses in the local cemetery marks the graves of the elderly who, in temperatures below zero, failed to scramble back out. The excrement overflowed onto the ground and it was impossible for Priscilla to keep her clothes clean.

A bugle call woke her at dawn. She had to climb down and up 100 concrete steps to fetch water, coal, and food. Of the liquid that passed as coffee, another inmate, Maybel Bayliss, wrote in an unpublished memoir: 'We drank it until one day we found a mass of tousled hair at the bottom of the can. Rats were frequent, some seemed as large as rabbits. These awful creatures would tear the sacks of dried vegetables before our very eyes.' Pricilla's gums turned black from the diet. Surviving on soup that was little more than warm water with bits of grass floating in it, she invited her room-mates to fictitious banquets.

At Le Coucou restaurant in rue Luc Breton, the patron's eyes widen when he learns of Besançon's English internees. 'No one ever told me – and I arrived here in 1960.' In 1972, as a 19-year old parachutist, Patrick Langlade spent four weeks' military service at the Caserne Vauban. 'Perhaps I slept in her bed!' But he doesn't altogether believe what I say. I've almost finished eating when there's an excited shout. 'Come over here!' He has Googled it. 'Look! Margaret Kelly. She was at Besançon. The Blue Belle girls were prisoners!'

Priscilla escaped after three months, this time by pretending she was pregnant. (In March 1941, mothers with children under 16 were released.) Either believing that Robert had not lifted a finger to help, or weary of a stifling existence, she left her husband and fell in and out of love, including with a Frenchman called Eugene who owned a factory in Annemasse making nylon stockings.

Annemasse is reached by train via Lyon, from where I take a two-hour bus journey. It lies tantalisingly close to the Swiss border. By day, you have a splendid view of Mont Blanc tossing off its cloud wrap, and, closer to town, Mount Salève where the teenage Borges went rock climbing with friends; at night, you look down on the clear lights of Geneva and the old taverns where Borges used to get drunk. It's a town of pharmaceuticals and chocolate-makers and women with absurdly small dogs. Quite why Priscilla should have sought a fleeting happiness here under another name is no less mystifying than her failure to escape into Switzerland. Was there nothing for her in England? Did she feel Germany's victory was so assured? Was she so in love with Eugene that she felt her future was in France? Or did she simply submit like a roulette ball, to roll wherever she was tossed?

Like my aunt, the writer Sybille Bedford had spent her formative years in France. Her father initiated nightly sessions of roulette, transforming their house into a gambling club. She remembered the family 'dicing with thoughts of ruin' while her father kept up a commentary about young men he'd seen lose all and shoot themselves at dawn in Monte Carlo. The image never abandoned her. 'The relation of the single man or woman to history,' believed Bedford, 'is that of victim or of escapee – and in that huge context which turn of the roulette-wheel determines the overlapping elements of circumstances, heredity and chance?'

There was a small brown piece of paper in my aunt's papers that is dated from this period. Typed on it, in French, an astrological portrait of her character carries the following warning. 'Gambling: play as little as possible because you will have bad luck. On the other hand, you will have better luck in love.' My aunt has underlined the last sentence in pencil, as well as the prediction: 'In your life you will experience difficult passages, but a moment will come when you will know perfect happiness.'

In Annemasse, I visit the Casino and watch a young woman lean her haughty body over the baize and smother it with blue chips. There's no alteration in her expression, whether she wins, whether she loses. The croupier flicks a white ball. I'm not a gambler, but in memory of my aunt, who liked a flutter, I place a single chip. The ball spins back around the lacquered rim, before rattling into slot 25. I've won two euros, not quite enough to buy a bottle of mineral water. 'You always win in Annemasse,' smiles the woman next to me.

AND POCKETS OF GENIUS . . .

YSENDA MAXTONE GRAHAM FINDS INSPIRATION STILL ALIVE AND WELL AT THE BR RESEARCH CENTRE IN DERBY

I took a train to Derby to find out what people at the British Rail research centre are actually doing on a Tuesday afternoon. What are they researching? How inspired are they? Does anybody notice if they invent anything?

The woman behind the reception desk was doing a quick crossword. She rang up Jackie Robertson for me. Jackie Robertson's job, poor thing, is to make sure that journalists don't find out anything secret. 'I'll be trolling around with you all afternoon,' she said, 'and this is Donna. She's just started working here so she'll be trolling around with us as well.'

Jackie was brisk and cheery and wore shoulder pads and a weighty gold necklace. She was as beady-eyed as the person who escorts you to the loo during an exam and no one, in her presence, dared say anything subversive or even cross. One man tried to, but he was sorry the moment he'd done it. 'That Stoneblower project was a bit of a saga,' he said. He looked up, saw Jackie's frown and amended his words. 'I mean, it was a long-term project.'

In a small and tiny office, the first of many, Jackie explained that there were five branches at the research centre: Scientific Services, Civil Engineering, Mechanical Engineering, E&S (Electronic Systems and Software) and Electrification. 'We've got some of the world leaders in their fields here.'

'Oh, have you? Who?' I asked.

'You've got me there. I can't think of any offhand. But anyway, it's not the individual person here, it's the team that matters.'

It is only an R centre here, not R and D. Once something has been researched and invented, its development and manufacture carry on elsewhere. The Stoneblower, for example, is now in what is called 'a tender situation', while a manufacturer is being sought. What is a Stoneblower? It is an automatic track-leveller. Three times during my short visit, the image of a cup of leaf tea either spilling or not spilling was used by the explainers as an illustration. David Round, in his tiny little office, told me how the Stoneblower, in the middle of the night, could crawl along a track, detect a dip in it, lift it up and blow small stones underneath it from a huge supply in its hopper.

The old method of track levelling was to use a track-tamping machine, but that was not nearly as good because instead of putting new stones in, it just squeezed the existing stones. That disturbed them. 'The wonder of the new machine,' David Round said, 'is that it leaves the solid stuff and adds more.'

He drew me a diagram, with his Biro, of a curve in a track. Spontaneous diagram-drawing is a healthy sign of enthusiasm and he explained, as he drew, about the automatic track-alignment system that was also being developed, to stop your cup of tea sliding along the table.

Bridget Eikoff, in Mechanical, also drew me a diagram – of a wheel head-on and coming out of the picture, so it didn't look like a wheel but like a breeze block. That was to explain rail-wheel contact and how the cross-section of the wheel is being developed so that it will change shape in a regular way with wear.

Bridget works in what is known as the VD Unit – Vehicle Dynamics – and she is a clever, donnish and happy woman, who uses a bit of rail as a paperweight. She is fascinated by the way in which train wheels go round.

The result of years of work from the VD unit is something called VAMPIRE, a particularly infuriating acronym because the second letter doesn't quite work. 'Vehicle dynAmics Modelling Package, In a Railway Environment,' boasts the brochure and, like so much at the British Rail research centre, it turns out to be a complex set of computer programmes.

It does seem to be the case that the real enthusiasts, the most inspired and excited people of all at the research centre, are the ones who sit at computer screens. 'You want to see some hands-on work going on, don't you?' Jackie said. 'Yes, yes, please.' But time and time again it was not hands-on work that I saw, but merely fingers-on. It was men at keyboards, clicking the mouse.

Once in the afternoon I saw something physical happening: a man in a white coat was making a drill a bit longer. Near him there stood an intriguing railway carriage covered in a huge red cloth like a bit of Christo art.

'What's going on under there? I asked. 'Secrets,' said Jackie. In the Electronic Systems and Software branch a sweet Chinese man called Eddie Liu explained what he was doing. 'I'm working on Control Centre of Future,' he said.

It is strange how everything in British Rail has to have a jingly name like that. We passengers have had to get used to it, with the Supersave, the Awayday, the We're Getting There campaign and, this week, the new Customer Comes First policy. But you might have thought that the highly intelligent employees at the research centre would be spared all this. Not at all. The jingly voice of British Rail seeps into their subtlest projects, giving them jolly names that are meant to boost everyone's morale.

'I came to the railway because I believe in trains. I like trains,' said Michael McGuire when we went to his office and were brought leaf tea with UHT milk in it, just as you get on a 125. Beneath us, out of the window, we could hear real trains screeching and screaming on the real tracks outside Derby station.

It is nice to know that the people who work at the research centre have a bit of the train-spotter in them and can't resist peeping out of the window to verify their guess as to which train is going past. The simple love of trains is a strong emotion; I detected quite a lot of it about. On their walls people had postcards not of blue seas and palm trees but of black railway tracks meeting at infinity.

'Now we're going to see something really exciting,' said Jackie. 'When I first heard about it I was amazed myself. Are you ready?' She led me along a corridor to a man called David Hill, another consultant in a shirt and tie.

'Come this-a-way,' he said. Where did this-a-way lead? Into another office with a computer. But David Hill was delightful and what he told me was, indeed, exciting.

'What we're working on here is Condition-Determined Maintenance. It's all about changing the way in which we maintain trains. In a population of diesel engines or cars, some will last 100,000 miles, some 200,000 miles, but most of them, 150,000. To be on the safe side, you have to service them all at 100,000. That's called Planned Preventative Maintenance. Now, when is a car most likely to go wrong?'

I didn't know what he wanted me to say, so I didn't say anything.

'The week after it's been serviced. It's called maintenance-induced failure. We're now moving towards a philosophy of 'If it's working, don't fix it.'

But you have to know whether a train is working or not. The idea of CDM is that the functioning and components are checked every few seconds. Every train will have a computer on board to do this. We're moving towards 'the intelligent train'.

We turned to the screen and saw an example of an intelligent train. There is only one in England at the moment. It is very small and runs between Euston and Birmingham. It can tell you everything about itself. It tells you, by weighing the carriages, how many people got out at Harrow. It tells you how long the second door took to open at Watford: 0.55 seconds after the person pushed the button, the movement was detected; 2.11 seconds later, the full opening was completed.

'But,' said David, 'it's not enough for a computer to be able to collect data. It has to have an automated analysis technique as well. That's what we're working on now.'

In the little computer room three brilliant computer scientists were working on exactly that. They talked in that mathematical way about n: their n is the smallest number possible to separate all the various conditions in a component's action. They had made a graph of the opening of an automatic door and had discovered that in the opening of a door there are 15 features that can be separated into 23 fault conditions, plus the faultless condition called 'good door'. 'Peak force in first second,' said the graph, at a jagged pinnacle. Then; 'positive area under force-time curve until door opens'. And doors, of course, are child's play compared with engines.

They were a fulfilled and excited bunch in that computer room;

they had a sense of humour and a sparkle in their eyes. At five o'clock, everyone went home, many of them by train, and all of them highly sensitive to sounds, bounces, jolts and small time-intervals.

RAIL DREAM PUTS EAST AND WEST ON THE SAME TRACK

JUST ONE 50-MILE TUNNEL WOULD REVOLUTIONISE GLOBAL TRAIN TRAVEL. AND, SAYS **JAMES LANGTON**, SOMEONE IS SERIOUSLY PLANNING TO BUILD IT

Imagine a world. Two continents follow the line of its equator for almost the entire circumference. One great ocean stretches south from the sub-equatorial coasts of both land masses, with another to the north. A tiny neck of water, almost invisible on the map, is all that divides East from West.

This is our planet, turned through 90 degrees as if the North Pole were on the line of the new Equator. Seen this way, from the tip of Tierra del Fuego to the Cape of Good Hope becomes an almost unbroken coastline. This extraordinary 20,000-mile trek, up the western seaboard of America, along the Pacific Rim, through southern Asia, and then down the eastern coast of Africa, involves travelling by sea just once. Across the 50 miles of the Bering Strait.

Now imagine yourself in the future, early in the next century. A morning train is leaving Waterloo International Station in south London. It rumbles through Kent at 80mph (the fast rail link is still not complete) before gathering speed among the drab fields of northern France. By the time lunch has been cleared from the dining cars, the train is arriving in Berlin. Poland flashes past in the afternoon. The passengers barely notice the click as the carriages' axles automatically expand to the wider Russian track gauge. It is night when the suburbs of Moscow approach.

For breakfast, passengers emerge to blinis, black tea and a view of the Urals. In the night, the train has joined the new fast track which follows the line of the old Trans-Siberian Railway. By the end of the second day, the twin electric engines are hauling through the foothills of the Sayan Mountains. Mongolia is only 300 miles to the south.

Day three brings the frozen emptiness of Siberia. At a dot on the map called Tynda, the railway divides, south to the port of Vladivostok, and north to a new line through some of the bleakest terrain on earth. Some time in the early hours of day four, the train crosses the Arctic Circle.

After breakfast, US customs and immigration officials come on board. The train is heading for the tip of the Chukchi Peninsula and the international date line. In less than an hour, it is a day later. The train has emerged from the eastern bore of the Bering Strait Tunnel and is now in Alaska. The new catering crew serve baked Vermont ham and pecan pie for lunch.

By night the train has reached the little town of Fort Nelson in British Columbia, where it joins the North American railway network. By the following evening, the 49th Parallel and the Great Lakes are on the horizon. On the sixth day, the London-New York transcontinental express glides over the East River and into Harlem. At the northern end of Central Park, it follows the commuter trains on the underground approach to Grand Central Station. In the heart of New York, it stops for the last time. Passengers wishing to stretch their legs can take a yellow cab to Battery Park, at the southern tip of Manhattan. There they can breathe in the sea air for the first time on their epic voyage.

What fantasy is this? Not a fantasy at all, according to the Interhemispheric Bering Strait Tunnel and Railroad Group. Its intention is to bring about the greatest engineering project the world has ever seen. Later this month, the Third International Bering Strait Tunnel and Railroad Conference was due to be held at the Savoy Hotel in London. So great is the interest that last week the organisers decided to postpone the event until February. The number of delegates has been increased from 200 to 500.

The aim is to construct a railway tunnel under the sea between Russia and the United States. The 50 miles of the Bering Strait once represented the ideological gulf between the Cold War enemies. Now it is all that separates them. The gap between the continents of Asia and North America is tantalisingly slim.

Never mind the problems. The vision is extraordinary. It would make possible not just a journey from London to New York, but a transcontinental network of railways running the length of South America to the shores of the Indian Ocean. There is already a plan to construct another railway tunnel under the Strait of Gibraltar to Africa. If so, it would, in theory, be possible to board a train in Britain and travel directly to almost anywhere in the world.

The problems are not technical. In 1905, an international consortium raised $6 million as initial capital for a railway from Siberia to Alaska. The project foundered not because of the eventual cost – estimated at $300 million – but because of the Russian Revolution. For the next 70 years, the Bering Strait became the front line of the conflict between Capitalism and Communism. While most Americans regarded the Soviet Union as a faraway place, its soldiers and aircraft manoeuvred only miles from the coast of the US.

Now Russians and Americans are cautious friends. The Bering Strait, however, remains as inhospitable as ever. In the winter, the sea between the two continents freezes. The climate is polar, with temperatures falling to −40C. There are few trees and fewer people. The population density on both sides of the strait is less than one person per square mile.

Yet none of this would seriously impede the construction of a tunnel. The granite and limestone underneath the sea bed poses far fewer problems than the geology of the English Channel. The technology for digging under the Bering Strait would be no more complex than that for the Channel Tunnel. Fortuitously, there are also two islands in the middle of the Strait. These could be used to drill ventilation shafts, and for access to the construction site.

Ah, but the cost. The price of the Channel Tunnel doubled from £4 billion to £8 billion. The bill – and a highly provisional one at that – for the Bering Strait project is £26 billion, of which £6 billion is for the tunnel. On the American side, nearly 1,200 miles of new railway line will have to be built. On the Russian side, the distance is nearly double that. With the continuing problems of Eurotunnel, who would want to venture into such a wilderness?

George Koumal, the chairman of the Bering Strait Tunnel and Railroad Group, believes that it can be done. Mr Koumal is Czech-born, an international mining engineer and now an American citizen.

For him, it is the 'noble project. It completes Columbus's dream of going west to reach the Orient. It will make it possible to say again "Go west, young man".'

There is also an economic case. There are vast natural resources largely unexploited on both continents: four trillion tons of coal in northern Alaska, uncalculated reserves of gas, oil and mineral deposits in Siberia. The concept of a transcontinental railway might be romantic for passengers, but it is freight that will make it pay, linking middle America with the rapidly expanding economies of Asia and the Pacific Rim.

In this world, distances can be deceptive. It would be quicker and shorter to ship grain from Kansas to Bombay by rail than by the current sea routes. Suddenly the division of the world into East and West becomes almost meaningless. The great economies – Europe, Japan, America and, increasingly, China – are only a train ride away.

Will it happen, then? The Russians are keen, it is said, but have no money. One of the purposes of the London conference is to bring the US and Canadian governments on board. And Capitalism, in the form of the City's huge financial resources. The keynote speaker at the Savoy will be the respected political economist Lord Skidelsky.

Mr Koumal says the Bering Strait tunnel is 'a project whose time has come'. Perhaps it would be a fitting way to open the 21st century. Ten thousand years ago, North America is thought to have been populated by tribes from Asia who migrated across the frozen narrows. Among other things, George Koumal has a vision of a tide of retired American couples in their camper vans recolonising in the opposite direction. Somehow, despite the scale of the Bering Strait project, the world seems a smaller place.

TOKYO FAIRY TALE

A Japanese plan for a Tokyo-Berlin railway, to be built after the war, was described yesterday in a Tokyo broadcast. The locomotives would be driven by rockets and airscrews. Starting from a point on the Korean coast linked with Japan by a tunnel, the railway would cross Mongolia, Afghanistan, Persia and Iraq to link up with a German line from Berlin to Istanbul and Baghdad.

The fantastic nature of this plan is shown by the fact that the distance from the Korean coast to Japan is some 200 miles.

A MYSTERIOUS WORK OF GIANTS
IN MIDDLE ENGLAND

ONE MAN'S BRITAIN
BYRON ROGERS

Just 30 years, that is all it takes for a disused railway to become a place of mystery. Who built those blue-brick bridges and why? What is that embankment out in the fields; the green road leading nowhere? Any longer than 30 years, and our children, like Anglo-Saxons in Roman ruins, may start thinking of that great viaduct as 'the work of giants'.

So it is, in your area, and in yours. And so, until now, it was in mine – only here in Northamptonshire something that seems barely credible looks about to take place. They are going to open the Great Central again.

It was the last mainline railway in Britain, built exactly 100 years ago to connect Marylebone Station in London with Sheffield, up the middle of England. Barbara Castle closed it in 1966, when it was losing £900,000 a year. But now there is a company, Central Railway, about to lobby Parliament for permission to lay rails along the old route, and connect a Midlands lorry terminal with Europe through the Channel Tunnel. It will be a freight line only.

But if it comes, its impact will be most dramatic in rural Northamptonshire, where, when the Central was closed, a way of life came to an end so abruptly that old men who had told the time by the trains still found themselves listening for them years later.

In his classic story of village life, *A Countryman's Tale*, Syd Tyrrell wrote: 'Today, busy grubbing up weeds in the garden, I pricked up my ears and said to myself: "Why, that's a train on the branch line in the cutting." It was only a combine-harvester working in a field half a mile away.' What was so extraordinary was that Tyrrell, whose book came out in 1975, not only saw the closure but was old enough to remember the navvies building the Great Central: for once the story of a mainline railway was crammed into a man's lifetime, so this included not only the age of Brunel, but that of British Rail.

Huge, legendary men crowded his childhood memories, red kerchiefs round their necks, who caused chaos wherever they went. Labourers left the farms to join them, the contractors paying twice the agricultural wage, and such men, when the track was laid, did not return to the fields. It was the last little flicker of the Railway Age.

But even more extraordinary was the little railway town at Woodford Halse, left high and dry by the closure, with terraces of industrial housing, and 91 acres of marshalling yards; even now a sort of frontier exists between it and the surrounding countryside. One moment you are in a rural landscape, and the next moment you could be in the North of England.

In its decline, bizarre businesses rose and fell. In a small antique shop, I was once offered the full dress silk uniform of a mandarin of the Chinese Empire. 'Nine hundred pounds, and it's a bargain,' said the woman, who did not explain how she came by it. In a shed, I met a young man trying to set up a business that turned out chessmen based on participants in the Battle of Waterloo.

Both are long gone, and I imagine the old Roman towns must have been like this towards the end. The Great Central, its rails sold off years ago, became a footpath, people blackberrying in its cuttings, cows walking slowly home against the sky along the lofty viaduct. And so it still is.

But now it looks as though the trains will come again. The irony is that Edward Watkins, the man who built the Great Central, always intended it to connect with Europe through a tunnel. Nothing quite like this has happened before.

A LINE GOING NOWHERE

THE BR SELL-OFF IS THE LAST ACT OF A VANDALISM THAT HAS BEEN GOING ON FOR YEARS, SAYS **BYRON ROGERS**

The break-up of British Rail starts in earnest this month. All that is known for certain is that for most people it will be a matter of indifference; for who can mourn a transport system brought to a halt by leaves and the wrong kind of snow? I can. I mourn not what it is but what it might have been.

To know what British Rail is like today, look down from Carmarthen Bridge at the town's railway station. I remember it with four platforms, but now there is just one, a whole line of offices and waiting-rooms having been pulled down, so that the wind howls through a halt as bleak as anything on the Great Plains. Carmarthen station is administered from a Portakabin now. The Roman Empire at its end was like this: a town like Wroxeter having shrunk to a fraction of what it had been within the ruined walls, its main building a sort of timber Portakabin. Rome was a dream of Universal Empire, just as the railways were a dream of the Permanent Way.

In his book *The Great Railway Bazaar*, Paul Theroux records a conversation with a South Vietnamese station master. The man's country had been blown apart but, remarkably, he talked only of what would result were the line to Loc Ninh reopened. For then all you had to do was lay a rail to Phnom Penh, and South Vietnam would be linked to the world, because beyond Phnom Penh was Bangkok, and beyond Bangkok was India, and beyond India, Turkey. The station master had heard that there was a railway in Turkey, and beyond Turkey was Europe.

For him it was a dream of order. His bible would have been the *Thomas Cook International Rail Timetable*, one of the most civilised books published. Wars break out, and the words 'service temporarily suspended' appear among the tables, for today's battlefields always become departure points again; the compilers of this book stand outside history, guardians of world order.

Among the timetables are yesterday's lost worlds: the 06.55 for Puno arriving in Cuzco at 17.35; and – yesterday's gold rush – the morning train for the Yukon leaving Skagway at 10. But what you will not find here is a timetable for that doomed little railway, the Central Wales Line. When Matthew Engel of the *Guardian* recently wanted to travel on that line from Shrewsbury to Swansea, he tried Paddington first, then Swindon, and finally a whole succession of stations before getting the times from the Portakabin on Carmarthen station.

In front of me are the memoirs of Raymond Carr, now 87, a retired station master and the son of a station master. To join the LNER (London and North-Eastern Railway) in the 1920s, he not only had to sit tests in maths, English and spelling; he also had to draw from memory a map showing the routes of the other companies, and all the country towns, coalfields and main ports.

The railway was a way of life and had its own folklore. On duty in the parcels office at Leeds station, the night-shift porter and Mr Carr inspected a livestock box; this contained a large cat en route for a championship show. As the box was opened, the animal sprang out and vanished into the night. The two men, at their wits' end, substituted the station cat. It was a good-looking cat, and they often wondered how it had done at the show, for they heard nothing more.

Like all railwaymen of his generation, Raymond Carr saw this way of life fall apart. There were 83 stations in the part of the country where I now live, and now there are only eight. Forty years ago I could have caught a train from my village and been in London quicker than I can drive now. And this was a branch line.

Eccentrics bloomed along it – like the engine driver who kept a shotgun in his cab that he used to shoot at rabbits, stopping the train whenever he got one. There was another driver who every month applied to the Home Office for the post of public hangman. The plate-layers knew about this and built a gallows in a cutting, so that each time his train went by there was a dummy swinging, while in the cab a man gibbered with rage.

But it was the men in charge of the little stations who fascinated me – all that crenellated wood, the yellowing photographs of seaside resorts in the waiting-room, and the flowers hanging in boxes or dragooned in plots – petunias, lobelias, asters, marigolds.

The station master was near retirement when I met him, and was surrounded by his trophies: first prize for 'Best Station Garden', first prize for 'Cleanliness and Tidiness'. He had been there 50 years and had seen history from his station: the 1920s when the industrial working class came on Sundays to rediscover the country their grandparents had left, and he watched their pale faces and the impossibly large bunches of flowers they had picked. Europe came apart in the 1930s and he noticed a sudden boom in goods traffic. I returned to the station the year after he retired, and all the flowers were dead.

So who killed the railways? Who killed the system of transport that would have kept heavy lorries out of our villages, and cars from town centres? Who killed all that pride and way of life? You could say it was the spirit of nationalisation, which used to retire its workers thus: 'The British Transport Commission hereby gives you notice that your service with the Commission is terminated as at the 22nd day of February . . .' – this to a man with 50 years' service.

You can cite the cynicism and indifference of governments from both parties; you can mention Dr Beeching, whom I once saw open a private branch line at Buckfastleigh. 'If I hadn't closed this,' said this large, jolly man, 'none of you would be here today.' But it was none of them, really.

Politicians and officials just lent their names to a process already under way. We killed the railways, you and I. In his memoirs Raymond Carr says he found that people who were protesting against the closure of branch lines had never used them. The local Women's Institute signed a petition against the closure of the Scarborough-to-Whitby line, but of the 30 signatories only three had made journeys more than once a year. At a meeting in Northallerton to discuss a branch-line closure, those attending were asked how they had come. Not one had come by rail.

But to use the railways was to accept all sorts of lunacy that were perpetrated upon us. We did not object to the disappearance of the compartments in which people had met and talked, and the open-plan carriages came, in which no man over six feet can sit in comfort. We did not object when the automatic doors came, which reduced us to so much travelling freight (on Network SouthEast this was supposed to be accompanied by the redundancy of train guards, but when the new doors came, the guards operated them). It was clear that the people running this transport system had long ago lost all pride in it, and we walked away from our birthright.

The result is that a mystery has come to the countryside. Our children do not know what these earth embankments are, or the viaduct that goes nowhere now but still dominates the valley, or all those bridges built so perfectly in blue brick. We pass them without a glance, for we know what they are, and are guilty that they are the remains of a railway system that once went everywhere.

The cruellest irony about the break-up is the timing, for it takes place on the eve of something so extraordinary that no one ever thought to see it in his lifetime. This year the rail link with the Continent will come, so it really will be the Permanent Way; but where in Britain will it go, and for how much longer?

ROAD TO RAIL

Sir — I find it ironic, given Byron Rogers's article ('A line going nowhere', April 3), that your spread in the Review section about the North Yorkshire Moors Railway and the railway museum at Darlington mentions only road access to these places.

B Land
Redcar, Cleveland

ENGINE DRIVER AGAIN IDOL OF SCHOOLBOYS

By **R H GREENFIELD**

Suddenly, small boys seem to want to be engine drivers again. Last week I found a group at Platform 8, Paddington, waiting to see the Great Man. One was taking a photograph of the locomotive.

The cause of all this excitement is British Rail's new HST (High-Speed Train), just introduced on the London-Bristol run. It is still running experimentally as a FHST (Fairly-High-Speed Train) working to normal timetables, hence the lack of publicity. It is not due to reach its intended 125mph till next month when, given agreement on manning by the locomen's union, it will cut 15 minutes off the journey to Bristol and 23 off that to Cardiff.

A trip on the 'Inter-City 125' is exhilarating. To get the full value you should travel, as I did, in the company of a railway expert such as David Hawkins, 12, of Hayling, Sussex, making his first run in the new train. We went forward to the front locomotive, a great streamlined beast with a projecting jaw like a diesel-electric Bob Hope. There the Great Man himself, the driver, Mr Sid White, took us into the aircraft-like cab and explained the workings of the mighty Paxman Valenta 12-cylinder, 2,250hp diesel-electric engine.

There are two power cars, front and back, their controls linked electronically to give a total power output of 4,500hp. The train has reached 143mph, a world record for a diesel-electric. 'It's a wonderful machine,' said Mr White, a stocky Somerset man who has been on the railways for 37 years.

For the passengers, all this technical wizardry manifests itself in air-cushioned suspension, full air-conditioning in every carriage and electrically operated automatic doors between the carriages. While one cannot actually balance a coin on its edge as the train zips through Didcot, the ride is a revelation to a refugee from the bone-shaking suburban cattle trucks of Southern Region. In my reclining seat I was able to do the crossword in blissful comfort. In the smart new buffet car I enjoyed a pint of draught bitter without spilling a drop.

When British Rail gets a proper kitchen/restaurant-car into service, a 125mph lunch beside the verdant banks of the Thames will be a memorable experience. At present, subduing a muscular gammon steak on a flimsy plastic tray with flexible plastic cutlery rather detracts from the luxury image.

TRAINS STILL CONTAIN THE ROMANCE OF TRAVEL, UNLESS YOU HAVE TO STAND THE WHOLE WAY

SAYS **SANDI TOKSVIG**

In 1895, when Auguste Lumière and his younger brother Louis (who died on this day in 1948) showed their one-minute film of a steam train arriving at a French station, urban legend has it that the audience panicked and ran out of the theatre. It was not siderodromophobia, or fear of trains and train travel (possibly from the Greek sideros – iron – and dromos – a racecourse), that caused the exodus, but the shock of the new medium showing a train approaching.

No doubt, as with the suggestion of refreshments being readily available on a train of today, the story has been exaggerated. I don't know if I would have panicked for I love trains and always approach the platform with misplaced enthusiasm. The other morning, I caught a commuter service from the seaside in Kent. I was not alone in thinking this was a good plan and the platform was strewn with those who were putting thoughts of oysters behind them and heading to make a crust in the city. The passengers were not at all like the Lumière audience, for they were calm as the train approached and they remained calm, which was surprising as many of them stood all the way to London.

It cannot have been an uncommon occurrence that people had gathered at that hour with the intention of travel, and I was reminded of a remark of W S Gilbert: 'Sir, Sunday morning, although recurring at regular and well foreseen intervals, always seems to take this railway by surprise.' I was en route from Whitstable, where the notion of commuting can't have been a surprise as it is where the idea first began. The Canterbury and Whitstable Railway, nicknamed the Crab and Winkle Line, opened in 1830 and in 1834 produced the world's first season ticket ferrying Canterbury workers to the sea. The line was only

10 miles long, but it rather marvellously required three stationary engines, several horses and a single locomotive to do so.

It also gloried in an unusually narrow tunnel. Apparently the committee who planned the line were appalled when the surveyor told them no tunnel was necessary as 'the line is practically level'. The committee insisted that they wanted to have a tunnel and so they got the railway's Rocket Man, George Stephenson, to create an alternative route that was 'undulating enough and picturesque enough to please anyone who did not mind paying for it' and which 'contained everything no complete railroad should be without'.

Of course a good train journey ought to include a tunnel. There is a wonderful story of George Bernard Shaw finding himself sharing a compartment with two rather prim middle-aged women who did not know him or each other. Silence reigned as the train chugged on until they passed through a tunnel and the compartment descended into darkness. Shaw immediately began loudly kissing the back of his hand. As the train re-emerged into the light the great playwright turned to his companions and inquired: 'To which of you charming ladies am I indebted for the delightful interlude in the tunnel?'

It was today in 1833 that Andrew Jackson became the first American president to ride on a railway train. He rode 12 miles on a Baltimore-and-Ohio train from Ellicott's Mill, Maryland, to the city of Baltimore. I have no idea what he thought of the trip, but as he was also the first president to be born in a log cabin he probably didn't have a high benchmark for service. I hope he was excited, for as E M Forster rightly declared: 'Railway termini are our gates to the glorious and the unknown. Through them we pass out into adventure and sunshine . . .' Last month, after a 60-year gap, the service between Bishop Auckland and Stanhope in County Durham reopened. It won't amaze you that it took volunteers to help get the thing going or that they had to build a new platform for the service after Northern Rail and the rail regulators couldn't agree about using the actual station. Nevertheless, for £5.50 you can once more travel through 16 miles of rolling countryside, passing villages that glory in names such as Witton-le-Wear.

With such enterprise to hearten the soul of a railway enthusiast, I refuse to be downhearted. It was the train that came through for us during the Iceland ash. It is the train that still carries the romance of travel, although I don't suppose we shall ever quite have the glamour of the past.

Years ago I worked with Evelyn Laye (born next month in 1900). I was 23 at the time and each evening after the show was commanded to her dressing room, where the still glamorous actress would dispense anecdotes and champagne in equal measure. She told me about touring the United States by train in the 1930s with Noel Coward. Each of the stars had his or her own railway carriage with name emblazoned on the side, which lit up as they passed through stations. That is glamour. That would be wonderful. Failing that, of course, a little actual beef in the Euston-to-Preston beef sandwiches would be nice.

A VIRTUAL STEPPE TOO FAR

LEADING ARTICLE

If you haven't yet booked a holiday, consider a 5,600-mile trip on the Trans-Siberian Railway. It's cheap – or it is if you travel by the newly available virtual route from Google. The experience is the opposite to the old interlude film of London to Brighton in four minutes. On this trip, you stare from the window for 150 hours, and it never seems to grow dark. True, no homely lady serves tea from a samovar, unless you have one at home, but you can hear the wheels' dum-de-dum, or if that palls, listen to an audiobook of *War and Peace*.

We confess we have not yet had a spare seven days for the whole journey, but we did sample highlights. After 1,200 miles, we're in Yekaterinburg, where the poor Tsar and his family were murdered. But there's not much to see except for sidings, and it looks like rain. Off we go. At last, the Ob, and over a wide bridge, Omsk. After 58 hours, there's a chance to stretch our legs at Krasnoyarsk, home of the amusing Monument to a Drunkard – a steam-driven hourglass – at Lovers' Square. See how the drunkard falls down!

Lake Baikal really is big, 395 miles long, and the train runs along the shore, rather as at Dawlish. The clouds break above the immense Zeisko-Bureinskaya plain . . . We must have dozed off, but we're still in the immense Zeisko-Bureinskaya plain. It's very soothing.

We've made it! We're drawing into Vladivostok.

Goodness, it looks a little like Croydon.

CHAPTER 9
STRANGERS (AND LOVERS) ON A TRAIN

---

14 DECEMBER 2002

RAIL LIFE AND THE MOVIES

TRAVELLING ACROSS AMERICA BY TRAIN, **JENNY DISKI**
WAS STRUCK BY THE FAMILIARITY OF IT ALL, BUT THEN
SHE'D SEEN IT BEFORE – IN THE CINEMA AS A CHILD

To travel any but the shortest distance by train is bizarre to most people in the United States. Why take three days to cross the country when you can do it in three hours by plane? A glossy American fashion magazine thought it so quaint that they commissioned me to write an article describing the journey I was about to make. When I returned to the UK I emailed the copy, and then got a call from the features editor. It was fine, but could I cut some of the stuff about the train and my fellow travellers and put in more landscape and scenery?

I did, of course, see a lot of landscape. I watched America go by inch by inch, staring for hours at a time out of the observation cars or the window of my sleeping compartments. My suitcase was weighted down with the books I had brought to read, but I didn't complete a single chapter while on the move because I couldn't keep my eyes on a page of print when every kind of the most extreme and extraordinary, changing and changeless landscape was rolling past my eyes. I often wished the train were slower so that I could examine the bayous, the rivers, the grasslands, the mountains and deserts in more detail.

But it became clear to me that the passage of landscape before my eyes was in itself a particular way of viewing the country. At any rate, a particular way of being in the country. Everyone knows the pleasure, even on the shortest train journeys, of staring out at the world that goes by beyond the viewer's control, to the accompaniment of the rhythm of the wheels on the rails and the swaying of the carriage. Hypnotic, the landscape forever approaching and passing, skimming along, the eye snatching a detail, noticing a cloud, a bizarre building, a blasted tree, a startled creature, but not being able to hold on to it as the view rolls by.

Our thought processes work more slowly than the speed of a train or the eye. There's as much relief as frustration in that. Thoughts can exist independently of what the eye is taking in; they can be allowed to take care of themselves. Alternatively, you can read a book or open your laptop and ignore the whole thing while you get from A to B. I, at any rate, couldn't tear myself away from the passing parade of America, and I let my thoughts do what they would.

Passive watching is an intense and private activity. It leaves a residue. The eyes look and take in the fleeting images, absorb them into the processor inside the head, which transforms them into a memory: the recollection of a split-second gone by that will become a memory of something seen yesterday, a week ago, a decade past, somewhere back in the mists of time. The flashing pictures remain, but they settle in beside other related images. And most of the related images are in Technicolor and wide-screen.

Was that image, that memory, from the train journey or a movie you once saw? American landscape is known, as speeches in Shakespeare's plays or phrases in the King James Bible are known. They are already read, so that when you come across them in their proper context they jar and falsify the moment.

In the auditorium, Macbeth's nihilism and despair are weakened as you overtake the actor in his assessment of life as full of sound and fury, signifying nothing. On the page 'In the beginning God created the heavens and the earth' slips by in a far too familiar rhythm, so you forget to wonder: what beginning? Created from what? Why? And as you actually pass through the boundless grasslands of Montana, or deserts of Arizona and New Mexico, a thousand Westerns complete with their wide-open background scores rush to clog the mind: *The Big Country, The Searchers, Stagecoach, The Man Who Shot Liberty Valance, Wagon Train, Red River* and, of course, *Blazing Saddles.*

John Wayne, Henry Fonda, Ward Bond, James Stewart, Montgomery Clift stride or lope into view and people the empty vista outside the window, filling it with human endeavour. There's a stored image for every inch of the landscape passing by. Gunslingers on galloping horses kick up the dust getting out of town fast ahead of the posse, cowboys bed down by the campfire, guns at the ready beneath the saddle under their head, ranchers locked in sullen, greedy conflict with immigrant farmers plan violent evictions, wagon trains full of pilgrims in search of a new life and the odd run-out-of-town whore circle as the Indians charge down from the hills to attack the intruders, the lonely hero walks away westward from the danger of being included in the civil society he has helped to bring about.

Each image comes complete with its own landscape. Every landscape comes with its own set of meaningful images, seen already in darkened cinemas and on television. We know the landscape of America, even if we have never been there. We've inhabited it, even if we've never set foot outside London, Delhi or Helsinki.

But what do I do with all this view? I can attempt to describe what the eye catches, and try to nail down the strobing images in an approximation of words. So. The sky is vast and vacuously blue, the empty deserts at sunset threaten the spirit with their scrubby grey-green dying light, the rivers wind from bare trickles in parched earth to thunderous rushing torrents, the canyons dismay and dizzy you as you stare down into them and try to make out the bottom, the mountains loom in anthropomorphic shapes of things seen best in dreams, the grasslands and wheatfields wave like an endless syrupy ocean tickled into motion by the breeze. You know, you've seen it in the movies.

What is remarkable, what is strange about passing through America, peering at it through the screen of the train window, is that everything is familiar. It is much more as if America is passing through you, what you are, what you've known.

Sitting there looking out at the landscape is like having a dye injected so that the tendrils of memory in the brain light up and trace the private history of your mind. As I sit and watch the weird rock formations, sagebrush, cactus and Joshua trees of the desert land go by, the cinema in Tottenham Court Road where I saw my first shootouts jumps vividly into my present. The smell and plush of the carpet underfoot comes flooding back to me, the tense anticipation as the lights begin to fade, the solid dark presence of my father sitting beside me, the blue smoke from his cigarette curling up into the bright beam on its way to the screen, which will light up with dreams and places and complexities of human joy and trouble that my striving six-year-old brain can barely imagine, let alone make sense of. That's what the landscape of America is like.

On sunny days in mid-1950s London, I went to Russell Square and played cowboys and Indians on a landscaped hill with a tarmacked path cut through it like a perfect canyon. When it rained, I went with my friend to the Egyptian Gallery of the British Museum and we played my favourite game. Surrounded by monumental stone fragments — an icy-smooth foot bigger than a bathtub, a marbled sinewy arm extending to a closed fist as broad as the front of a bus — we would sit on a bench intended for weary or thoughtful culture-seekers and pretend in loud voices and almost certainly execrable accents to be American children on holiday — no, vacation.

With our voluminous knowledge based on the films and television we had seen, we discussed the incredibly luxurious and automated homes we had left behind, what we thought of little England (cute, very cute), the contents of our wardrobes (bobby socks, real denim jeans) and the shimmering stars who dropped in regularly for tea. We could think of nothing more glamorous to be, nowhere more extraordinary and magical to persuade people we were from, while genuine American tourists — more crisp and matronly than glamorous — passed by smiling at our unconvincing twang and improbable fantasies. That is what the landscape of America is like: being a child in 1950s London.

But there is another way of looking at the journey. The fact is, I am not in any of the places the train passes through, I am on the train. That is my place, that is the real landscape. The extraordinary thing is not the difficulty of knowing what I am experiencing as I look through the window, but that my real landscape is filled with strangers who are thrown together by the accident of travel and who, because of being human, or American, or not English, or not me, are busily making themselves known to each other before they go their separate ways.

Just because we all happen to be going in the same direction, an 'us' has been formed. And I discover that however much I wish to justify my private daydreaming and pleasurable alienation with thoughts of the difficulty of having the experience of what has been already experienced, this random collection of strangers has become a group to which I belong, here and now and unavoidably.

And I discover I don't want to avoid participating in this group. Not that I could if I want to smoke or eat or drink or see the landscape through the big picture windows in the viewing car. But I am enjoying being a stranger among strangers on a train making contact with other strangers.

Of course, that movie has been made, too. The American dream or nightmare journey is as known as the dream landscape. But the people on the train are undeniably of my present as well as echoing my past. The bonding is fast. We do begin to look suspiciously at newcomers entering the smoking coach after the previous stop, feeling all the more like an us as these new strangers arrive. But soon they are regulars, assimilated, and they look askance at the next strangers to our group who enter our space. We are evidently a group to the outside world.

People who do not smoke look curiously through the glass of the door as they pass by. Enviously, even. One woman braves the fug, opens the door, coughs, blinks and says to us all, 'I wish I smoked. You all look as if you're having so much fun.'

We know we are a temporary agglomeration, a group whose elements are always leaving, arriving, re-forming, but I have the oddest, and rarest, sense of belonging in this smoking coach and more generally on the train. A kind of clarity of what kind of creature I might be that usually eludes me.

I see myself reflected in the company of these people who know nothing about me, and who will never think about me again once they have got back to their real lives. I sense I am seen. It may be true (it feels true to me) that only by being alone can I experience myself fully, but being a stranger on a train – at least for a little while – gives me a view of myself here and now, and of others, now and then, which, sitting solitary and staring, I rarely achieve.

CARRIED SIDEWAYS THROUGH THE NIGHT

IN A CHAPTER FROM *THE DOG WHO CAME IN FROM THE COLD*, AN ONLINE NOVELLA BY **ALEXANDER McCALL SMITH**, BARBARA AND HUGH DODGE DRUNKEN FOOTBALL FANS IN READINESS FOR THE LONDON-TO-EDINBURGH SLEEPER

'That's our sleeper train,' said Hugh, pointing along the platform. 'See it?' Barbara Ragg nodded, momentarily distracted by the sight of a group of staggering football fans being searched by a contingent of transport police before they were allowed on the platform. The search was being conducted in good spirits, it seemed, even though it was proving productive. At the side of the concourse was steadily growing a motley pile of bottles and cans, taken off the fans by the police. Barbara did not want to stare, but found it difficult to tear her gaze away. For a moment she was consumed with shame; where else in Western Europe could such sights be seen? Where else was public drunkenness so manifest? On the streets and in the cafés of France? She thought not; such places always had a light, civilised air, even if the statistics showed that the French consumed vast lakes of wine. But they drank it with food, while engaged in pleasant conversation, not like this. Nor, she imagined, did they have mobs of drunken young women, screeching hen parties, tottering in high heels and short skirts from bar to bar, fuelled by sweetened vodka concoctions.

And in Germany? The Germans got drunk at beer festivals, in large tents, to the strains of oompah music – again, all very different from this. And yet if you said anything about it to anybody, they merely shrugged, or smiled at you as if to imply that you were some sort of killjoy.

Hugh did not appear to have noticed.

Perhaps, being Scottish, he was inured to such sights. 'I like sleepers,' he said as they made their way down the platform. 'Do you?' 'I don't really think very much about them,' she said.

Hugh quoted Norman McCaig. 'There's a Scottish poet,' he said. 'He wrote a poem about the Edinburgh-to-London sleeper. He said something about not liking being carried sideways through the night. That's such a powerful image, isn't it? Being carried sideways through the night.'

Barbara agreed. 'Sometimes,' she said, 'when I look up and see an aeroplane overhead, I think of all the people in it. All those people being carried in the sitting position through the air. If you just took the outer skin of metal away, imagine what it would look like. Rows of people shooting through the air.'

Hugh smiled. 'Yes, very odd. I think I probably prefer being carried sideways through the night to being carried through the air like that. One is less of a hostage to fortune when one is only a few feet off the ground, don't you think, rather than, what is it, four miles above it?'

Trains were normally of little interest to Barbara, except as a means of getting from place to place, but this one was different. At first, it seemed to her that it had no windows, a sealed train, of the sort in which Lenin travelled from Switzerland to Russia; then she saw that there were windows, but ones rendered opaque by drawn blinds.

'I can hardly remember when I last took a sleeper train,' she said. 'As a teenager I did some travelling on the continent. We were in a wagon-lit, I think.' It was a hazy recollection: a vague memory of sounds, of being rocked through the night on the way down to Italy; the slightly acrid smell of sleeper carriages, a smell redolent of batteries and stuffiness, and slightly sour milk.

'I want to go on the Orient Express one day,' said Hugh as they neared their carriage. 'To Istanbul. I've always wanted to. It's such a romantic idea, isn't it?' 'I suppose so,' said Barbara. 'Shall we do it?' asked Hugh. 'Should I book?' She laughed. 'Perhaps.' He had started to say 'we' now, quite frequently, and she was still getting used to it. It touched her. Oedipus Snark had never said we; her life with him had never been a shared one. With Oedipus, it was always I.

They boarded. A diminutive woman with a strong Glaswegian accent showed them to their compartments, two single-bed cabins with a communicating door between. For a moment Barbara felt a twinge of disappointment, but then asked herself what she had expected. Sleepers did not have double bunks, of course, because that was not the point of a sleeper. You were meant to sleep when on a sleeper – as the name suggested.

The woman took their order for morning tea, which would be served just before they drew in to Glasgow. Then it would be on to Fort William, arriving shortly after 10. Then, with a smile, she left them.

Barbara put her case on the rack and raised the window blind, catching sight of her blurred reflection in the blank glass of the window. I am on a train with my fiancé, she thought. I am going to Scotland. I am with the most beautiful man I have ever met – yes, he really is that – and it is I, Barbara Ragg, who has him.

It was an unexpected thought, a form of stocktaking in which we all engage from time to time. We contemplate our situation and say to ourselves, 'Here am I, doing this; me, of all people, doing this – who would have thought?' We ask ourselves how we got what we have got and why Nemesis does not yet appear to have noticed. It is not a matter of desert. It was not that now, at least in Barbara's case; for her it was more of a feeling of wonder that it had happened at all. It had not been in her script. It was not meant to be like this.

She turned around. Hugh was standing behind her.

'My darling, beautiful, wonderful Barbie,' he whispered.

The first part of this was fine; the latter not quite. He had never called her Barbie before. She made light of it. 'Barbie™?' He put his arms around her. 'Barbie. Well, it's short for Barbara, isn't it?' 'Yes. But . . . but do you know who Barbie™ is?' Hugh looked puzzled. He planted a kiss on her brow.

He was wearing some sort of cologne; there was the scent of sandalwood. 'No.'

'She's a doll.' Hugh smiled. 'I knew somebody who called his girlfriend "doll". She seemed to like it. She was one of those blondes, you know, not a great intellectual. Doll seemed to suit her.'

The train gave a sudden shudder. 'We're on our way,' said Hugh. Then he whispered, 'To be in love and to be on the sleeper. Bliss.'

Barbara closed her eyes. 'Oh, Hugh . . .' And then she thought: Barbie. Few mistakes were genuinely without meaning – Professor

Freud had told us that, and the lesson still stood. So was Barbie Barbie™ or another Barbie? Or even her? Or was she Barbie™? It was enough to confuse even a semiotician.

'I have a surprise for you,' said Hugh.

THE OTHER ME: CHRIS'S VERY INTERESTING HOBBY

ED MARRIOTT FINDS THAT THE EDITOR OF *VIZ* IS A LIFELONG TRAIN-SPOTTER

Long before Chris Donald made his fortune as creator of the Fat Slags, Sid the Sexist and Felix and his Amazing Underpants, he was 'copping' trains, ticking them off in his book of train numbers. The editor of the adult comic *Viz* has come a long way from the house above the railway line in Jesmond where he grew up. But, BMW and holidays in the West Indies notwithstanding, his heart remains in the railway sidings.

He lives in a former station; in his drive sits a guard's van. On every door are enamel plaques saying 'ticket office' or 'waiting room'. On the walls hang black-and-white prints of steam engines. Once a train-spotter, it seems, always a train-spotter.

It began as a childhood disease that involved looking at old railway stations, says Donald, now 32. 'If the station was open I wasn't interested in it. It had to be closed and falling to bits. Whenever we went on picnics I'd be in the back of the car with my Ordnance Survey map of old railway lines begging my dad to stop.'

By the age of 12, Donald was afflicted with the full-blown train-spotting virus, largely the result of peer pressure. 'When we first moved to Jesmond I was the only one of my friends who wasn't a train-spotter. I didn't want to be the odd one out, so I became one too. I never felt embarrassed about it. We did it for all the right reasons. Anyway, ours was an elite group of train-spotters. We didn't talk to the others because they all had social inadequacies.'

Train-spotting, however, ended when he was 16 and for 10 years his passion for trains remained squirrelled away. During those wilderness years there were few kindred spirits, although occasionally he would come across people who would find out he was interested in trains. 'Out of the blue they'd start making train noises at me.'

In 1989, he felt he had shelved his love affair long enough. Deciding it was time to move out of Newcastle with his wife and two young children, he placed a wanted advertisement in a local newspaper for a railway station and spent the next few months touring the countryside before finding the right one. He would rather the name was not printed because 'train-spotters are funny folk. If it got out where I live they might come down here and swipe all the stuff I've been collecting. It's highly desirable, if you know what you're looking for.'

Suffice it to say that the station nestles in hills not far from Berwick-upon-Tweed, on a branch line that was closed in 1965 after a career that could generously be described as sedate. Donald estimates that the line stopped carrying passengers in the 1930s, and bore cattle and grain for its final years.

Donald is the third occupant of the station since 1965, and the first to take a real interest. At the moment he is restoring the verandah that ran along the back of the building. Being a former railway station, the house is long and thin – about 150ft by 30ft. Behind it is a lawn, where once the rails ran. The track will remain buried.

Since he moved in he has met a few fellow train fans. 'Jools Holland [the musician and television presenter] has a station. We met a few weeks ago and he enthusiastically noted down my address. We weren't in when he was up here last time but we'll meet up one day and exchange interesting train stories.'

The house takes up most of Donald's spare time. He has just bought a metal detector, hoping to turn railway archaeologist. So far all he has found is a pram. When he has finished decorating the house he will start work on his studio. It will be a replica of the original signal box and will be built on its foundations. This will bring Donald halfway to living out his *Railway Children* fantasy – as a signalman in a sleepy country station. 'It would be fantastic – me and Jenny Agutter.'

In reality, however, he understands that life on the railways might be a little more prosaic. 'I once met a signalman. He said it was the most boring job in the world. He ran away and joined a rock band. You imagine railway people to be all cosy and enjoying their work, like Bernard Cribbins. But take a look in my guard's van. It's covered in graffiti inside – all the guards calling each other bastards.'

Donald says his wife, Dolores, 'likes the house, but she couldn't care less that it was once a train station'. She is relaxed about his extravagances. 'Three months ago I bought a train. I asked Dolores what she thought. She just said, "Go on then." So I bought it, for about the same price as a family car. I will bring it back here and put it in the garden. I know I should look after it, but I like rusty things. I go on holiday and take photographs of rusty things lying in the grass. I'm looking forward to seeing it turn into a flower bed.'

If Donald had had his way, he would have been a train driver. *Viz* fans should thank his careers adviser, who dissuaded him. 'She shook her head and said, "You'll need A-levels in Maths and Physics and then you'll have to study engineering at university." I was gobsmacked. I'd seen train drivers and I knew they didn't have degrees in engineering.'

Shorn of this idea, Donald left school with undistinguished A-level results and started *Viz* with his 'baby brother', Simon. The first few issues cost £60 to produce. Now it sells one million a month.

Trains have made only a fleeting appearance in *Viz*, in the form of Timothy Potter the Train-Spotter. 'The joke was that he was short-sighted. He would go into newsagents and mistake the checkout for a train.' Perhaps it was too close to the bone. Timothy Potter never lived to see another issue.

Donald avoids questions about the future. Will he ever tire of *Viz*? 'I'm bored already.' While he continues to edit the comic, he daydreams wildly. One idea is to start a high-class pornographic magazine. 'It would have a scientific typeface and would have no pretensions to being a men's magazine about cars. It would be a scientific publication for people with a medical need. Our publisher, John Brown, isn't too happy about the idea. I don't think his wife approves. Failing that, I would like to write a book about converted train stations in Northumberland. Or I could write a column on train-spotting for a Sunday newspaper. It would sell a lot of copies, you mark my words.'

GOING MY WAY?

ANTHONY PEREGRINE, ON A TRAIN TRIP
ALONG THE ROUTE NAPOLÉON, MEETS A LADY
IN NEED OF COMPANY

'You seem to be a nice man.' I smiled. When you look like I do, you take compliments where you can. This one came on the train from Fontainebleau to Paris, courtesy of an older lady on the seat opposite. In a belted raincoat and sensible woollen hat, she was the sort of woman you see peering closely at things in museums, or sitting quietly in the salon-de-thé.

We got talking – which, if you are familiar with trains, you will know is neither common nor generally desirable. But she seemed nice, too. 'What were you doing in Fontainebleau?' she asked.

I had been alone for nine days and had hardly talked at all. Now I talked far too much. What I'd been doing in Fontainebleau was rounding off a railway trip along the Route Napoléon, the one Bonaparte took on his escape from exile in Elba. He had been intent on marching up France to re-establish himself as emperor. I had been intent on following him by public transport.

'Why?' asked the lady (we'll call her Marthe). 'Because that's the sort of thing I'm paid to do,' I said. 'Some reporters dodge gunfire in the Middle East. Others ride trains through France.' It had been an excellent trip, too – perhaps the finest way of getting from the charged light of the Mediterranean to the softer greys and greens of Burgundy and beyond.

As I didn't need to tell Marthe – she knew her stuff – Napoleon had stepped ashore at Golfe Juan in March 1815. With 1,200 men, he was aiming to recapture Paris and power, from both of which he had been chased the year before. Thus started the Hundred Days. First, though, he nipped five miles down the coast. 'We will march on Cannes!' he cried. This was like marching on Lytham-St-Annes. Cannes has never resisted much, and didn't in 1815.

After an overnight stay, the Emperor and I, a couple of centuries apart, set off for Grasse . . . in my case, a 35-minute bus ride, there being no train service. The bus was packed, so I entered the capital of French perfume squashed up against the fattest woman in Provence. My stop came before hers. Disembarking involved mountaineering more intimate than either she or I appreciated.

Grasse was a delight – sweet-smelling and beautiful, with skirts of trees and flower-fields, and a tight-packed centre of secret places. The town's perfume museum had 19th-century fragrance dispensers in the shape of little boys having a pee. 'My grandmother had one of those,' said Marthe. 'But it was for herbal tea.'

From Grasse, Napoleon moved upwards into Haute Provence, relying on mules. I settled back into another bus (still no trains) for the three-hour trip to Sisteron. Here were real, rocky mountains, which the driver tackled as if party to a suicide pact. It was with relief that we came upon sudden, straggling hamlets before surging off towards another precipice.

In these remote regions, Napoleon had halted at an auberge and ordered an omelette. He had been mighty surprised by the price. 'Are eggs scarce round here, then?' he asked. 'No,' said the aubergiste, 'But emperors are.' Marthe echoed the response as I gave it. I thought I'd dug up a telling anecdote, but it was a well-worn piece of Napoleonic folklore.

Sisteron perches at that point where, alongside the Durance river, Provence squeezes itself into the Dauphiné through a gap between sentinel rocks. It worried Napoleon. If royalist opponents of his return had blown the river bridge, he would have been stuck. But they hadn't. Neither, incidentally, did US bombers in August 1944 when trying to cut off the German retreat. In the attempt, they killed 300 villagers.

The locals are, though, used to battling. Perched on one of the huge rocks is Provence's final, finest citadel. From the top, and given a couple of chums, you could hold off the North Korean army. Down below, the town is so tight, the streets so narrow that you're effectively edging through the population's domestic life.

All these rocks, of course, mean rock climbing. On the train the next day, I sat behind a Californian chap with his leg in plaster from thigh to toe. 'Fell off the second day,' he said. Across the aisle, his wife smiled indulgently, which was sweet of her. This was, after all, their honeymoon.

Moving on to Grenoble, Napoleon single-handedly faced down an entire royalist army. Having persuaded them to his side, he entered the city in triumph. I entered on the 10.45 a.m. from Sisteron. Grenoble being the Gateway to the Alps, I took the cable car from the town centre, across the Isère river and up the nearest mini-Alp. I wanted an idea of what the city looked like from on high. What I actually got was an idea of what it is like to go into outer space in a Christmas tree bauble.

At an inconveniently huge distance from the earth's surface, the contraption paused for something like a couple of hours to change gear. I knew for certain that we were in a disaster movie remake and that I'd have to climb out and edge back down the cable, hand over hand, with my neighbour and at least three of her children on my back. Then it started moving again – but I still preferred Grenoble from ground level. It is airy, open and cultured, with trams and boulevards. The influence of the Alps is omnipresent. Indeed, it is just the sort of city that would go skiing, if that were the sort of thing cities did.

Napoleon stayed over in Grenoble, regrouping, recruiting, planning his onward progress and firing off irritable notes to his treacherous second wife, Marie-Louise. ('Faithless trollop,' said Marthe, with conviction, when M-L's name cropped up.) Then he moved on to Lyon. I caught a train and followed, but couldn't face France's second city – too big, too much altogether. So I caught another to Villefranche-sur-Saône, the economic capital of the Beaujolais region, where the emperor had had lunch.

This wasn't such a smart idea – my stopping, I mean, not Bonaparte's lunch. Like Rochdale, Villefranche is certainly loved by those who live there but neither expects visitors nor knows what to do with them if they should arrive. It has, however, conserved a vigorous French attitude to breakfast. Sneaking down to my hotel's café/bar at 6.45 a.m., I burst in upon a smoke-filled scrum of *la France profonde* stoking up for the working day on wine, beer and brandy.

I am easily led – and so, a little later, slept as my train tracked the Saône into the plump farmland of Burgundy, awakening for Mâcon and again for Chalon-sur-Saône, two riverside towns that were almost certainly as well-fed and prosperous in 1815 as they are today. In the place-St-Vincent, Chalon has all urban Burgundy distilled into one square – steep and uneven grey roofs, eyrie windows, half-timbered façades and portly folk studying vintages in the wine-shop window. There never seems any good reason to stop eating and drinking in Burgundy so, in my experience, people don't.

The route now darted west, through the Mercurey vineyards, to Autun. This was a town with resonance for Napoleon: he had been at military college there 30 years earlier. It's a good, unsung place for the rest of us, too. ('I've never been,' said Marthe. 'You should go,' I said. 'Do you know how to make the number 20 using just French town names?' she asked. 'No,' I said. 'Sète Foix Troyes Autun,' she said.)

On the fringe of the Morvan granite uplands, Autun has ramparts, city gates and large chunks of a 12,000-seater Roman theatre, from the time it was Augustodunum. Up in the Romanesque cathedral, what is left of St Lazarus is crammed into a cask in a side-chapel. By the look of him, I fear he's not going to be rising a second time.

This bit of Burgundy is also home to Charolais cattle – difficult to meet in town centres. So I hired a bike and was soon rolling through pasture-land where the broad white cows looked as serene and replete as everyone else in the region. Pausing on a little hump-backed bridge, I thought for a moment that I was in rural north Lancashire and might stop and stay forever.

But I had a train to catch . . . in the wake of Napoleon, to Saulieu. A pleasant enough little town etched along the Route Nationale 6, Saulieu had the great good fortune to be half-way between Paris and Lyon in the pre-motorway days when much traffic south took the RN6. It became the gourmet stop-over. With a population of fewer than 3,000, it still has a dozen or more restaurants – prime among them La Côte-d'Or, which has three Michelin stars and charges more for a meal than the common man can easily pay.

I ate elsewhere and then hurried to the St Andoche basilica, where the town's English-language leaflet promised that, among the exceptional collection of column-topping capitals, was one entitled

'The Bear's Fart'. In the event, the work featured two indeterminate beasts – perhaps bears or wolves or even lions – on their back legs and, I think, fighting rather than farting. Much less disappointing was the work of the local-born sculptor François Pompon, a friend of Rodin. His signature animal sculptures combined roundness and amplitude with power and grace. There was a fantastic bull in bronze outside the basilica – and a museum full of his works nearby (though his finest piece, a polar bear, is in the Musée-d'Orsay in Paris).

By the time Napoleon reached Saulieu, Paris was panic-stricken. Louis XVIII – placed on the throne by the European powers who had earlier defeated Bonaparte – was preparing to flee. By the time Napoleon reached Fontainebleau, Louis had indeed flown, for Ghent. The royalist cause was (temporarily) lost. Napoleon had thus completed a triumphant round trip, back to the château from which he had left for exile almost exactly a year earlier. To the north, the capital was open and waiting.

By the time I arrived at Fontainebleau, it was mid-afternoon and raining. The château – preferred by Napoleon to Versailles – loomed across the enormous park. In one set of buildings, it seemed to sum up the complex, decorative and fragile grandeur of French history. I paused to ponder this on the horseshoe staircase in the main Cours-d'Adieu – and stayed motionless a touch too long. The end of my journey would thus be recorded in at least half-a-dozen Japanese photo albums.

'They do like taking photographs, don't they, the Japanese?' said Marthe. We were now arriving in Paris and I was feeling guilty at having been the sort of travel bore whom people hurl themselves off trains to avoid. 'That was most interesting,' said Marthe. Then, finch-like, she leaned forward and put her tiny, bony hand on my knee.

'But you must be tired. Perhaps you would like to come back to my flat, to relax . . . and maybe enjoy a little relief?' She said this quite straightforwardly, as if asking me to help her with her bags. Across the aisle, other passengers were studying puzzle books or screens, murmuring into mobiles or staring out of the window. Outer Paris ceded to inner Paris. So I hadn't fallen through a gap in the time-space continuum. I was indeed on a train and being solicited by someone's gentle, cultured great-aunt.

Little in my life had prepared me for this change in gear of our conversation. One moment we were talking historical tourism, the next moment . . . well, we weren't. It would have been easier to handle if she'd wanted me as a hit-man. ('Sorry – never could shoot straight.')

By now, we had pulled into the Gare de Lyon. I helped her down from the train – it was one of those double-deckers, with steep steps – and, to stall for time, invited her for a coffee. Sipping briskly, Marthe explained that she took the train from Paris to Fontainebleau most working days. On the return trip, she would approach decent-looking men – in the hope of eking out her public services pension. 'I have a season ticket,' she said.

Her success rate was, she said, good. She rarely had two fruitless journeys consecutively. All this explained why she had put up with my account of the Route Napoléon. But it didn't get me out of the fix. By monopolising her attention, I had deprived her of the chance of meeting a more promising decent man and, therefore, of earning her daily bread. And Louis XVIII thought he had problems . . .

In the event, I shook her hand, wished her well, then abruptly kissed her cheek and left. Marthe turned towards the platforms, doubtless to find another train to Fontainebleau. I walked sharply out of the station, feeling as much of a rat as I'd felt for some time.

'You feel bad about not deceiving me with a prostitute you met . . . on a train?' said my wife when, that evening, I recounted the episode on the phone. Put that way, it did sound a bit daft. Things often do when women re-explain them for you. 'You're right, of course, dear,' I said. Back-tracking was essential. Otherwise, having trailed Napoleon from the Côte-d'Azur to Fontainebleau and now Paris, I, too, would have been facing my Waterloo.

CHAPTER 10
STEAMED UP

---

12 JULY 1992

A RAIL PASSION IN RUSSIA

WESTERN TRAIN BUFFS MAY SAVE THE EAST'S OLD LOCOS,
SAYS **DUFF HART-DAVIS**

We could scarcely believe our eyes. For days and nights we had hunted in vain, and we had begun to believe that, like the Snark, it might not exist. But now here it was, at 2.30 on a blazing hot afternoon, on a branch line in the foothills of the Caucasus: a Russian E-type steam locomotive, black as night, built about 1955 and bearing the number 774-97.

The driver, Alexei, a big man with a shock of grey hair and a mouthful of silver teeth, beamed down at us from the cab. With minimal fuss, he coupled up our saloon carriage, lent to us for the duration of the trip by the North Caucasus Railway Company, and away we went, with dense black smoke belching from the funnel. Even for me, a novice in steam, it was quite something to stand in the furnace-like cab and feel the old engine pant heavily, inclining fractionally to right and left each time it started to strain.

The track wound between low, green hills, with the outlying peaks of the Caucasus showing majestically on the horizon. At the end of the line – a stone-cutting factory – we were preparing to return when disaster struck. The diesel engine that had been pulling us on the main line came up behind and took our wagon in tow again, to save the old loco; but hardly had it started when − crunch − down went its front bogie into shingle, derailed by a hand-set point.

Ye gods! With 80 tons of dead diesel between us and home, we had visions of spending the night on the steppe − but we had under-estimated the diesel driver, a man of incredible strength and resource, who for the next hour wrestled with heavy lumps of metal, jamming them beside the rails to lift the wheels when the engine moved backwards.

When all was set, he went back up to his cab and put his engine into gear . . . but its wheels just squealed and ground uselessly. In the end it was the steam loco that, with one gentle heave, pulled its modern companion back on to the rails.

That evening, in a siding at the spa town of Mineral'nyye Vody, we invited Alexei and his fireman to dine in our saloon. Showered and changed, they looked different men, but their thirst remained powerful. I swear that when the first glass of neat vodka went down Alexei's throat, there was a whoosh as of water hitting red-hot coal.

Both men, we learnt, were retired. They had brought the steam engine out as a special favour to us, and had driven it all the way from Armavir, 125 miles up the line. Down went the glassfuls − vodka, iced mineral water, vodka. Alexei talked so fast that he had little time to eat. He snatched the odd mouthful of smoked fish, but otherwise maintained a torrent of anecdotes.

Suddenly he rose to his feet and began to declaim, in a deep, booming baritone, flinging out bear-like arms to left and right. 'What's he reciting?' I whispered to Sasha, our guide from Moscow. 'His own poems.'

'The driver loves his engine,' Alexei bellowed. 'He loves her so much that he treats her like his bride. He strokes her. She is a living being. To him, her noises are a song. He grooms her every morning as if she were a mare, feeds her with coal, gives her water to drink. Then his steel mare races over the steppe, and even the wind cannot catch her.'

It was tremendous stuff, and it lasted late into the hot southern night. But in the end, the poet's ardour was such that we had to pull the cord on him: as his feet returned to earth, they seemed a little unsteady, and it needed two human shunters to steer him away along the tracks into the dark.

For my companion, Tim Littler, that day last summer was something of a triumph. Tim had come to Russia in the hope of arranging steam tours for his own firm, GW Travel, and although our hosts, the North Caucasus Railway Company, had put themselves out to look after us, they had not at first realised that steam was a vital ingredient – indeed, the life-blood – of the enterprise.

Thus, they had put at our disposal a fine coach, equipped with air-conditioning, a panelled saloon, a full-sized bath and shower, sleeping compartments, a kitchen, and two *provodnitsy*, or stalwart ladies, to look after us. They had hitched us to the back of overnight expresses as they came through from magically distant places such as Tashkent and Samarkand, and taken us on a most agreeable tour of the North Caucasus. But at first they had not done anything about laying on a steam engine, and it was only after Tim had exerted heavy pressure that the E-type finally appeared.

We were there in July 1991, only a few days before the coup that knocked Soviet Communism on the head. At first, railway officials tried to play the line that steam was old, dirty and outmoded, and had no place in a go-ahead, up-to-date society such as the Soviet Union. There were very few steam engines left, they said. Most had been broken up for scrap. Only by degrees did we discover the falsity of these claims. Since then, steam engines have been coming out of the woodwork all over Russia, many of them P-36s, renowned for their power and endurance – locomotives to set the hearts of Western connoisseurs racing.

One of the most astonishing finds was no fewer than 300 E-types at a depot on the frontier with Poland. Built by slave labour just after the Second World War, and hardly used, these E-types have the European gauge (slightly narrower than Russian) and were intended to haul supply trains in support of the planned Soviet invasion of Europe.

In spite of the reluctance of our hosts to produce what we wanted last summer, the message that Western fans are mad for steam evidently went home, for now the North Caucasus Railway Company has combined with GW Travel to set up a tour in the south for September, with accommodation in renovated vintage coaches, and a variety of engines, including a P-36, which has been hauled all the way from Siberia and is now being restored. Considering the generally moderate standard of Russian hotels, it is clearly an excellent idea to sleep and eat on board as much as possible.

I cannot guarantee the performance of the engines, but I can recommend the scenery of the north Caucasus, and of the eastern coast of the Black Sea, down to which there is a wonderful run through wild, wooded gorges. The mountain spa towns that the tour will visit are set in grand country. Pyatigorsk is rich in memories of Mikhail Lermontov, the romantic rebel poet of the early 19th century, and Kislovodsk is a jewel: it has a splendid old station, and the town has been compared, by no means ridiculously, with Bath.

WEEPIE THAT WILL NEVER RUN OUT OF STEAM

IT IS 100 YEARS SINCE *THE RAILWAY CHILDREN* WAS
WRITTEN AND 40 YEARS SINCE IT WAS MADE INTO
A TEAR-JERKING FILM. NOW THE TALE IS BEING
STAGED AT WATERLOO STATION – COMPLETE
WITH REAL STEAM ENGINE. **DAVID GRITTEN**
TALKS TO THE NEW SHOW'S CREATORS

It's a story that was written more than 100 years ago, and it has enough anachronisms to make it an unlikely survivor. Yet E Nesbit's *The Railway Children* commands the affections of the British people like few other fictions; something about it clearly chimes with our national psyche.

This has been a good year for *The Railway Children*. The late Lionel Jeffries' celebrated 1970 film of Nesbit's novel, starring Jenny Agutter and Dinah Sheridan, recently celebrated its 40th anniversary and it was re-released in cinemas in April. Much fuss was then made of special commemorative editions of the film on DVD and Blu-ray in May.

Now there's more. A site-specific theatrical production of *The Railway Children*, staged with great success in 2008 and again last year at the National Railway Museum in York, is about to be seen in London for the first time, employing a brilliantly original venue: the disused Eurostar terminal and platforms at Waterloo Station. A 1,000-seater auditorium has been created at Waterloo especially for this production, with a railway track running through the middle of it, and with the audience divided in two, facing each other from either side of the track. Even better, a real steam engine will appear in the production (a GNR Stirling Single 4-2-2, built in Doncaster in 1970). During each performance it will pull a single saloon carriage, known as the Old Gentleman's Carriage, built in 1971. It is the very same one used in Jeffries' film.

I visited Waterloo this week, went through an unobtrusive door next to Platform 19 and re-entered the old Eurostar terminal for the first time in a decade. On the converted platform, Jenny King, the producer, let me clamber into the cab of the gorgeous Stirling Single. I then lounged in the saloon carriage, with its comfy sideways-facing armchairs, decorative ashtrays and silver tea service. Ah, the luxury. But I'd gone to Waterloo to ask about *The Railway Children*. Why has it lasted this long? Why do we British love it so much? Mike Kenny, a playwright who specialises in writing for children and families, has adapted this production from Nesbit's novel, while Damian Cruden, artistic director of York Theatre Royal for 12 years, has directed it.

On the face of it, the story's longevity is unexpected. Nesbit herself would be an obscure name if not for *The Railway Children*. Of her other works, *Five Children and It* and *The Treasure Seekers* are known and well liked, but *The Railway Children* was by far her biggest success. It tells the story of three sheltered siblings, Roberta (Bobbie), Peter and Phyllis, who suffer a huge upheaval when their father, who works for the Foreign Office, is taken away from their London home for questioning. (He is accused of selling state secrets to the Russians.) The children and their mother, now penniless, move to Three Chimneys, a cottage in rural Yorkshire near a railway line. Their mother stoically refuses to tell them about the circumstances that brought them there. The children befriend Perks, the local railway porter, and wave each day at The Old Gentleman, who passes them on the 09.15 London train.

The three siblings have more adventures than they ever did in London. They help avert an accident by halting a train after a landslide sends rubble and foliage crashing down on to the track, a scene that provokes the immortal cry: 'Get off the line, Bobbie!' They encounter and informally adopt a Russian exile, Mr Szczepansky, who is searching for his family.

'It's phenomenally contemporary when you read it,' Mike Kenny says. 'It has the wrongful arrest, the selling of state secrets. There's a mother taking the children a long way away, and not communicating with them about it. They're poor. The story is obsessed with the economics of all that. The children end up building relationships with people they'd normally never have met, so there's an interesting class tension there. They spend a lot of time on their own, because their mother has to work. They have a freedom they've never had before. They go from being in the nursery, essentially, to wandering round railway tracks. And they find a refugee and take him into their home.'

Damian Cruden thinks Nesbit's story is 'fantastically well constructed. Everything knits together, so the presence of the refugee in the story echoes the children's plight as refugees.'

Edith Nesbit was a socialist, one of the founders of the Fabian Society, and her political sympathies find subtle expression in the text. 'People put themselves out when they don't have to,' observes Kenny. 'They do the right thing. It's all about being communal. It's a story that generates incredible warmth.'

Cruden adds: 'There's a big thing in *The Railway Children* about surrogacy – adults being asked to be responsible for children who aren't their own. And if adults take that on, there's a security and safety in a world that can be threatening to children. I think there's something terribly British about that – together, if we all behave appropriately, we can make things right.'

Again, Nesbit's life provides a clue to this theme: she had three children with her husband Hubert Bland, but also raised two children as her own whom Bland had fathered with his mistress.

All these things are true. Yet there's surely another psychologically potent element in *The Railway Children*: the role of the absent father. It's a factor that has real resonance for audiences today. So many children are being raised by single mothers, with a father figure nowhere in sight. And the poignancy of families trying to hold things together without a father is reinforced each time we see television footage of British troops returning from Afghanistan or Iraq. Some fathers, of course, never return from these combat zones.

The power of the absent father in story-telling was brought home earlier this year by the phenomenal success in Britain of the film *Nanny McPhee and the Big Bang*. It grossed a surprisingly strong £16 million in eight weeks. As scripted by Emma Thompson, it owes much to the spirit of *The Railway Children*; it deals with a working mother and two children in rural Britain trying to cope while the father is away at war.

One could dismiss this as mere theorising were it not for the fact that it has echoes in Nesbit's own life: her father, John Collis Nesbit, died when she was three years old. 'She resurrects her father in *The*

Railway Children,' says Cruden. 'There's phenomenal potential wish-fulfilment in the story.'

Whatever the validity of the theory, Bobbie's famously plaintive cry at the end of *The Railway Children* ('Oh, my daddy! My daddy!') is extraordinarily moving. It's the emotional payoff of the whole story.

The lasting popularity of *The Railway Children* is clearly due in part to Jeffries' film, with its radiant performance by Jenny Agutter as Bobbie. Kenny concedes the point, but has his reservations about the film. 'It's a product of its time – the Sixties, when steam was on its way out. There's a kind of nostalgic haze about it. I saw it in my late teens, and it seemed this was an England where the sun always shines. And the mother was always kind and perfect – though you had the sense she was struggling. But looking back on it now, it was lovely stuff, and the ending is sublime.'

Still, Kenny's adaptation goes back to the original source: 'This production is closer to Nesbit's book. I'd say it's grittier than the film. We've taken one big liberty. We tell it from the point of view of the three kids, recalling it now they're young adults. That announces it as a piece of theatre, story-telling, and allows for a little playfulness in that story-telling.'

And then, of course there's the real railway track and the real steam engine, which will give the Waterloo production such immediacy. The two men have seen it work night after night to great effect in York. 'The ending's a killer,' Cruden says, smiling. 'That's right,' Kenny agrees. 'Audiences will weep.'

THE REV W AWDRY

CLERGYMAN WHO CREATED THE CLASSIC CHILDREN'S
CHARACTERS THOMAS THE TANK ENGINE
AND HIS FRIENDS

The Reverend W Awdry, who has died aged 85, was the creator of Thomas the Tank Engine, Gordon the Grumpy Express, the Fat Controller and the whole group of human-faced rolling stock whose adventures celebrated the golden sunset of steam railways.

Their stories – recounted in some 30 books which led to television series and numerous commercial spin-offs – began in 1944, when Awdry's three-year-old son Christopher was ill with measles. Nursery rhymes had palled with repetition. So Awdry, although no artist, drew some engines with faces to illustrate the lines, 'Early in the morning, down at the station,/All the little engines standing in a row.' To go with them he wove a few tales which the child, long after he had recovered, insisted be repeated word for word.

The first engine Awdry named Edward ('It was the first name that came into my head'), and he jotted the stories down on the backs of old circulars. He saw little value in the stories, but at his wife's suggestion they were sent to Edmund Ward, a fine art printer in Birmingham, who paid £40 for the copyright and commissioned an indifferent illustrator.

The Three Railway Engines was published in 1945; it sold remarkably well, and over the next year was reprinted four times. *Thomas the Tank Engine* appeared in 1946, and a steady flow of additions appeared every autumn for the next 24 years. By then Awdry found the task of coming up with new stories too onerous, and handed over to Christopher.

One part of the Awdry books' success was that they came out in small, easy-to-handle volumes; another was the fine work of the later illustrators whose bright, brochure-style pictures showed a world of well-kept stations, neatly dressed passengers and overalled work-men.They also appealed for the way the narrative was crafted to trip off parental lips with the rhythm of rolling stock. James the Red Engine puffs, 'Come along, come along,' as he struggles up a steep hill, while his coaches say encouragingly, 'You're pulling us well, you're pulling us well.' As Gordon is made to haul some trucks, he complains, 'A goods train, a goods train' in disgust.

For all their simplicity, each of the stories was based on a real incident, such as the loss of some trucks, a derailment, or a fish found in an engine's boiler. Sometimes Awdry's readers questioned the likelihood of such events. In one story, Percy is forced down a gradient by his loaded trucks and collides with the rear of a stationary train at the bottom, ending up perched precariously on top of a wagon. Railway enthusiasts by the score wrote to Awdry claiming that such an event or anything like it was quite impossible. 'My reply', said Awdry, 'is that it actually did happen on April 13 1876, on the London, Chatham & Dover Railway, and that a photograph of the accident is to be found on page 31 of Volume XXXIV of *Model Railway News.*'

Wilbert Vere Awdry was born on June 15 1911 at Ampfield, Hampshire, where his father, a railway enthusiast, was vicar. Every Wednesday afternoon, young Wilbert went for a walk with his father that ended with their climbing an embankment to see the engines of the London and South East Railway pass on the way from Romsey to Eastleigh. If it was raining they were admitted to the platelayers' cabin, where there was always talk of steam engines and their ways.

Awdry went to Dauntsey's School, Devizes, and St Peter's Hall, Oxford, before completing his training at Wycliffe Hall, Oxford. He spent three years teaching at St George's School, Jerusalem, before being ordained at Winchester Cathedral in 1936. He first took a curacy at Odiham, Hampshire, and then moved to West Lavington in the same county. During the Second World War his pacificism led him to take charge of the large parish of King's Norton, Birmingham. He next became vicar of Elsworth with Knapwell in Cambridgeshire, where he proved a diligent pastor in the moderate evangelical tradition, and was a great favourite with the children of the parish.

In 1951 Awdry became Rural Dean of Bourn. Two years later he moved to the larger parish of Emneth, near Wisbech, where he ministered faithfully for another 12 years before retiring to Stroud, Gloucestershire, to give part-time assistance in local parishes.

Inevitably problems ensued as the stories became international bestsellers. Pressing inquiries from eager children were fielded by placing his railway on the mythical island of Sodor, located somewhere between the Isle of Man and Barrow-in-Furness. For Sodor Awdry designed, with the help of his children, an entire fictional landscape crisscrossed by a network of railway lines.

Awdry halted the first television series in 1959 because the BBC wrote in a scene that he believed inauthentic. Thirty years later he was pleased by a new animated production put out by Central Television, using the voice of Ringo Starr. But he was exasperated when Central started to write their own story-lines.

In 1951, Awdry published *Our Child Begins to Pray*. Besides his children's books, he edited *Industrial Archaeology in Gloucestershire* (1973), which ran to three editions, and was joint editor of *A Guide to Steam Railways in Great Britain* (1979). In 1987 he was joint author of a history of the Birmingham and Gloucester Railway.

In his last years, Awdry looked back philosophically on his two callings. 'Railways and the Church have their critics,' he would say. 'But both are the best ways of getting man to his ultimate destination.'

He married, in 1938, Margaret Wale, who died in 1989; they had a son and two daughters.

TUNNEL OF LOVE

AS THOMAS THE TANK ENGINE MARKS HIS 65TH ANNIVERSARY, A BOX OF DOCUMENTS SHEDS NEW LIGHT ON HIS ORIGINS. **LORNA BRADBURY** REPORTS

It is the autumn of 1942 and a two-year-old boy is recovering from a bout of measles. His father entertains him by singing his favourite nursery rhyme, 'Down at the Station Early in the Morning'. Bored and itchy, the child soon loses interest, so his father sketches out a sad railway engine and makes up a story to go with it. A couple of months later, for Christmas, the child receives an engine, carved by his father from a piece of broomstick. As the boy's game starts to flag, he demands a story. 'We need to name the engine first,' his father tells him. 'Why don't we call it Thomas the Tank Engine?' The bare bones of this story may be familiar to enthusiasts of the children's series by the Rev W (Wilbert) Awdry. His best-selling books are this year celebrating their 65th anniversary, and their appeal remains constant, bolstered by the long-running television series narrated for a time by Ringo Starr and by the spin-off toys and games (which now include an iPhone application). But the contents of a box of documents, including Thomas the Tank Engine manuscripts from the Forties and Fifties, shed new light on the early years.

Recently unearthed in the offices of the production company that makes the TV series, the box contains Awdry's original sketches, drawn on the back of old parish circulars in late 1944 or early 1945. He produced them to guide the illustrators of his first book of stories, *The Three Railway Engines*. Wilbert, a railway obsessive and a stickler for accuracy, tried out two illustrators until one, E Reginald Dalby, finally met his approval. We can clearly see notes in what would seem to be Wilbert's hand stuck over the writing on the back of these sketches. '3 R Engines. Story 4. Page 5,' reads one. 'Fat Director [he became the Fat

Controller in the third book] orders Henry to be released from tunnel,' reads another.

There is the original manuscript of *Edward's Day Out*, the first story in the first book, in which Awdry's text appears on the left-hand pages and his sketches on the right. There are various promotional postcards, including one for the fifth book, *Troublesome Engines* (1950), by which time Thomas was a best-seller and a household name. And there are some early pop-ups, illustrated by Clive Spong, with paper engineering by Roy Laming, including the story *Henry and the Elephant* from *Troublesome Engines*.

Christopher Awdry, now 69, the measles-afflicted child for whom the stories were first conceived, is surprised at the contents of the box. 'They must be the original materials my father sent to his publisher,' he says, recalling the early months of 1943. Towards the end of 1942, Christopher says, his mother tried to buy him some books, but was so dismayed by what was on offer that she set about persuading her husband, exempt from fighting in the war because of his job as a clergyman, to publish the stories with which he had entertained his son. A distant cousin, a junior producer at the BBC, was then roped in to hawk them around various publishing houses. The following year, the publisher Edmund Ward agreed to take them on – on the condition that Wilbert wrote a fourth one 'to provide a happy ending for the set'.

Paper and colour printing shortages stopped the book from being published during the war, but it came out just four days after VE Day in May 1945 and was an immediate success. 'I suppose you could say it's never looked back since,' Christopher says, with typical understatement. Interestingly, this early collection contained stories about the sad engine, Edward, and about Gordon and Henry, but Thomas didn't appear in print until Wilbert's second book, in 1946.

Christopher's father was, by all accounts, an unassuming clergyman who knew little of life apart from his job and was surprised at the literary fame he achieved shortly after the war, and Christopher retains something of this unworldly air. Though Thomas the Tank Engine is now an enormous business – most of whose profits reside with the television production company – and a global brand that stretches from the United States to Japan, its success has not gone to his head.

His abiding childhood memory is of the year he was sent to boarding school, aged nine. His father sent him a copy of his new book, *Tank Engine Thomas Again*, the fourth in the series. 'My father had told me stories throughout my childhood, but that was the first time I was aware of him as a writer,' Christopher says. 'I remember my friends were impressed, too – though I suppose that only lasted for a few days.'

Wilbert passed on his enthusiasm for storytelling to his son, who carried on the series from 1983, with his father's blessing, shortly after his own son was born. Wilbert also passed on a deep love for the railways. Theirs is a family in which the mystery of steam trains looms large. Christopher's grandfather was a clergyman and a railway enthusiast, like Wilbert, whose interest in trains grew out of his visits to parishioners who worked on the railways. Christopher is a railway historian first and foremost, and both he and his father have always been keen that their stories remain accurate in railway terms.

Christopher says that neither he nor his father was surprised that children identify so strongly with the series. 'A steam engine is the nearest thing to a human being that has actually been created by man,' he says. 'You can see all the moving parts. You can see all the smoke. In a way, it's more logical to give a steam train a name than an animal.' These stories carry on appealing to fresh generations of children, despite the fact that they are so much of their time. They convey a safe, structured, deeply moralistic world, which may explain why autistic children particularly love them.

Next year marks the centenary of Wilbert's birth, so there will inevitably be more spin-offs. The brand lives on, as strong as ever. Christopher is working on a new book in the series, the 42nd, but he won't reveal any of the details. 'I haven't put pen to paper yet,' he says. But in this age of high-speed railways, you can be sure it will still feature boilers, funnels and the world's favourite tank engine.

THOMAS THE TANK ENGINE REACHES THE END OF THE LINE

COMMONS SKETCH BY **ANDREW GIMSON**

Thomas the Tank Engine is dead. The announcement was made yesterday afternoon by Alistair Darling, the Transport Secretary, and those of us who formed our knowledge of railway management from the works of the Rev W Awdry cannot help feeling a bit disorientated.

Awdry as a prose stylist was reassuringly — some would say intolerably — dull, but his books were full of incident. Thomas and the other engines were continually leaving the tracks, usually because they had disobeyed orders or indulged in petulant rivalries. The death toll was low but the punctuality record must have been the worst in the entire history of railways.

The strange thing was that almost everyone seemed quite happy with this state of affairs. Awdry captured the tolerance, even the love of failure that seemed to have become one of our national characteristics. We much preferred it when things went wrong, and even the Fat Controller, Sir Topham Hatt, who had to sort out the worst calamities, appeared to consider this a perfectly normal part of his duties. For while he punished the worst offenders by refusing to let them work, it never seemed to occur to him that his own style of management might be at fault.

Mr Darling, who appeared in the chamber wearing a grey tie on which a faint red pattern could be discerned, envisages a system in which petulant rivalries are a thing of the past, where the people who run the trains and the people who look after the track actually get on with each other. It is not a very British idea, but I suppose we shall have to get used to it.

In pursuit of this plan, Mr Darling said he was abolishing the Strategic Rail Authority. As soon as he said this, it was quite impossible to think why Mr Darling's predecessor but one, John Prescott, had invented the SRA in the first place. The manner in which Mr Darling said farewell to Richard Bowker, the head of the SRA, was masterly: 'For the past two-and-a-half years he has shown outstanding leadership and relentless determination to improve the railways. He has made a substantial contribution to the railways and leaves with my strong support and good wishes.'

The minister was no less ruthless in dealing with Tim Yeo, his ineffectual opponent on the Conservative front bench: 'If the honourable gentleman could contain himself for once, he might learn something. I appreciate he's got nothing to say.'

Mr Yeo did have a number of things to say, but he said them rather badly. He asked why the train operators would not be allowed to decide when the trains should run, and he complained about the state of two of his local stations, Colchester and Manningtree, where according to him 'conditions have hardly changed in half a century. No airport expects its customers to stand around in the wind and the rain awaiting departures.'

What Mr Yeo failed to do was to make the case that the railways are carrying more passengers than for 40 years, and 45 per cent more freight than in 1995, because the Conservatives had the wit to privatise them, albeit in a cackhanded way. The railways are a growing success, but we have yet to cast off the habit of thinking of them as a failure.

John McDonnell (Lab, Hayes and Harlington) sought to congratulate Mr Darling on renationalising the railways by inventing a much-improved version of British Rail. But Mr Darling was far too canny to accept the compliment, and claimed instead that he is tackling 'the remaining flaws left over from privatisation' by setting up a workable form of partnership between the train-operating companies and the state.

Mr Darling declined to remark, as he might have done, that he was tackling the remaining flaws left over from his immediate predecessor, Stephen Byers, and from Mr Prescott.

One wonders whether a future Prescott or Byers will be able to rush us back to the world of Thomas the Tank Engine, in which things continually go wrong.

CHINESE HUFF AND PUFF OVER STEAM HERITAGE

BY **JOHN GASKELL**

Zheng, Xu, Liu and Dong stood on the locomotive's cab floor shrouded in smoke and wreathed in smiles. The Chinese delegation was conducting a week's investigation into England's unquenchable nostalgia for the age of steam. Here, at the Bluebell Railway, near Haywards Heath, Sussex, they had reached the end of the line.

Their quest had taken them off the usual tourist trail and out to the wilds of East Lancashire, along the shining path to mysterious Keighley and down the Worth Valley. Officially, the purpose of the visit was to meet steam fans, exchange views and ideas, and discover how steam train history should be preserved.

China is in no danger of losing its railway heritage for many years yet, with four in five trains running on coal. The country still lives in the steam age. To the Chinese, the concept of volunteers preserving steam trains as a hobby is a joke, akin to Britons devoting their lives to the adoration of, say, the Vauxhall Cavalier, with fans clutching souvenirs and queuing for rides at special weekends. But Zheng, Xu, Liu and Dong are looking to the future. In their home city of Datong, the Crewe of the Orient, production of steam engines stopped three years ago in favour of diesel and electric models.

Their mission had a secondary purpose: to drum up visitors for the Third Chinese International Steam Locomotive Festival at Datong. Overseas travellers with sufficient currency are warmly welcomed in China and Datong does its bit by attracting the world's railway buffs. Who else goes there? Mr Xu, the interpreter, translated for Mr Dong. 'Very important persons come, like the Queen from Holland and Edward Heath. Those kind of people.'

Mr Dong, the eldest and obviously the leader of the team, presented his business card, packed with details of his many grand titles but omitting the fact that he is the chairman of Datong Communist Party. Thus his presence on the trip perhaps owed less to his knowledge of railway engineering than it did to firm execution of timetables.

He may have been angered that their visit to a railway engineering works at Loughborough had to be cancelled owing to their BR connection being one hour late. But, as with all questions, he was exquisitely polite. What did Mr Dong think of British Rail? 'Very good.' Had they tried the famous British Rail sandwiches? Mr Xu put the question to the group at some length. The group chortled and had a long discussion. Someone, it seemed, had an amendment to the answer. More debate, a referral to standing orders and then the reply.

'Yes.'

'Yes?'

'Very nice,' waxed one.

Thus did the heavy curtains of opposing cultures inch apart. Mr Dong was better at the set pieces: his What To Do In And Around Datong was flawless; Datong's coal mining history, a joy.

The group had a different kind of minder in the shape of Bob John, a civil servant from the Department of Transport and a member of the Bluebell Railway Society. He led a British delegation to Datong's first steam festival and in return acted as their host on their tour of Britain, in loco parentis, as it were.

'I suspect it's been a very severe culture shock for old Dong, but the others have been out of China before,' Mr John said. 'Before they arrived they asked to be put in first class on British Rail, which anyone who has travelled by train in China will understand. But when they experienced second class they thought it would have been adequate. They have been very well received. They have generated interest among British enthusiasts to go over there.'

Despite Tiananmen Square? 'That will put some people off, but steam enthusiasts tend not to look beyond the steam locomotive. After all, plenty of them make trips to South Africa.'

On their last day, the Chinese presented plaques to their Bluebell hosts, before T-shirts, silk handkerchiefs and railway workers' badges were opened – gifts for the running-dog lackeys of the capitalist press, honourable friends for the day.

NO, CARS AREN'T NECESSARILY BETTER THAN TRAINS

JAMES MAY HAS A CONFESSION TO MAKE . . .

Last week, on *Top Gear*, you'll have seen me beat a Forties steam locomotive with a Forties car in a fair-and-square, not-just-for-television race between London and Edinburgh. So we proved that, even 60 years ago, and as we've known ever since, cars are better than trains. Therefore, it must follow that Dr Beeching was right and that the notion of trains as a panacea-in-waiting is just a lot of misty-eyed nonsense.

Or is it? I have to admit that, much as I loved that old Jag XK120, a part of me felt a bit churlish about beating the Tornado. A steam locomotive is a noble beast and an honest expression of industrial toil. There's a reason why a five-year-old in 2009 loves Thomas the Tank Engine, even though such a thing hasn't been seen in regular employment since before his parents were born. And never had a face.

We know, as we do with mechanical wristwatches, that a steam engine can't really be as good as the modern equivalent, but that doesn't detract from the simple fact that it's just more beautiful. A steam engine is so open to understanding; so downright comprehensible in its workings. I stand next to a steam engine on a preserved railway line and, even though I would struggle to pick up any one component of it single-handed, I can conceive of making one myself. I never feel like that about a gas turbine or rocket motor.

Here's what surprises me most, though. The XK120 beat the 4-6-2 by no more than 10 minutes, even though the train was limited to 75mph and, because it is, in the end, an inefficient steam engine, had to stop for coal and water far too often.

Despite what many people like to claim, our races are run in real time and the results are genuine. We go back and film pretty pictures to help tell the story later. This was a damn near-run thing.

And it took place, nominally, in 1949. In the intervening six decades, the car hasn't really become any faster. Obviously, my Fiat Panda will now cruise along the A1 as quickly as the then-supercar Jag would, but if you have any sort of respect for the law, then it must be recognised that by 1949 the car was already as fast as it would ever be in Britain. Yes, I realise that advances in road design mean that the car will now go faster more of the time, but for practical purposes the outside of the envelope was reached a very long time ago.

Supercars are hilariously good fun, but I've yet to be convinced that they take you anywhere more quickly.

Meanwhile, there was still room for improvement on the railways. It seems to me that we hung on to the steam engine for far too long; that the cheapness and ready availability of coal left us wedded to it long after we should have moved on. The world steam locomotive speed record was set in 1938, and steam survived on the railways for another 30 years without improving on that.

Steam power, for all its romance, was astonishingly dirty. When I was a boy, Westminster Abbey, York Minster and the Albert Hall (both of them) were black buildings, because of coal. It's why shirts had detachable collars. Steam was also, on the whole, pretty slow. Mallard astonished, but most trains simply ruined your clothes.

But this week, I took a train from London to Durham, and the journey took less than two and three quarter hours – and that in a country where trains are considered slow. I couldn't have done that in the car. I've also taken a train from Lille to Calais, and it went so fast I thought, like passengers on Stevenson's Rocket, that I would stop breathing. As far as I can make out, the only thing limiting the top speed of Japan's bullet trains is the problem of running out of Japan before they can be brought to a halt.

Getting to the station and working out which train you can take with the exact ticket you have is an astonishing bore, but there's no denying the simple fact that, once you're on one, a train is a fantastic way to travel the length of the country. To be honest, it sometimes seems to me that Beeching struck before the railways could show what they were really made of. So yes, the car beat the train, but overall, I'm not entirely sure that the result stands up.

Let's just keep quiet about this one, shall we?

20 SEPTEMBER 1998

HOW STRESS WAS DISCOVERED ON VICTORIAN TRAINS

BY **ROBERT MATTHEWS**

Travelling by train can often be a test of mental and physical stamina. Delays, cancellations, over-crowding: it's enough to drive one in search of trauma counselling – which, curiously, is a profession whose origins can be traced back to the early days of rail travel. The concept of 'post-traumatic stress disorder' emerged not from the shattered lives of Vietnam veterans or even the 'shell-shocked' soldiers of the Great War, but during investigations into the cause of a bizarre ailment suffered by passengers involved in the earliest railway collisions.

With commuters now insouciantly reading their papers within feet of trains passing at 125 miles an hour, it is hard to imagine the awe and fear inspired by the advent of steam engines. In 1829, Stephenson's Rocket managed 29mph, a speed easily attainable by a galloping horse. But within 10 years the speed of the fastest train had doubled, and by 1854 engineers on the Bristol and Exeter Railway had broken the 80mph barrier. As the speeds crept up so, inevitably, did the number of accidents. By the 1860s, the railway companies were losing fortunes as passengers sued for compensation. Questions started to be raised about the authenticity of some of the claims being made.

Many were of course perfectly genuine: broken bones, burns, scalding and the like. But then there were the claims from people who had emerged from major accidents without a scratch – only to succumb to a host of more or less vague symptoms, such as giddiness, headaches and 'nervousness'. Medical opinion at first favoured the idea that the victims were suffering the after-effects of severe deceleration caused by the accident. The syndrome soon acquired the quaintly Victorian appellation of 'railway spine'. Its origins have now been investigated in fascinating detail by Dr Ralph Harrington, a historian at the University of York.

According to Dr Harrington, acceptance of the reality of railway spine began around 1860, with the publication of a book on railway injuries by an influential London surgeon, John Erichsen. Before long, Erichsen was making regular appearances in the witness box in compensation cases, arguing that the outwardly unharmed passengers were suffering from 'chronic and sub-acute inflammation action in the spinal membranes, and in chronic myelitis'. Such gobbledegook could not hide an awkward fact, however: Erichsen had found no evidence of damage to the spine. This led him to hint at another possibility – that railway spine was linked to psychological trauma.

Other doctors spoke out rather more forcefully in support of the idea that the 'psychical shock' of a railway accident played a major role in railway spine. As so often, however, fashions in medical thought prevented that theory from gaining much ground: at the time Erichsen was writing, physical diseases were ineluctably linked to physical causes.

By the 1880s, Erichsen's views had come under attack from Herbert Page, a railway company surgeon. In these cynical times, one naturally assumes that Page was simply trying to dismiss the claims of litigious passengers. Surprisingly, he insisted that he did not believe that the claimants were mendacious malingerers. Rather, he believed that the medical profession was at fault by paying far too much attention to the body, and not enough to the mind. Railway accidents, he said, were quite capable of providing the conditions needed for 'profound exhaustion of the nervous system or traumatic neurasthenia', the cause of which was 'very largely fright and alarm'.

To modern eyes, Page's explanation is strikingly reminiscent of the concept of post-traumatic stress disorder, whose reality is now widely recognised. As Dr Harrington points out, Page was led to his psychiatric explanation of railway spine not solely by the absence of physical injury. To his Victorian eyes, the awesome power of the train was proof enough of its ability to cause 'psychic' damage.

Only historians talk of railway spine today, but remnants of the thinking that produced it still exist, in the form of the great Victorian stations such as St Pancras. According to some, these were deliberately designed in the image of vast cathedrals: to soothe passengers as they embarked upon their journeys to far-off places at terrifying speed.

EMBLEMS OF MOTION AND POWER

ANDREW GRAHAM-DIXON REVIEWS
'ART IN THE AGE OF STEAM'

H G Wells wrote that 'the 19th century . . . will, if it needs a symbol, almost inevitably have as that symbol a steam engine running upon a railway'. The Walker Art Gallery's new exhibition, 'Art in the Age of Steam', takes Wells' thesis as its starting point while travelling a good few years past his chronological terminus of 1900. Its subject is the way in which painters and photographers responded to the railway, both as fact and emblem, from the middle years of the 19th century to the early 20th.

Logically the show should have begun with Turner's great paean to the power of steam-powered locomotion, 'Rain, Steam and Speed' (1844). With its abbreviated forms and rushing, headlong perspective, Turner's vision of a dark, thrusting, tubular train piercing the misty air is the quintessential 19th-century picture of train travel – matched, in the work of the painter's contemporaries, only by the word-painting in Dickens's *Dombey and Son*: 'Roaring, rattling, tearing on, spurning everything with its dark breath . . . shrieking, rolling, rattling through the purple distance!' Sadly, Turner's evanescent masterpiece has been deemed too fragile to travel to Liverpool. It has been replaced by a digital projection, like a stained-glass replica of a hallowed relic. Its absence is pretty much the only disappointment in what is otherwise a fascinatingly broad-ranging exhibition, especially strong in loans from collections in France and America.

'Type of the modern! Emblem of motion and power! Pulse of the continent!' The American poet Walt Whitman's enthusiasm for the steam train, encapsulated in his 'To a Locomotive in Winter', was echoed by the work of American painters. In 1865, Jasper Francis Cropsey hymned the grandeur of the Starrucca Viaduct, Pennsylvania, isolating it against the wide horizon like a giant emblem of order brought to the wilderness. Five years earlier, Thomas Proudley Otter had distilled his own idea of American progress into a picture called 'On the Road', a work of art structured around the blatant contrast between old-style, horse-drawn wagon and the new Iron Horse, thundering its way across the continent, accelerating the pace of conquest and settlement.

In Europe, the spread of the railway was greeted with more evidently mixed feelings. Adolph von Menzel's small, breezy oil sketch of 'The Berlin-Potsdam Railway' (1847) is a vision of pastoral peace and quiet eruptively disturbed. Perched high above the track, Von Menzel looks down at a small black locomotive hurtling so furiously through the landscape that he feels compelled to render it as a hectic black blur. Nearby hangs the fine watercolour 'The Night Train' (1849) by the rather underrated English painter David Cox. Under a gaseous, cloudy night sky, a distant train relentlessly puffs its way through a bare landscape. In the foreground, a group of horses, thoroughly spooked, bolts in all directions. The implacability of the train's advance, ordained by tracks like lines of indefinite extent drawn across the landscape, is set against the haphazardness of nature.

Most Victorian British painters simply turned their backs on modern industrial subject matter, such as the railway, leaving it to cartoonists, caricaturists and print-makers to fill the void. Thomas Talbot Bury's acquatints of the Liverpool-and-Manchester railway nakedly celebrate the triumph of technology. His broad-shouldered navvies, toiling on a deep cutting, might almost be the troops of Leonidas defending the pass at Thermopylae. When John Cooke Bourne was commissioned to commemorate the engineering feats of Isambard Kingdom Brunel, he managed to make the railway bridges and viaducts of the 19th century appear like the triumphant monuments of a new imperium, a second Egypt or Rome. But Bourne is also capable of finding something sinister in the inexorable advance of the railway network. 'Great Ventilating Shaft, Kilsby Tunnel' (c. 1835-6) is a view of black, cavernous tunnels and sediment-stained walls evoking the labyrinthine prisons of a Piranesi nightmare.

The fine artists of 19th-century Britain might have shied away from depicting the effects of railway travel on the landscape, but they found in carriage and station lively mises-en-scène for social and psychological dramas. W P Frith's 'The Railway Station' (1862) remains one of the most arresting paintings of Victorian England because of its spiralling sense of unease. For all the painter's ostensible attempt to order the seething crowd that is his subject matter – whether by age, morality or class – what he conjures most vividly is the potential for anarchy and confusion in the new world of the 19th-century metropolis.

For his part, inspired perhaps by the new phenomenon of the prolonged chance encounter made possible by railway travel, Augustus Egg painted one of his most haunting pictures, 'Travelling Companions' (1863). The work shows two identical girls in identical clothes sitting opposite each other in a carriage. One of them has a basket full of apples by her side and, cheeks flushed, seems to be dreaming a sensual dream. The other, with a virgin's fresh blooms beside her, sits upright and reads an improving book. Their forms have been arranged so symmetrically as to evoke the images that can be made by folding a piece of inked blotting paper in half. What looks at first sight like a picture of two people is best understood as two speculative (albeit stereotypical) fantasies about a single inscrutable girl. Is she virgin or temptress? These are the daydreams of a fellow traveller, implicitly male, given a palpable form and shape.

Egg's painting calls to mind a brief note by the great essayist Walter Benjamin, in which he refers gnomically to 'railroad tracks, with the peculiar and unmistakable dream world that attaches to them'. Other painters to whom the remark might aptly be attached are the Italian proto-Surrealist Giorgio de Chirico, whose stilled and phantasmagoric paintings of sunlit piazza and echoing arcade are often haunted by lurking phallic locomotives; and the pre-eminent artist of American anomie, Edward Hopper, whose melancholia disposed him to find a metaphor for life itself, as he disconsolately saw it, in the long and lonely wait of a passenger watching the sun flare and fade in the early evening sky.

The railway fostered new experiences. But more than that, it can be said to have altered the very nature of human perception; or at least to have accelerated the tempo of life to the extent that life itself seemed different as a result. Ford Madox Ford, writing in 1905, noted the peculiar sensation that he had at the end of a railway journey – the feeling of having experienced the world, at speed and through the windows of a train carriage, as though fractured into a thousand pieces. 'One sees . . . so many little bits of uncompleted life.' What might be described as a form of steam-driven relativism took its time to filter into the forms of art, but eventually – or so it might be argued – it shaped the most fundamental revolutions in modern painting.

For all their declared determination to embrace modernity and change, the French Impressionists portrayed trains and train stations in a surprisingly static fashion. Monet's paintings of the Gare Saint-Lazare, despite their billowing clouds of tinted steam, are among his stillest and most monumental images of the modern city. It was not until the era of the yet more iconoclastic Cubists and Futurists that the stuttering, broken form of seeing enhanced by railway travel worked its way into the very language of art. So it is with the brittle kaleidoscopes of modern painting – mosaics of form within which trains and their travellers survive only as abbreviated glimmers and glimpses – that this show rushes to its aptly violent end.

LAST WHISTLE FOR RAILWAY BISHOP

BY **R H GREENFIELD**

The requiem for a soldier may be the Last Post and for a Highland chieftain a piper's lament. But at a memorial service yesterday to 'the Railway Bishop' the sound that marked the one minute's silence was the haunting whistle of British Rail's last steam locomotive, Evening Star.

The service, attended by several thousand people, was held at the station of Appleby-in-Westmoreland, where Bishop Eric Treacy had gone to photograph Evening Star before he died in May aged 71. Two special steam trains brought to the service his widow, Mrs Mary Treacy, former members of his flock and fellow railway enthusiasts from Halifax and London.

The former Bishop of Wakefield, who retired in 1976, was a talented photographer and had been a train lover since his days as a parish priest in the railway district of Liverpool in the 1930s. He travelled long distances to photograph locomotives, becoming a familiar figure to hundreds of railwaymen. The Settle-to-Carlisle was one of his favourite lines.

The memorial service was arranged by British Rail and the Steam Locomotive Operators' Association. The train from Halifax, drawn by Evening Star, was named 'The Bishop Treacy', and the London train, drawn by The Flying Scotsman, was named 'The Lord Bishop'.

After yesterday's service in the station yard, Mrs Treacy unveiled a memorial plaque to her husband on the down platform. About 4,500 people attended, almost double the population of Appleby itself. In addition to the special trains, 14 coaches came by road and some people camped overnight in tents.

Throughout, Evening Star stood at the platform, in gleaming green livery and with steam up. When her whistle gave a mournful blast during the service she seemed to those who were gathered to be bidding her own farewell.

NOTES ON CONTRIBUTORS

JOLYON ATTWOOLL wrote guidebooks to Latin America, a region with strangely few great railway trips, before joining the travel desk of the *Daily Telegraph* in 2008. Since then, he has made up for lost time with various enriching, infuriating and bizarre train journeys – many of them on his daily commute from Lewisham to Victoria.

JAMES BEDDING's great-grandfather built the railway line through the marshes fringing Lake Maggiore in Switzerland, his foreman giving him a daily tot of rum to ward off malaria. Many years later, James's father worked for British Rail as an architect; he now runs the family train set. James, meanwhile, is a journalist who hopes that the Swiss Federal Railways clock on his desk will one day improve his relationship with deadlines.

GAVIN BELL is a former foreign correspondent of the *Times*, who has found that travel writing makes an agreeable change from reporting on wars and *coups d'état*. He won the Thomas Cook/*Daily Telegraph* Travel Book of the Year Award with *In Search of Tusitala: Travels in the Pacific after Robert Louis Stevenson*, and his latest book is *Somewhere Over the Rainbow: Travels in South Africa*. He is still travelling hopefully.

JOHN BETJEMAN (1906–84) loved trains; and railway stations, or journeys to and from them, inspired some of his best poems. There is a statue to him at St Pancras Station in London, a building he helped to save from demolition, and which, along with his writing, will be his monument.

LORNA BRADBURY is a literary journalist who has worked and written for the *Daily Telegraph* for the past 10 years. She has taken the odd train around Britain and eastern Europe, but most of what she knows about engines and steam she has learned from her son, who is three, and a keen student of *Thomas the Tank Engine*. He is called Percy – a name he shares with the cheeky engine who was allowed to run the branch line while Thomas was otherwise occupied.

ADRIAN BRIDGE, a former Berlin correspondent of the *Independent*, covered central and eastern Europe in the 1990s. He is now a commissioning editor on the travel desk of the *Daily Telegraph* and takes the train as often as possible.

CON COUGHLIN, executive foreign editor of the *Daily Telegraph*, is a world-renowned expert on the Middle East and Islamic terrorism and author of several critically acclaimed books. His latest book is *Khomeini's Ghost* (Macmillan).

HUGO DAVENPORT worked for the *Observer* – where among other things he covered Northern Ireland and went to the North Pole with Ranulph Fiennes – and the *Mail on Sunday* before joining the *Daily Telegraph*. He was on the staff from 1987 to 1996, first as a feature writer, then as film critic. He is the author of *Days That Shook The World* (BBC Books).

MICHAEL DEACON is a columnist and commissioning editor at the *Daily Telegraph*. He believes passionately in the importance of train travel, partly because of what it teaches us about the boundless majesty of the world we live in, and partly because even at the age of 30 he can't drive.

JOHN GASKELL (1951-2008) deployed his wit and charm to great effect in reporting offbeat stories for the *Daily Telegraph* and *Sunday Telegraph*. He was at his best with tales verging on the unbelievable: a collection of Christmas memorabilia that was being sent to a Japanese museum; children in St Paul's in Bristol who were said to prefer watching riots to television; a party of patriotic strippers who were offering to rally the battered spirits of American troops during the first Gulf War.

ANDREW GILLIGAN has reported from about 50 countries for the *Daily Telegraph* and *Sunday Telegraph*, the BBC and the London *Evening Standard* and tries, in every country he visits, to make at least one journey by rail. He has never spent more than 24 hours on a train – it only feels like that.

ANDREW GIMSON writes the parliamentary sketch for the *Daily Telegraph* and is the author of *Boris: The Rise of Boris Johnson* (Pocket Books).

ANDREW GRAHAM-DIXON, one of the leading art critics and presenters of arts television in the English-speaking world, is a columnist for the *Sunday Telegraph*. His six series for the BBC include the acclaimed *A History of British Art*, *Renaissance* and *Art of Eternity*. His most recent book, *Caravaggio: A Life Sacred and Profane* (Penguin), was longlisted for the 2011 Samuel Johnson Prize.

R H GREENFIELD (1934–2005) was defence correspondent and later a feature writer for the *Sunday Telegraph*. He was famously disinclined to open post, which piled up on his desk to form a barricade. Once Sebastian Faulks, one of his colleagues at the time, pulled an envelope from near the bottom of the heap, opened it and said: 'Ah, Harry, I see Mafeking has been relieved.' After his departure from the newspaper, Greenfield became involved in paganism and his former colleagues heard tales of his dancing naked at stone circles. He was 65 before he had his first tattoos and he told a friend that what most embarrassed him about his past was that he had worn a tie-pin.

ELIZABETH GRICE has been a feature writer for *the Daily Telegraph* since 1992. She is the author of *Rogues and Vagabonds*, the story of nineteenth-century travelling players on the Fisher Circuit of theatres in East Anglia. Her hobby, yet to be committed to print, is tracking down and documenting medieval dovecotes.

DAVID GRITTEN, a film writer/critic for the *Daily Telegraph*, proudly admits he was an avid train-spotter from age 10 to 12, in the dying days of steam. He stood for entire days on freezing platforms at Birmingham Snow Hill and Lichfield Trent Valley, with a duffel bag packed by his mother containing an orange, a bottle of Lucozade, and egg-and-cress sandwiches. Even now he forsakes easyJet's dubious lure and travels to the Cannes Film festival by train: Eurostar to Lille, then a gloriously languid journey through rural France and beside the sun-flecked azure Mediterranean before arriving in Cannes itself.

DUFF HART-DAVIS was associated with the *Sunday Telegraph* from its launch in February 1961, joining as a junior in the literary department and rising to be assistant editor of the paper. His books include novels, a biography of Peter Fleming, histories of deer-stalking and of the *Telegraph* (*The House the Berrys Built*) and *Hitler's Games*, a study of the 1936 Olympics. His latest is *The War That Never Was* (Century), the story of the British covert war in Yemen.

CHRIS HEATH has been working for the past seven years as a correspondent for *American GQ*; he also contributes travel articles to the *Telegraph Magazine*, and he has written books about the Pet Shop Boys and Robbie Williams, including the bestselling biography *Feel: Robbie Williams*.

SIMON HEFFER was born in 1960 and at the time he wrote the piece included in this anthology was the parliamentary sketch writer of the *Daily Telegraph*. He subsequently became the paper's deputy editor, and a political columnist, and wrote a number of books, mainly about history. He still travels by train on the rare occasions he can afford it.

CHRISTOPHER HOWSE is an assistant editor of the *Daily Telegraph* and a regular contributor to the *Spectator* and the *Tablet*. His books include *How We Saw It: 150 Years of The Daily Telegraph* (Ebury Press) and *A Pilgrim in Spain* (Continuum).

PETER HUGHES, founding editor of ITV's *Wish You Were Here . . .?*, once travelled from Wick, in Scotland, to Vladivostok by train under the misapprehension that it was the longest continuous railway journey in the world. He has nevertheless won a number of awards for travel writing.

BRIAN JACKMAN is a freelance writer. The son of a railwayman, he first travelled on the Cornish Riviera Express at the age of three and has since crossed the Tamar at least once every year. He is best known for his abiding interests in wildlife and wild places – especially Africa where he has undertaken almost 100 safaris. His books include *The Marsh Lions* and *The Big Cat Diary* (with Jonathan Scott), and *The Countryside in Winter*. He now lives three miles from the sea in Dorset with his wife, two cats, nine chickens and a donkey.

JAMES LANGTON has been news editor of the *Sunday Telegraph* and New York correspondent. He is now deputy editor of the *National on Sunday* in Abu Dhabi. He is the author of *Your Pedigree Chum* (Faber and Faber), an examination of the history, and possible future, of man's best friend.

ALEXANDER McCALL SMITH is the author of *The No 1 Ladies' Detective Agency* books and of four other series of novels. He is also the writer of short stories, plays and lyrics for opera and song. His books have been translated into forty-six languages and have won numerous awards. He lives in Scotland and enjoys writing on trains.

FIONNUALA McHUGH is much fonder of trains than planes (despite having been born in an RAF hospital in Wiltshire). As she has never learned to drive, or to cook, anything with a dining-car attached has to be ideal. She has been travelling in Asia since 1986, and has lived in Hong Kong since 1993 (from where she used to write a pre-handover column for the *Telegraph Magazine*). Her favourite book about train travel, and Asia, is Kipling's *Kim*.

STEPHEN McCLARENCE is an award-winning travel writer who, as a non-driver, depends on trains (and buses) to get around. He regularly visits India and enjoys reading *Trains at a Glance*, the Indian railway timetable, though he has never been seen wearing an anorak. Some years ago, he was forced to cancel a long-planned trip on the Trans-Siberian Railway, but found consolation in the spectacular line from Sheffield to Huddersfield.

BONNIE MALKIN covers Australia and the Pacific for the *Daily Telegraph* and also works as an assistant news editor for the foreign desk. Since arriving in Sydney in 2008 she has covered, among other stories, the 2009 Victorian bushfires, the Samoan tsunami and the 2010 Federal Election.

EDWARD MARRIOTT is the author of four works of non-fiction (*The Lost Tribe*, *Wild Shore*, *The Plague Race*, and *Claude & Madeleine*, all published by Picador) and now works as a psychodynamic psychotherapist in private practice and the NHS.

ANDREW MARTIN is the author of nine novels, including a series of thrillers with a background in the railways of the early twentieth century. The first in the series was *The Necropolis Railway*; the latest is *The Somme Stations*.

ROBERT MATTHEWS (www.robertmatthews.org) was the science correspondent of the *Sunday Telegraph* from 1990 to 2005, and dreamt up many of his weekly columns while staring out of the window of the dreadful little trains that run between London Paddington and his home town of Oxford. His latest book is *Why don't spiders stick to their webs? And other everyday mysteries of Science* (Oneworld).

YSENDA MAXTONE GRAHAM is an author and journalist living in London. Her book *The Real Mrs Miniver* was shortlisted for the Whitbread Biography

Award, 2002. Her latest book is *Mr Tibbits's Catholic School*, published by Slightly Foxed editions. Her two eldest sons knew the entire London Underground network by heart by the age of six.

JAMES MAY co-presents *Top Gear* on BBC Two and has been a regular contributor to the *Daily Telegraph* since 2003. His collected thoughts on cars, bikes, pies, poetry and much more can be read in *Notes from the Hard Shoulder* (Virgin Books) and online at telegraph.co.uk/motoring.

CHRIS MOSS was born in Lancashire, educated in London, Liverpool and Leeds, and lived for 10 years in Buenos Aires, where he worked for the *Herald*. He is travel and literary editor of *Time Out* magazine and writes for the *Daily Telegraph* and *Condé Nast Traveller*. He is the author of *Patagonia: A Cultural History* (Signal Books/OUP).

DERVLA MURPHY (born Lismore, County Waterford, 1931) was determined to write, not to marry and to travel to India. She realised two of these ambitions in *Full Tilt*, her first book, which describes her exuberant bicycle ride from Lismore – where she still lives – to India, through Iran and Afghanistan. It has been followed by some 20 further titles, including an acclaimed memoir, *Wheels within Wheels*. Her most recent book is *The Island That Dared*, an account of a series of journeys through Cuba with her daughter Rachel and her three grand-daughters. www.dervlamurphy.com

KEVIN O'FLYNN has lived and worked as a journalist in Moscow since 1996. He has written at one time or another for all of the broadsheets and for *Newsweek*, Agence France Presse and the *Moscow Times*. One of his first train journeys in the former Soviet Union required him to bribe his way on to a packed carriage. He spent the overnight journey from Minsk to Vilnius sleeping on a luggage rack with a crate of oranges.

JAMES OWEN failed in his ambition to grow up to be a tank engine like his childhood idol Thomas and had to settle instead for becoming a journalist and author. He does much of his travelling by train, preferring it to venturing on to the roads of Italy, where he lives. His books include *Danger UXB: The Heroic Story of the WWII Bomb Disposal Teams*. *Commandos* is due to be published in 2012.

ANTHONY PEREGRINE left Lancashire for Languedoc 20 years ago and has since travelled, eaten and drunk his way round Europe for a living. His work has appeared in the *Daily Telegraph*, the *Sunday Times*, the *Daily Mail* and other publications too obscure to mention. Some still owe him money. He reckons there's nothing more exciting than settling into a first-class seat on the TGV – unless it be the exploring of a new destination at the other end.

PAMELA PETRO grew up in the New York City area, and cut her travelling teeth on the trains of Amtrak's East Coast Corridor. Since then she has travelled around the world for publications from the *New York Times* to the *Daily Telegraph* and *Granta*, and has written three books of travel literature: on

France, the American South and Wales – where she went to graduate school, in Lampeter. Pamela is also a visual artist who works with environmental installations of photography.

NIGEL RICHARDSON was on the staff of the *Daily Telegraph* for 13 years. He has written five books, including a bestselling travelogue, *Breakfast in Brighton*, and a critically acclaimed novel for teenagers, *The Wrong Hands*, as well as radio drama. He continues to contribute to the *Telegraph* and to other leading publications.

BYRON ROGERS has been a feature writer for the *Daily Telegraph*, the *Sunday Times*, the *Guardian*, the *Evening Standard* and *Saga* magazine. His eight books include several that collect his journalism, such as *An Audience with an Elephant* and *The Bank Manager and the Holy Grail*; two acclaimed biographies, of the idiosyncratic novelist and publisher J L Carr and the Welsh poet and vicar R S Thomas; and *Me: The Authorised Biography* (all published by Aurum). His latest is *Three Journeys* (Gomer).

NICHOLAS SHAKESPEARE (born in Worcester, 1957) grew up in Paris, the Far East and South America. His novels are translated into 20 languages. They include *Snowleg*, longlisted for the Booker Prize, and *The Dancer Upstairs*, chosen by the American Libraries Association as the best novel of 1997. He is also the author of an acclaimed biography of Bruce Chatwin. His longest train journey (five days) was from Buenos Aires to Cuzco.

SANDI TOKSVIG, following a first-class degree from Cambridge, went into the theatre as a writer and performer. Her latest play, *Bully Boy*, premiered in May 2011. Well known for her television and radio work as a presenter, writer and actor, she has also written 20 books, including fiction and non-fiction for both adults and children. She is a regular columnist for the *Sunday Telegraph* and for *Good Housekeeping* magazine.

CATH URQUHART, after three years travelling and reporting for the *Daily Telegraph* and ten as travel editor of the *Times*, changed tracks to retrain as a lawyer, and is currently a pupil (trainee) barrister at a set of chambers in London. She now spends more time on the train than ever, as she heads off to court in Bromley, Slough and Milton Keynes. In her backpacking days, she spent a week on the Trans-Siberian from Beijing to Moscow, and made several 30-hour-plus train journeys across India and China.

JOHN WELLS (1936-1998) was a humorist, journalist, linguist, translator, novelist, historian, actor and playwright. His best-known role was as Denis Thatcher in *Anyone for Denis?* – the spin-off from his 'Dear Bill' letters in *Private Eye* – which he wrote and starred in. He never drove a car, and the farmhouse where he lived in his later years was conveniently near a station.

BENJI WILSON writes features, profiles, columns and criticism for a wide range of publications, from the *Daily Telegraph* to *Private Eye*. He caught the prose bug watching Ivor the Engine as a six-year-old and trying to write down the distinctive sound of Ivor chugging away voiced by Oliver Postgate ("Psssscht-ee-coff"). He then completed a school project on bullet trains and ever since then has been a train-spotter, in spirit if not in deed.

ACKNOWLEDGEMENTS

A *Telegraph* anthology, like a *Telegraph* newspaper, is the product of teamwork. I should like to thank all those writers, staff and freelance, who boarded new trains for this one, and all the others who gave permission for me to draw on pieces they had written that were in the archives.

My thanks, too, to Graham Coster, my publisher, and Caroline Buckland, his counterpart at the *Telegraph*; to Gavin Fuller in the *Telegraph* library; to Mick Brown and Nigel Richardson for helpful suggestions; and, as always, to my wife, Teri.